# Big Book of SAT® Practice Tests

© 2016 by Kaplan, Inc.

Published by Kaplan Publishing, a division of Kaplan, Inc.
750 Third Avenue
New York, NY 10017

Printed in the United States of America

10 9 8 7 6 5 4 3 2

ISBN-13: 978-1-5062-0718-6

# Table of Contents

Practice Makes Perfect ............................................................................. v

Practice Test 1 ...................................................................................... 1

Practice Test 2 ..................................................................................... 51

Practice Test 3 ..................................................................................... 99

Practice Test 4 ................................................................................... 151

Answer Grids and Essay Practice Test Comment Forms ..................... 199

# Practice Makes Perfect

Don't be scared of the SAT. Why? Because we know what's on the exam, and we know exactly how you should prepare for it. Kaplan has been teaching kids how to succeed on the SAT for more than 75 years—longer than anyone else, period.

This book contains your four course practice tests. Each exam mirrors the SAT you will see on Test Day and will provide you with plenty of practice as well as opportunities to assess your strengths and weaknesses before you take the real thing. Taking practice tests is important, but just as important is understanding why you got a particular question right or wrong. So when you're done, check out the detailed answers and explanations in your online center. These provide you with thorough explanations for the correct answers as well as strategic advice, all of which will help you practice thinking like an expert! In addition, every explanation includes the difficulty level of each question. All of this practice is geared toward one thing—getting you the most points on Test Day!

## HOW TO USE THIS BOOK

This book is filled with over 600 practice questions to help you master the SAT.

Follow these steps to get the most out of these practice tests:

1. Bring this book, a pencil, and a calculator to every class!

2. Follow the proctor's instructions for each test. It's important that your Kaplan test experience be as close to the real thing as possible.

3. Assess your strengths and weaknesses. After you finish each test, go online and check out your score AND read the explanations for questions you missed as well as for questions on which you guessed.

4. Complete the required homework in your Course Book.

5. Log into your online center at least two to three times a week and work on the assignments from your personalized recommendations. These recommendations are based on your strengths and weaknesses and will help you improve your score in the least amount of time.

## SCORING YOUR TEST

You gain one point for every question you answer correctly. You lose no points for answering a question wrong OR for leaving a question blank. This means you should ALWAYS answer EVERY question on the SAT—even if you have to guess.

## SAT TEST DATES

As a general rule, students take the SAT at least once in their junior year, often taking it for the first time in March. The SAT is administered on select Saturdays during the school year. Sunday testing is available for students who cannot take the Saturday test because of religious observances. Check the official College Board website at collegeboard.org for the most up-to-date test dates.

## SAT REGISTRATION

To register for the SAT by mail, you'll need to get an SAT Paper Registration Guide from your high school guidance counselor.

- You can register online at sat.collegeboard.org/register. Note: Not all students are eligible to register online, so read the instructions and requirements carefully.

- Register early to secure the time you want at the test center of your choice and to avoid late registration fees.

- Students with disabilities can go to collegeboard.org/services-for-students-with-disabilities to learn how to apply for accommodations, or call (609) 771-7137 (TTY: (609) 882-4118) for more information.

- In the United States, the fee for the SAT is $54.50 with the essay, and $43 without the essay. This price includes reports for you, your high school, and up to four colleges and scholarship programs. To get the most up-to-date information on test fees, please check collegereadiness. collegeboard.org/sat/register/fees.

- You will receive an admission ticket at least a week before the test. The ticket confirms your registration on a specified date, at a specified test center. Make sure to bring this, along with proper identification, to the test center. Some acceptable forms of identification include photo IDs such as a driver's license, a school identification card, or a valid passport. (Unacceptable forms of identification include a Social Security card, credit card, or birth certificate.)

- Your SAT scores will be available online approximately three weeks after the test.

- Remember to check with the College Board for all the latest information on the SAT. Every effort has been made to keep the information in this book as up-to-date as possible, but changes may occur after the book is published.

- Finally, bookmark the College Board's website: collegeboard.org.

# SAT®
## Practice Test 1

# READING TEST

### 65 Minutes—52 Questions

Turn to Section 1 of your answer sheet to answer the questions in this section.

**Directions:** Each passage or pair of passages below is followed by a number of questions. After reading each passage or pair, choose the best answer to each question based on what is stated or implied in the passage or passages and in any accompanying graphics (such as a table or graph).

**Questions 1-10 are based on the following passage.**

This passage is adapted from *A Study in Scarlet*, Sir Arthur Conan Doyle's first story in his acclaimed Sherlock Holmes series. In this excerpt the narrator, Dr. Watson, observes Mr. Holmes, with whom he has recently entered into a shared housing arrangement, although he knows very little about this new room-mate as of yet.

As the weeks went by, my interest in him and my curiosity as to his aims in life gradually deepened and increased. His very person and appearance were such as to strike the attention of the most
*Line*
(5) casual observer. In height he was rather over six feet, and so excessively lean that he seemed to be considerably taller. His eyes were sharp and piercing, save during those intervals of torpor to which I have alluded; and his thin, hawk-like nose gave his
(10) whole expression an air of alertness and decision. His chin, too, had the prominence and squareness which mark the man of determination. His hands were invariably blotted with ink and stained with chemicals, yet he was possessed of extraordinary
(15) delicacy of touch, as I frequently had occasion to observe when I watched him manipulating his fragile philosophical instruments. . . .

He was not studying medicine. He had himself, in reply to a question, confirmed Stamford's[1]
(20) opinion upon that point. Neither did he appear to have pursued any course of reading which might fit him for a degree in science or any other recognized

portal which would give him an entrance into the learned world. Yet his zeal for certain studies
(25) was remarkable, and within eccentric limits his knowledge was so extraordinarily ample and minute that his observations have fairly astounded me. Surely no man would work so hard or attain such precise information unless he had some
(30) definite end in view. Desultory readers are seldom remarkable for the exactness of their learning. No man burdens his mind with small matters unless he has some very good reason for doing so.

His ignorance was as remarkable as his knowledge.
(35) Of contemporary literature, philosophy and politics he appeared to know next to nothing. Upon my quoting Thomas Carlyle,[2] he inquired in the naïvest way who he might be and what he had done. My surprise reached a climax, however, when I found
(40) incidentally that he was ignorant of the Copernican Theory and of the composition of the solar system. That any civilized human being in this nineteenth century should not be aware that the earth travelled round the sun appeared to be to me such an
(45) extraordinary fact that I could hardly realize it.

"You appear to be astonished," he said, smiling at my expression of surprise. "Now that I do know it I shall do my best to forget it."

"To forget it!"

(50) "You see," he explained, "I consider that a man's brain originally is like a little empty attic, and you have to stock it with such furniture as you choose. A fool takes in all the lumber of every sort that he comes across, so that the knowledge which might

---

[1]Stamford is the mutual acquaintance who introduced Dr. Watson to Mr. Holmes. In a previous scene he told Watson that Holmes was not a medical student.

[2]Thomas Carlyle was an influential writer and philosopher whose work was well known at the time of this novel's publication.

GO ON TO THE NEXT PAGE ▷

(55) be useful to him gets crowded out, or at best is
jumbled up with a lot of other things so that he
has a difficulty in laying his hands upon it. Now
the skillful workman is very careful indeed as to
what he takes into his brain-attic. He will have
(60) nothing but the tools which may help him in doing
his work, but of these he has a large assortment,
and all in the most perfect order. It is a mistake to
think that that little room has elastic walls and can
distend to any extent. Depend upon it there comes
(65) a time when for every addition of knowledge you
forget something that you knew before. It is of the
highest importance, therefore, not to have useless
facts elbowing out the useful ones."

    "But the solar system!" I protested.
(70)    "What the deuce is it to me?"

1. According to the passage, as time passes, Watson
   finds Holmes
   
   A) increasingly intriguing.
   B) frequently irritating.
   C) somewhat snobby.
   D) occasionally generous.

2. As used in line 5, "casual" most nearly means
   
   A) impulsive.
   B) comfortable.
   C) relaxed.
   D) occasional.

3. As presented in the passage, Sherlock Holmes is
   best described as
   
   A) very secretive and hard to understand.
   B) an excellent companion to Watson.
   C) highly regarded by his peers.
   D) an unusual and extraordinary man.

4. As used in line 8, "torpor" most nearly means
   
   A) agitation.
   B) sluggishness.
   C) alertness.
   D) illness.

5. The passage most strongly suggests that which of
   the following is true of Holmes?
   
   A) He tried, but failed, to become a doctor.
   B) He was an excellent student at the
      university.
   C) He studies things he is passionate about.
   D) He is considered an expert in philosophy.

6. Which choice provides the best evidence for the
   answer to the previous question?
   
   A) Lines 12-17 ("His hands were . . .
      instruments")
   B) Lines 18-20 ("He was not . . . that point")
   C) Lines 24-28 ("Yet his . . . astounded me")
   D) Lines 28-30 ("Surely no man . . . in view")

7. The passage most strongly suggests that Holmes
   believes which of the following about learning?
   
   A) People should study broadly to know
      something about everything.
   B) Philosophy is not a valid field of study to
      pursue.
   C) The brain is limited in capacity, so you
      should prioritize what you learn.
   D) The Copernican Theory is unfounded and
      therefore should not be studied.

8. Which choice provides the best evidence for the
   answer to the previous question?
   
   A) Line 34 ("His ignorance . . . his knowledge")
   B) Lines 35-36 ("Of contemporary . . .
      nothing")
   C) Lines 42-45 ("That any . . . realize it")
   D) Lines 66-68 ("It is of the . . . ones")

GO ON TO THE NEXT PAGE ▷

9. The comparison of the brain to an attic mainly serves to

A) demonstrate Holmes's unique views on how a person should make use of knowledge.

B) illustrate Watson's combative nature.

C) provide an alternate explanation for why Holmes doesn't know about Copernicus.

D) resolve the conflict between Watson and Holmes.

10. The decision to tell the story from Watson's point of view suggests that the author

A) wants the reader to dislike Holmes.

B) needed a sympathetic narrator.

C) will focus the rest of the story on Watson's actions.

D) hopes the reader will share Watson's curiosity about Holmes.

**Questions 11-20 are based on the following passage.**

This passage is adapted from a speech given by President Woodrow Wilson to Congress on January 8, 1918. Here Wilson proposes a 14-point program for world peace. These 14 points became the basis for peace negotiations at the end of World War I.

It will be our wish and purpose that the processes of peace, when they are begun, shall be absolutely open and that they shall involve and
*Line* permit henceforth no secret understandings of any
(5) kind. The day of conquest and aggrandizement is gone by; so is also the day of secret covenants entered into in the interest of particular govern-ments and likely at some unlooked-for moment to upset the peace of the world. It is this happy fact,
(10) now clear to the view of every public man whose thoughts do not still linger in an age that is dead and gone, which makes it possible for every nation whose purposes are consistent with justice and the peace of the world to avow now or at any other
(15) time the objects it has in view.

We entered this war because violations of right had occurred which touched us to the quick and made the life of our own people impossible unless they were corrected. . . . What we demand in this
(20) war, therefore, is nothing peculiar to ourselves. It is that the world be made fit and safe to live in; and particularly that it be made safe for every peace-loving nation which, like our own, wishes to live its own life, determine its own institutions, be assured
(25) of justice and fair dealing by the other peoples of the world. . . . The programme of the world's peace, therefore, is our programme; and that programme, the only possible programme, as we see it, is this:

    I. Open covenants of peace . . . with no private
(30)    international understandings of any kind but diplomacy shall proceed always frankly and in the public view.

    II. Absolute freedom of navigation upon the seas . . . alike in peace and in war, except as
(35)    the seas may be closed in whole or in part by international action for the enforcement of international covenants.

    III. The removal, so far as possible, of all economic barriers and the establishment of
(40)    an equality of trade conditions among all the nations consenting. . . .

    IV. Adequate guarantees given and taken that national armaments will be reduced to the lowest point consistent with domestic safety.

(45)    V. A free, open-minded, and absolutely impartial adjustment of all colonial claims. . . .

    VI. The evacuation of all Russian territory and such a settlement of all questions affecting Russia as will secure the best and freest
(50)    cooperation of the other nations of the world.

    VII. Belgium . . . must be evacuated and restored, without any attempt to limit the sovereignty which she enjoys in common with all other free nations. . . .

(55) VIII. All French territory should be freed and the invaded portions restored. . . .

    IX. A readjustment of the frontiers of Italy should be effected along clearly recognizable lines of nationality.

GO ON TO THE NEXT PAGE ⇨

(60)     X. The peoples of Austria-Hungary . . . should be accorded the freest opportunity to autonomous development.

    XI. Rumania, Serbia, and Montenegro should be evacuated; occupied territories restored; (65) and Serbia accorded free and secure access to the sea. . . .

    XII. The Turkish portion of the present Ottoman Empire should be assured a secure sovereignty, but the other nationalities (70) which are now under Turkish rule should be assured an undoubted security of life. . . .

    XIII. An independent Polish state should be erected which should include the territories inhabited by indisputably Polish populations (75) . . . . [The state] should be assured a free and secure access to the sea. . . .

    XIV. A general association of nations must be formed under specific covenants for the purpose of affording mutual guarantees (80) of political independence and territorial integrity to great and small states alike.

11. Based on the first two paragraphs, which choice best identifies Wilson's purpose in making this speech?

A) To build an international military and political alliance

B) To declare the sovereignty and independence of the United States

C) To outline ways to maintain peaceful relations in the world

D) To reform governments in aggressor nations bent on conquest

12. Which choice provides the best evidence for the answer to the previous question?

A) Lines 1-5 ("It will be . . . of any kind")

B) Lines 5-6 ("The day of . . . is gone by")

C) Lines 16-17 ("We entered . . . occurred")

D) Lines 26-27 ("The programme . . . is our programme")

13. As used in line 31, "frankly" most nearly means

A) in an honest manner.

B) in a blunt manner.

C) in an abrupt manner.

D) in an outspoken manner.

14. Based on the information in the passage, it can reasonably be inferred that in the past,

A) the United States avoided alliances.

B) some nations formed private pacts with one another.

C) wars usually involved only two nations.

D) the borders of France and Italy were not well-defined.

15. Which choice provides the best evidence for the answer to the previous question?

A) Lines 1-5 ("It will be . . . of any kind")

B) Lines 16-19 ("We entered . . . corrected")

C) Lines 55-59 ("All French . . . of nationality")

D) Lines 77-81 ("A general . . . states alike")

16. As used in line 44, "consistent" most nearly means

A) dependable.

B) continuing.

C) agreeable.

D) rigid.

17. In lines 45-46 ("A free . . . colonial claims"), Wilson argues that to preserve peace, nations must

A) engage in free, open, and fair trade with colonies.

B) give up all aspirations for territorial and economic expansion.

C) provide constitutional protections for colonies.

D) work to resolve conflicts originating from imperial conquests.

GO ON TO THE NEXT PAGE ⟶

18. Points VI through VIII serve as evidence to support which claim made by Wilson throughout the speech?

   A) Democratic nations ought to sign pacts of economic and political cooperation.

   B) During the war, aggressors damaged property that they should be required to repair.

   C) In the past, nations violated one another's territorial sovereignty.

   D) Current colonies are entitled to establish free and democratic governments.

19. Which of the following approaches to international relations is most similar to Wilson's approach?

   A) Economic sanctions against ideological enemies

   B) Joint efforts to mediate conflict among nations

   C) Nongovernmental organizations to regulate trade

   D) Unilateral military action against unfriendly regimes

20. Which choice best describes the developmental pattern of Wilson's argument?

   A) A statement and restatement of the argument

   B) A statement of the argument followed by specific examples

   C) Initial claims followed by counterclaims

   D) Specific examples leading to a concluding argument

**Questions 21-31 are based on the following passages and supplementary material.**

The following passages are concerned with meditation, particularly the practice of mindfulness. Passage 1 provides an overview of meditation, while Passage 2 focuses on a particular practitioner, Congressmen Tim Ryan.

**Passage 1**

Meditation has been around for thousands of years, starting as a religious practice. Hindu scripture from around 1500 BCE describes meditating on
*Line* the divine, and art from this time period shows
(5) people sitting cross-legged and solitary in a garden. In China and India around the fifth century BCE, other forms of meditation developed. Several religions, including Taoism, Buddhism, Islam, and Christianity, have meditative rites. In 20th-century
(10) Europe and America, secular forms of meditation arrived from India. Rather than focusing on spiritual growth, secular meditation emphasizes stress reduction, relaxation, and self-improvement.

Although it still isn't exactly mainstream,
(15) many people practice meditation. Mindfulness meditation, in particular, has become more popular in recent years. The practice involves sitting comfortably, focusing on one's breathing, and bringing the mind's attention to the present.
(20) Concerns about the past or future are let go of. An individual can picture worries popping like a bubble or flitting away like a butterfly.

Mindfulness is about increasing awareness and practicing acceptance. To be present is to
(25) have sharpened attention, or to be in a state of heightened consciousness. Practitioners of mindfulness report having a better quality of experience, deeper engagement, and greater measure of fulfillment.
(30) There are also health benefits. According to the Mayo Clinic, "Meditation can give you a sense of calm, peace and balance that benefits your emotional well-being." Among the emotional benefits are reducing negative emotions, increased
(35) self-awareness, and stress management skills.

GO ON TO THE NEXT PAGE ⟶

Asthma, depression, and sleep disorders are all
conditions worsened by stress. Several studies have
shown that patients with these conditions benefit
from meditation.

(40) Dr. Robert Schneider, director of the Institute
for Natural Medicine and Prevention, says, "I have
been researching effects of meditation on health
for thirty years and have found it has compelling
benefits. The benefits of meditation are coming to

(45) be widely accepted by health professionals, business
leaders, and the media. It is now time for the
medical profession to catch up."

**Passage 2**

In 2008, hoping to relax from his stressful job,
Congressman Tim Ryan took a weekend retreat

(50) where he first practiced mindfulness meditation.
"I came out of it," he says, "with a whole new way
of relating with what was going on in the world."
Now Ryan is an advocate for the benefits of
meditation on health, performance, and social aware-

(55) ness. In the busy and aggressive world of Washington
politics, he's a voice for calm consideration.

Every week Ryan, a Democrat representing
the 13th congressional district of Ohio, hosts
a meditation session for his staff and any other

(60) members of Congress who want to join. Despite
the fact that Republicans and Democrats are considered politically opposed, Ryan believes that the
benefits of meditation ought to appeal to members
of both parties. Meditation promotes self-reliance

(65) and fiscal conservation because it's a health practice
that can be self-sustained and doesn't require costly
memberships or equipment.

In 2010, Ryan wrote the book *A Mindful Nation:
How a Simple Practice Can Help Us Reduce Stress,*

(70) *Improve Performance, and Recapture the American
Spirit,* in which he advocates increased mindfulness in many disciplines and professions. After
its publication, kindergarten classes in his Ohio
district started using deep-breathing techniques;

(75) now teachers rave about their students' improved
behavior. "Mental discipline, focus, self-reliance,
deep listening—these are fundamental skills that
are essential to kids' education," Ryan says. "We yell
at kids to pay attention, but we never teach them

(80) *how* to pay attention."

Word seems to be spreading around Capitol Hill.
"I've had members of Congress approach me and
say, 'I want to learn more about this,'" Ryan says.
"Between the fundraising, being away from fam-

(85) ily, (and) the environment of hyperpartisanship,
Washington is really stressing people out."

Ryan supports legislation that puts meditation to
good use for everyone. Among other bills, he has
sponsored one to increase the holistic-medicine

(90) offerings of the Department of Veterans Affairs.
"And I haven't met anyone in the country that isn't
feeling a high level of anxiety right now, given the
economy and what's going on in the world. So
mindfulness is for everyone."

(95) Mr. Ryan is quick to point out that mindfulness
is not a religious practice, but rather a secular
mental technique that can be effective regardless of
spiritual beliefs. He compares it to his grandparents
praying and to athletes working out until they feel

(100) "in the zone."

"Your mind and body sync up into a flow state,
without a lot of mental chatter," Mr. Ryan says.

GO ON TO THE NEXT PAGE

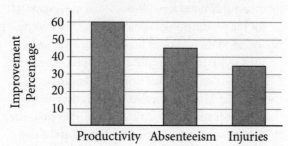

**Improvements After
Employee Meditation Program**

After the third year of its employee meditation program, a Detroit chemical plant reported these improvements.

21. The central idea of Passage 1 is that meditation and mindfulness

A) were first practiced as religious rites.

B) are becoming more accepted because of their benefits.

C) are valuable tools for psychologists.

D) help practitioners focus on their inner lives.

22. Passage 1 most strongly suggests that which of the following is true?

A) Individuals who practice mediation are less likely to develop illness.

B) Meditation helps people advance in their careers.

C) Not many studies have been done on the results of daily meditation.

D) Many medical professionals embrace the benefits of meditation.

23. Which choice provides the best evidence for the answer to the previous question?

A) Lines 2-5 ("Hindu scripture . . . in a garden")

B) Lines 15-17 ("Mindfulness meditation . . . in recent years")

C) Lines 24-26 ("To be present . . . consciousness")

D) Lines 30-33 ("According to . . . well-being")

24. As used in line 43, "compelling" most nearly means

A) creative.

B) judicial.

C) persuasive.

D) adaptable.

25. In Passage 2, what can be inferred about the author's point of view on meditation?

A) The author is uncertain about its value.

B) The author likes it but acknowledges its limits.

C) The author appreciates its value.

D) The author is devoted to it.

26. Passage 2 most strongly suggests that which of the following is true of Mr. Ryan?

A) He acts on his beliefs.

B) He is afraid to try new things.

C) He likes to try new things.

D) He is concerned about bipartisanship.

27. Which choice provides the best evidence for the answer to the previous question?

A) Lines 48-50 ("In 2008 . . . mindfulness meditation")

B) Lines 64-67 ("Meditation promotes . . . or equipment")

C) Lines 88-90 ("Among other bills . . . Affairs")

D) Lines 95-98 ("Mr. Ryan . . . spiritual beliefs")

28. As used in line 96, "secular" most nearly means

A) nonreligious.

B) serious.

C) impersonal.

D) pristine.

**GO ON TO THE NEXT PAGE**

29. In Passage 2, the author's use of the word "chatter" (line 102) implies that

    A) having an inner dialogue is a useful tool.

    B) people enjoy imagining themselves in various situations.

    C) meditation supporters talk about its surprises.

    D) much of what people think is relatively unimportant.

30. Both passages support which generalization about mindfulness meditation?

    A) It has become an acceptable way to show spirituality.

    B) It is making inroads into U.S. culture.

    C) It should be utilized in public institutions.

    D) It will soon be embraced by the American public.

31. Data in the graph provide most direct support for which claim from the passages?

    A) Meditation improves a person's focus and discipline.

    B) Children benefit from learning deep-breathing techniques.

    C) Meditation makes a person more generous.

    D) Health professionals are open to the idea of meditation being healthful.

**Questions 32-42 are based on the following passage.**

The following passage describes possible causes and impacts of colony collapse disorder, the mysterious disappearance of honey bee colonies.

Colony collapse disorder, sometimes referred to as CCD, is a phenomenon that has garnered much attention over the past few years from both the scientific community and the media alike. The
*Line*
(5)  disorder, which causes entire honey bee colonies to mysteriously disappear, is a major threat to both the environment and the economy. Honey bees are the world's natural pollinators, and are responsible for the production of about one-third of everything
(10) we eat. Without honey bees, produce that we're used to having in our diets, like apples, blueberries, strawberries, and nuts, would no longer be available. Honey bees also have an effect on the meat industry in the United States. They pollinate
(15) the various types of feed used by beef and dairy farmers. The services of the honey bee population are invaluable, and the survival of many different species depends on their well-being.

When colony collapse disorder was first
(20) recognized, beekeepers and scientists assumed that a pathogen was to blame. For example, there are several known viruses and pests that can kill off entire hives of honey bees quickly and be extremely hard to prevent. Mites, fungus, and bacterial
(25) infections are all common killers. Because of how often they're seen in hives, farmers assumed that these common plights were responsible for colony collapse disorder. However, as time passed and the disorder was studied, researchers noticed some-
(30) thing odd. In many cases, there were simply no dead bees to discover. While common killers of the honey bee left telltale signs, colony collapse disor-der left nothing behind but empty hives.

Scientists attributed the rapid disappearance of
(35) the bees to a form of altruistic behavior. When a bee gets sick, it flies away from the hive so as not to spread its illness to the other bees. It naturally prioritizes the overall health of the hive over its own. Although this behavior explained the bees'
(40) disappearing act, the cause of the disorder is yet to be understood and the list of possible explanations just keeps getting longer.

One team of researchers hypothesized that fluctuations in the earth's magnetic field might
(45) be doing damage to the magnetoreceptors, or built-in homing devices, that bees use to find their way home to their hives after flying all day. Honey bees, as well as birds and fish, use the earth's magnetic field to identify their location. Sunspots,

(50) which cause the strength of the earth's magnetic field to fluctuate, might be damaging the honey bee's biological tools.

While solar activity is outside the control of humans, another theory about the cause of colony

(55) collapse disorder points to the human invention of pesticides. Pesticides, which are chemicals used to prevent pest infestation of crops on a large scale around the world, are often picked up by honey bees during their foraging and pollination flights.

(60) Scientists have found that more than one pesticide can be found in the honey of one hive. They are currently studying the interaction of two or more pesticides, which travel into the hives and are stored by the bees in the pollen they use for protein.

(65) While the presence of one pesticide in a hive would certainly limit the life spans of bees and impair their navigational skills, it could be that it is the interaction of two or more pesticides that cause the entire colony to collapse. There are many ingredi-

(70) ents in pesticides that are not regulated by world governments, and this leaves a lot of ground for bee scientists to cover when doing their research.

Research over time usually helps to narrow down the field of possible causes of a disorder, but in the

(75) case of colony collapse disorder, scientists feel farther away than ever from finding the root cause and a cure. Many people around the world are taking up the cause of keeping honey bees alive by keeping bees in their backyards or on their roofs. Some

(80) cities and towns have relaxed regulations on beekeeping in response to the honey bee population crisis. Hopefully, community initiatives and research can both help to save the world's honey bee population.

32. The primary purpose of the passage is to

A) show that honey bees require certain conditions in order to live.

B) instruct the reader on how to increase the number of honey bees.

C) explain the relationship between sunspots and colony collapse disorder.

D) alert the reader to the impending crisis of decreasing numbers of honey bees.

33. The author's point of view is most similar to

A) an advocate for honey bee survival.

B) an environmentalist concerned about toxic materials.

C) a naturalist who researches changes in animal populations.

D) a concerned citizen who hopes to raise honey bees.

34. The author uses the word "mysteriously" (line 6) to emphasize

A) that fluctuations of the earth's magnetic field are uncontrollable.

B) how little is known about why colony collapse occurs.

C) that the reason a bee leaves its hive when it is sick is unknown.

D) why researchers are studying the effect of pesticides on honey bees.

35. As used in line 27, "plights" most nearly means

A) causes.

B) promises.

C) intentions.

D) troubles.

36. The author uses the fact that no bees are found in a hive after a colony collapses to

A) examine the extent of damage to the honey bee population that has occurred.

B) emphasize the ways in which honey bees relate to human beings.

C) refute the possibility that pathogens are the reason for the collapse.

D) show that pesticides are not to blame for the decrease in the honey bee population.

GO ON TO THE NEXT PAGE

37. Which choice provides the best evidence for the answer to the previous question?

    A) Lines 4-7 ("The disorder . . . the economy")

    B) Lines 21-24 ("For example . . . to prevent")

    C) Lines 31-33 ("While common . . . empty hives")

    D) Lines 37-39 ("It naturally . . . its own")

38. As used in line 59, "foraging" most nearly means

    A) rejecting.

    B) offering.

    C) watching.

    D) searching.

39. The passage most strongly suggests that

    A) the author is cautiously optimistic about the future existence of the honey bee.

    B) the author thinks that scientists have not tried hard enough to find the reason for colony collapse.

    C) one team of scientists believes that they will have an answer to the problem of colony collapse very soon.

    D) scientists have ruled out the theory that pesticides are at fault for colony collapse.

40. Which choice provides the best evidence for the answer to the previous question?

    A) Lines 7-10 ("Honey bees . . . eat")

    B) Lines 25-28 ("Because of how . . . disorder")

    C) Lines 53-56 ("While solar . . . pesticides")

    D) Lines 82-83 ("Hopefully . . . population")

41. According to the passage, which of the following events has occurred in response to colony collapse disorder?

    A) Concerned citizens have fought to ban certain pesticides.

    B) Some towns have relaxed their regulations on beekeeping.

    C) Farmers have resorted to other means of pollinating their feed.

    D) Scientists are working to control the use of electromagnetic devices.

42. Based on information in the passage, which statement best describes the relationship between honey bees and human beings?

    A) Human beings depend on honey bees to keep the environment and economy healthy.

    B) Human beings depend on honey bees to keep the effects of sunspots to a minimum.

    C) Honey bees depend on human beings to provide them with food.

    D) Honey bees depend on human beings to protect them from solar flares.

**Questions 43-52 are based on the following passage and supplementary materials.**

The following passage describes the potential problems caused by debris that humans have left behind in space.

In the first days of space exploration, one concern was the possibility that astronauts or spacecraft might be hit by meteoroids. Scientists
*Line* calculated that this possibility was extremely
(5) small because meteoroids are rare. Astronauts and spacecraft, on the other hand, would almost certainly encounter micrometeorites, which are about the size of grains of dust and much more common.
    However, in the 60 years since the beginning of
(10) space exploration, large quantities of human-made

orbital debris have accumulated. Much of the debris consists of satellites that have stopped functioning or rocket booster sections that separated from the main spacecraft during a mission. Some of (15) the debris consists of items lost by astronauts, such as tools or space suit parts. Still more of the debris is the result of collisions, such as when one satellite collides with another or with a large piece of debris.

NASA estimates there are millions of debris (20) particles that are too small to be tracked. These circle Earth at speeds up to 17,500 miles per hour, making even the smallest particles dangerous. One scientist calculated that a chip of paint hitting the window of a spacecraft at orbital speeds will hit (25) with the same amount of force as a bowling ball traveling at 60 mph. Such an impact occurred on the space shuttle *Challenger*'s second flight, chipping the windows and causing minor damage to the protective tiles on the spacecraft. While the damage (30) was not immediately dangerous, it led to the fear that any craft in orbit for long periods of time could accumulate enough damage to cease functioning.

Larger objects are even more dangerous, but they can be monitored and avoided. NASA tracks (35) about 500,000 pieces of debris larger than a marble, about 20,000 of which are larger than a softball. When NASA was still flying shuttle missions, it would often have to direct the shuttle to maneuver to avoid collisions with the larger debris. This could (40) usually be planned and accomplished in a few hours, but moving the International Space Station to avoid a collision takes up to 30 hours of advance notice.

Many satellites have the ability to adjust their (45) course slightly and can be remotely directed to avoid collisions with larger objects that would damage or destroy the satellites. NASA and the European Space Agency (ESA) have departments of scientists and engineers dedicated to cataloging, (50) modeling, and predicting the movements of space debris.

Some debris falls back to Earth, and most of it is burned up in the atmosphere. However, a large piece will survive long enough to get through (55) the atmosphere and crash. In 1979, the obsolete Skylab fell out of orbit, and much of it withstood

the trip through the atmosphere, crashing in the Australian outback. Space agencies also monitor debris to predict if and when any particular piece (60) might fall. Although they can issue warnings, there is currently nothing that can be done about pieces that might get through the atmosphere.

To avoid adding to the aggregation of debris, future satellites may need to be able to take (65) themselves out of orbit as their usefulness comes to an end. Until a way to remove these remains is implemented, however, those 500,000 pieces of large fragments, along with the millions of smaller pieces, will continue to orbit Earth.

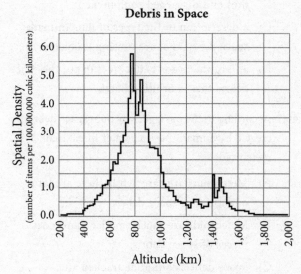

**Debris in Space**

Spatial Density (number of items per 100,000,000 cubic kilometers)

Altitude (km)

Adapted from NASA: U.S. Satellite Catalog.

43. The passage is primarily concerned with the

A) unintended consequences of space exploration.

B) composition of the space debris that orbits Earth.

C) dangers posed by space debris created by humans.

D) causes and consequences of collisions in space.

GO ON TO THE NEXT PAGE

44. Which choice provides the best evidence for the answer to the previous question?

    A) Lines 3-8 ("Scientists calculated . . . common")

    B) Lines 20-22 ("These circle . . . dangerous")

    C) Lines 33-34 ("Larger objects . . . avoided")

    D) Lines 44-47 ("Many satellites . . . satellites")

45. The second paragraph helps support the central idea of the passage by providing

    A) an explanation of why space debris left by humans is more dangerous than meteors.

    B) a summary of problems caused by old satellites and discarded equipment.

    C) a description of the types of human-made space debris that are causing problems.

    D) an argument for better tracking of the space debris that is orbiting Earth.

46. According to the passage, why does space debris created by humans pose a greater threat than meteoroids?

    A) Meteoroids are rare, while there are large quantities of space debris.

    B) Meteoroids are much smaller than most pieces of space debris.

    C) Space debris cannot be tracked and monitored, but meteoroids can.

    D) Space debris is only found in a narrow band around Earth.

47. Which of the following pieces of evidence most strengthens the author's central claim?

    A) An explanation of early concerns about space collisions in paragraph 1

    B) Information about how space debris is tracked in paragraph 5

    C) An example of space debris falling to Earth in paragraph 6

    D) The suggestion that obsolete satellites take themselves out of orbit in paragraph 7

48. As used in line 55, "obsolete" most nearly means

    A) displaced.

    B) redundant.

    C) excessive.

    D) outdated.

49. Based on information in the passage, which conclusion can reasonably be inferred?

    A) One way to prevent space debris from causing injuries on Earth is to warn people to avoid the predicted impact site.

    B) The smallest pieces of space debris can be removed by astronauts while they are working in space.

    C) Most space debris is not dangerous to space travelers because of its small size and relatively low speed.

    D) Pieces of space debris will become more of a problem as spacecraft travel farther into outer space.

GO ON TO THE NEXT PAGE

50. Which choice provides the best evidence for the answer to the previous question?

   A) Lines 19-22 ("NASA estimates . . . dangerous")

   B) Lines 33-34 ("Larger objects . . . avoided")

   C) Lines 34-36 ("NASA tracks . . . softball")

   D) Lines 60-62 ("Although . . . atmosphere")

51. As used in line 67, "implemented" most nearly means

   A) employed.

   B) investigated.

   C) prevented.

   D) appointed.

52. Based on the passage and the graphic, if NASA were to place a new satellite into orbit, which altitude range would pose the greatest danger?

   A) 500-700 kilometers

   B) 700-900 kilometers

   C) 1,400-1,600 kilometers

   D) 1,800-2,000 kilometers

IF YOU FINISH BEFORE TIME IS CALLED, YOU MAY CHECK YOUR WORK ON THIS SECTION ONLY. DO NOT TURN TO ANY OTHER SECTION IN THE TEST. **STOP**

# WRITING AND LANGUAGE TEST

### 35 Minutes—44 Questions

Turn to Section 2 of your answer sheet to answer the questions in this section.

**Directions:** Each passage below is accompanied by a number of questions. For some questions, you will consider how the passage might be revised to improve the expression of ideas. For other questions, you will consider how the passage might be edited to correct errors in sentence structure, usage, or punctuation. A passage or a question may be accompanied by one or more graphics (such as a table or graph) that you will consider as you make revising and editing decisions.

Some questions will direct you to an underlined portion of a passage. Other questions will direct you to a location in a passage or ask you to think about the passage as a whole.

After reading each passage, choose the answer to each question that most effectively improves the quality of writing in the passage or that makes the passage conform to the conventions of standard written English. Many questions include a "NO CHANGE" option. Choose that option if you think the best choice is to leave the relevant portion of the passage as it is.

**Questions 1-11 are based on the following passage.**

## A Sweet Discovery

[1] Like most chemists, a laboratory was where Constantin Fahlberg worked on his research. However, the discovery for which he is famous occurred not in the laboratory, but at supper.

1.  A) NO CHANGE
    B) Like most chemists, Constantin Fahlberg worked on his research in a laboratory.
    C) Constantin Fahlberg worked on his research, like most chemists, in a laboratory.
    D) A laboratory, like most chemists, is where Constantin Fahlberg worked on his research.

GO ON TO THE NEXT PAGE

**2** Chemical compounds are derived from coal tar, which is what Fahlberg began working on as a research chemist in a laboratory at Johns Hopkins University in early 1878. Coal tar was a by-product of steel manufacturing, and compounds derived **3** from them had been used as medicines and in dye formulations. Fahlberg, and others in the laboratory, were studying ways to add different chemicals to molecules found in coal tar to see if the new compounds formed had other useful properties.

One night in June, Fahlberg finished a long day of work; he had been so **4** demanding in his research that he forgot to eat lunch, so he hurried to his supper without stopping to wash his hands. He might have

2. A) NO CHANGE
   B) Johns Hopkins University is where Fahlberg began working as a research chemist in a laboratory, making chemical compounds derived from coal tar in early 1878.
   C) Coal tar creates chemical compounds. This is what Fahlberg began working on as a research chemist in a laboratory at Johns Hopkins University in early 1878.
   D) In early 1878, Fahlberg began working as a research chemist in a laboratory at Johns Hopkins University, making chemical compounds derived from coal tar.

3. A) NO CHANGE
   B) from it
   C) from these
   D) from him

4. A) NO CHANGE
   B) delayed
   C) engrossed
   D) excited

**GO ON TO THE NEXT PAGE**

considered hand washing unnecessary because he had not handled any toxic chemicals that day, or he might have just been so hungry he did not think about it. **5**

The bread tasted so sweet that Fahlberg thought he might have picked up some cake by mistake. He rinsed out his mouth with water and then patted his mustache dry with a napkin. He was surprised to find that the napkin tasted sweet as well. He took another sip of water and realized that the water now tasted sweet. **6** The bread, napkin, and glass of water had something in common. He then tasted his thumb, and it tasted sweeter than any candy he had ever had.

5. At this point, the writer wants to create an ideal transition to the next paragraph. Which choice most effectively accomplishes this goal?

A) Later, hand washing would become a critical protocol in the laboratory.

B) Thankfully, he didn't, or he never would have discovered what came next.

C) Fahlberg had not eaten any cake, or indeed anything sweet, that day.

D) Either way, he picked up his bread in his unwashed hands and took a bite.

6. A) NO CHANGE

B) Was there something that the bread, napkin, and glass of water had in common, he wondered?

C) In fact, everything Fahlberg touched seemed to taste sweeter than usual, which intrigued his scientific mind.

D) Fahlberg quickly realized that the one thing the bread, napkin, and glass of water had in common was that they had all touched his fingers.

GO ON TO THE NEXT PAGE

[1] Fahlberg rushed back into the lab and began to taste the contents of every beaker he had used that day. [2] Fortunately, he had not worked with anything poisonous or corrosive, or the story **7** may have a different ending. [3] **8** He had discovered saccharin, which he named for its intense sweetness. [4] He found a sweet-tasting mixture of chemicals and worked for weeks to isolate the sweet substance from the rest and to determine its chemical composition. [5] Although it is many times more sweet tasting than sugar, it cannot be used for energy by the body and therefore does not contribute to calories consumed or energy use. [6] Soon after Fahlberg started **9** making saccharin commercially in 1886, it became popular with people who needed to lose weight and with diabetic patients who needed to avoid sugar. **10** **11**

7. A) NO CHANGE
   B) would have had
   C) might have
   D) could have had

8. Which choice most clearly and effectively conveys the central idea of the paragraph?
   A) NO CHANGE
   B) The substance was saccharin, and it became known as an artificial sweetener.
   C) Instead, the substance was a harmless sweetener called saccharin.
   D) Interestingly, the substance was extremely sweet and would later be known as saccharin.

9. A) NO CHANGE
   B) inventing
   C) creating
   D) producing

10. To make this paragraph most logical, sentence 4 should be placed
    A) Where it is now
    B) Before sentence 1
    C) Before sentence 3
    D) Before sentence 6

11. Which of the following sentences would provide the best conclusion for the passage?

A) Clearly, Constantin Fahlberg's legacy of research, along with his accidental discovery, continues to have lasting effects on society even today.

B) If Fahlberg had stopped to wash his hands that day, he might have continued his experiments on coal tar derivatives, never knowing that an important substance sat at the bottom of one of his laboratory beakers.

C) In addition to his discovery of saccharin, his work on coal tar proved that Constantin Fahlberg was a talented scientist whose work has applications in the present day, even though a number of new artificial sweeteners have been developed.

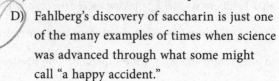
D) Fahlberg's discovery of saccharin is just one of the many examples of times when science was advanced through what some might call "a happy accident."

**Questions 12-22 are based on the following passage.**

## René Descartes: The Father of Modern Philosophy

Throughout history, philosophy has shaped culture in pivotal ways. From the ancients to the postmoderns, great philosophers have spoken powerfully within **12** there respective contexts. For modern Western culture, one philosopher's formative impact surpassed his contemporaries: France's René Descartes. Called "the father of modern philosophy," Descartes crucially influenced Western perspectives on knowledge and rationality.

This 17th-century philosopher ushered Western thought through an era of great public doubt and upheaval and into the age of self-reliant rationalism. Political and religious tradition and authority—the **13** obvious premodern sources of truth and knowledge—were being questioned and rejected as new ideas identified potential inconsistencies. **14** Because foundations of truth seemed to be crumbling, Descartes's writings proposed an alternative foundation: individual reason.

12. A) NO CHANGE
    B) their
    C) its
    D) it's

13. A) NO CHANGE
    B) makeshift
    C) innovative
    D) reigning

14. A) NO CHANGE
    B) In a time when foundations of truth seemed to be crumbling, Descartes's writings proposed an alternative foundation: individual reason.
    C) Despite the fact that foundations of truth seemed to be crumbling, Descartes's writings proposed an alternative foundation: individual reason.
    D) Although foundations of truth seemed to be crumbling, Descartes's writings proposed an alternative foundation: individual reason.

[15] An expert in many fields, Descartes's work would on many levels serve to establish foundations for modern culture and science. [16] This emphasis on reason, as opposed to traditional or authoritative bases for certainty, would become the modern mechanism for determining truth and knowledge.

[17] Modern culture would come to cherish this as an intellectual ideal. In his most famous project, Descartes sought certainty by mentally stripping away every layer of knowledge that was remotely possible to

15. A) NO CHANGE
    B) Expertise in many fields, Descartes created work that
    C) An expert in many fields, Descartes would create work that
    D) With his expertise in many fields, Descartes's work

16. At this point, the writer wants to add specific information that supports the central claim of the paragraph. Which choice provides the strongest support?
    A) Even so, his most impressive contribution was his advocacy for the individual's rationality.
    B) Unlike Descartes, other philosophers argued that reason alone could not provide the basis for knowledge.
    C) The idea known as "Cartesian dualism" posited that in the world there exists only mind and matter.
    D) His work on philosophy has proven to have more importance than his ideas about anatomy, many of which have since been disproven.

17. Which sentence should be added in front of sentence 1 to clarify the topic of the paragraph?
    A) Descartes's contributions to philosophy were seen as threatening to religion.
    B) Descartes focused his work on the pursuit of fact-based certainty.
    C) The foundation for the ideas of many other philosophers is Descartes's work.
    D) Descartes's ideas were rooted in his Jesuit training.

GO ON TO THE NEXT PAGE ⟶

doubt. Descartes arrived at his memorable [18] conclusion, "I think, therefore I am," he could only be certain of the fact that he was thinking. [19] Building from there, he could work toward rational certainty in other areas of knowledge.

Emphasizing the importance of building knowledge on certain evidence, Descartes modeled a reversal of the reigning scientific processes (which typically worked backward from observation to explanation). Descartes founded the modern scientific method, in which research and study could be reliably conducted based on certain evidence. Scientific method, and the emphasis on human reason, would become standard elements of modern thought. Though reimagined by ensuing culture and philosophy, [20] these changes propelled by Descartes's initial contributions to that conversation.

18. A) NO CHANGE
    B) conclusion "I think, therefore I am" he could only be certain of the fact that he was thinking.
    C) conclusion, "I think, therefore I am" he could only be certain of the fact that he was thinking.
    D) conclusion, "I think, therefore I am." He could only be certain of the fact that he was thinking.

19. Which choice most logically follows the previous sentence and sets up the information that follows?
    A) This revelation came as a shock to many people.
    B) However, he believed that this certainty offered evidence to confirm his existence.
    C) Still, it was a place to start.
    D) This was a radical new way to think about thinking.

20. A) NO CHANGE
    B) these changes being propelled by
    C) these changes having been propelled by
    D) these changes were propelled by

Some people may argue that it is impossible to separate what Descartes accomplished from the things his contemporaries did. Certainly, most scientists and philosophers influence and build from each other's work. But Descartes was the crucial voice in early modern dialogue. His expertise drew trusted readership, and his well-read ideas pointed culture down the road to modern understanding—a road

paved with reason, modernism's great intellectual virtue. Shifts 22 begun by Descartes's work would influence the very structure of ideas and systems in the modern world, from research methods to public processes like government and health systems.

21. A) NO CHANGE
    B) Some may argue that it is impossible to separate Descartes's accomplishments from those of his contemporaries.
    C) Some people may argue that it is impossible to separate Descartes from his contemporaries.
    D) Some may argue that what Descartes accomplished is no different from what his contemporaries did.

22. A) NO CHANGE
    B) foreseen
    C) initiated
    D) evolved

**Questions 23-33 are based on the following passage.**

## The Novel: Introspection to Escapism

Art is never 23 immovable, nor is it meant to be. A poem written today looks and sounds vastly different from a poem by Shakespeare, and a modern symphony no longer resembles one by Beethoven. So it is with the novel, that still relatively young member of the literary family (many consider *Don Quixote*, published in 1605, to be the first). The novel is evolving to reflect the 24 changing world; for better or for worse.

23. A) NO CHANGE
    B) sluggish
    C) static
    D) stationary

24. A) NO CHANGE
    B) changing world—for better
    C) changing world: for better
    D) changing world for better

[25] The novel, while well regarded, would never match the poem as the ideal form for conveying the struggles of humanity. A few quotations from acclaimed novelists of the past illustrate how [26] loftily the form was once regarded. G. K. Chesterton said, "A good novel tells us the truth about its hero; but a bad novel tells us the truth about its author." English writer Ford Madox Ford believed the novelist played an important role as a recorder of history. [27] Ford said of his friend Joseph Conrad, "We agreed that the novel is absolutely the only vehicle for the thought of our day."

It's not that over centuries writers of novels have shed these ambitions; novels today still address complexities and intricate social dynamics. [28] However, in recent decades, popular novels and their film adaptations have driven the novel market in a broader direction.

25. Which choice most effectively establishes the main topic of the paragraph?

A) NO CHANGE

B) The novel was once sacred ground, meant to capture and reveal universal truths, to depict society and all its ills, to explore and expound upon the human condition.

C) Both poetry and novels enjoyed a resurgence of popularity in the early 1900s due to the notoriety of many of the prominent authors of the day.

D) By the early 1900s, novels had evolved into something entirely different from the form Cervantes pioneered with *Don Quixote*.

26. A) NO CHANGE

B) broadly

C) haughtily

D) pretentiously

27. Which choice best improves the sentence?

A) Ford said of his friend, the novelist Joseph Conrad,

B) Ford said of his great friend, Joseph Conrad,

C) Ford said of Joseph Conrad,

D) Ford said of his friend, Joseph Conrad, a Pole who moved to Britain,

28. A) NO CHANGE

B) However: in recent decades,

C) However in recent decades,

D) In recent decades however;

**[29]** Novels are considered just another entertainment medium, which are now available on digital devices, one that ought to enthrall its passive reader and relieve him or her of the stress and tedium of life. The difficulties, challenges, and triumphs of real life are **[30]** less often the subject of popular novels; instead, escapist tales of fantastical lands and escapades are more popular. **[31]**

29. A) NO CHANGE
    B) Novels, which are now available on digital devices, are considered just another entertainment medium,
    C) Novels are considered just another entertainment medium, now available on digital devices,
    D) Novels, just another entertainment medium which are now available on digital devices

30. A) NO CHANGE
    B) less often the subject of popular novels instead, escapist tales of fantastical lands and escapades are more popular.
    C) less often the subject of popular novels, instead, escapist tales of fantastical lands and escapades are more popular.
    D) less often the subject of popular novels: instead, escapist tales of fantastical lands and escapades, are more popular.

31. At this point, the writer wants to add specific information that supports the ideas presented in the paragraph. Which choice provides the most relevant detail?
    A) Novels exploring deep social issues remain the most heavily decorated books come literary award season.
    B) Director James Cameron remarked recently about the "inherent difficulty" of adapting novels with fantasy themes.
    C) Writing in the *New Yorker* magazine in 2014, critic James Woods stated that readers now want novels that, like popcorn, are "easy to consume."
    D) The "slice of life" novel remains tremendously popular among books targeting younger readers.

GO ON TO THE NEXT PAGE

It is rare today for a novelist to attempt to ask, "What does it mean?" Instead, [32] we strive to provide the reader with an answer to the question, "What happens next?"

"Publishers, readers, booksellers, even critics," critic James Woods wrote, "acclaim the novel that one can deliciously sink into, forget oneself in, the novel that returns us to the innocence of childhood or the dream of the cartoon, the novel of a thousand confections and no unwanted significance. What becomes harder to find, and lonelier to defend, is the idea of [33] the novel as—in Ford Madox Ford's words—a 'medium of profoundly serious investigation into the human case.'"

**Questions 34-44 are based on the following passage and supplementary material.**

## Interning: A Bridge Between Classes and Careers

Kelli Blake, a chemical engineering major, recently [34] excepted a summer internship with BP, an international energy company, to gain career experience. Some argue against the value of internships, claiming they pay very little and can involve performing [35] boring tasks, yet Kelli feels her internship is critical to helping her discover whether engineering is right for her.

Kelli wants a real-world perspective on information she has gained in her classes. Her internship with a corporate leader is affording her the opportunity to apply her conceptual knowledge to tasks inside a major

32. A) NO CHANGE
    B) they strive
    C) it strives
    D) he or she strives

33. A) NO CHANGE
    B) the novel as, in Ford Madox Ford's words—a 'medium of profoundly serious investigation into the human case.'"
    C) the novel as, in Ford Madox Ford's words: a 'medium of profoundly serious investigation into the human case.'"
    D) the novel as, in Ford Madox Ford's words; a 'medium of profoundly serious investigation into the human case.'"

34. A) NO CHANGE
    B) accepted
    C) adopted
    D) adapted

35. A) NO CHANGE
    B) skilled
    C) menial
    D) challenging

GO ON TO THE NEXT PAGE

oil company. **36** <u>During this internship, for example, Kelli is working on a glycol dehydration project; she will be using the classroom skills she learned from thermo-dynamics, organic chemistry, and more.</u> She can later add this project to her résumé and portfolio, giving her an edge over other college graduates.

**37** <u>Offshore engineers have many rules and regula-tions.</u> Helicopter underwater egress safety training is required of employees traveling to offshore facilities, so she will **38** <u>stand out</u> from other applicants by already being safety certified. "I have a new appreciation for the protocols followed by engineers at refineries," she states. Kelli believes that gaining new skills and showing she can apply her classroom knowledge to real situations will give her an advantage over her competition should she decide to join BP.

36. Which choice best supports the central idea of the paragraph?

A) NO CHANGE

B) Kelli can use the materials from her intern-ship in a professional-quality presentation; she can then deliver the presentation to her classmates when she returns to college after her internship.

C) In addition, Kelli is designing the next internship proposal for her classmates after she completes her own and graduates.

D) Kelli is hoping to formulate her project results as a professional published document to sell to BP.

37. Which choice provides the most appropriate introduction to the paragraph?

A) NO CHANGE

B) Kelli admires the engineers who administer the safety training.

C) The skills Kelli acquires can be applied to existing knowledge.

D) Kelli will also earn an underwater safety training certificate.

38. A) NO CHANGE

B) stand down

C) stand up

D) stand alone

Everyone has **39** their own reason for wanting to become an intern. Kelli has several other reasons behind her decision. **40** For example, Kelli wants to meet people to learn about the variety of careers available, from entry level to senior engineer. She will accomplish all of her intern goals **41** by working on technical projects, attend "lunch and learn" meetings, watching webinars, and shadow coworkers.

39. A) NO CHANGE
    B) your
    C) its
    D) his or her

40. A) NO CHANGE
    B) For example; Kelli wants to meet people to learn about the variety of careers available, from entry level to senior engineer.
    C) For example, Kelli wants to meet people—to learn about the variety of careers available, from entry level, to senior engineer.
    D) For example, Kelli wants to meet people to learn about the variety of careers available; from entry level to senior engineer.

41. A) NO CHANGE
    B) by working on technical projects, attending "lunch and learn" meetings, watching webinars, and shadowing coworkers.
    C) by working on technical projects, attend "lunch and learn" meetings, watch webinars, and shadow coworkers.
    D) by working on technical projects, attending "lunch and learn" meetings, watch webinars, and shadowing coworkers.

What are some further benefits of internships? Besides gaining exposure in the field, Kelli is networking. The most important person to her now is her mentor, Dan, a senior engineer who can help her grow professionally by answering her questions. Gaining valuable contacts and [42] good role model. These are other reasons she has pursued this internship.

Kelli is now an acting member of a corporate team. She realizes she will be learning a lot about the industry and will benefit from adopting an entirely new vocabulary. She views her internship as an adventure, one in which engineering teams worldwide must work collaboratively and efficiently. [43] It is worth it to give up her summer, Kelli argues, because though she is losing her summer she is doing the job of an actual engineer through her internship. Moreover, she views the experience as one of the best ways to learn about her field and industry, which typically offers around [44] 35 internships per 1,000 hires.

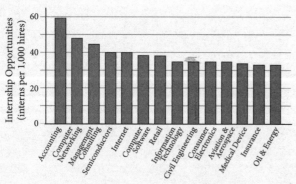

Industries Likely to Hire Their Interns

Adapted from Kurt Wagner, "Which Internships Really Pay Off?" ©2014 by Revere Digital LLC.

**42.** A) NO CHANGE
B) a good role model, these are other reasons
C) a good role model; are other reasons
D) a good role model are other reasons

**43.** A) NO CHANGE
B) It is worth giving up, Kelli argues, because though she is losing her summer, she is doing the job of an actual engineer through her internship.
C) It is worth it to give up her summer, Kelli argues, because she is doing the job of an actual engineer through her internship.
D) It is worth it to Kelli to give up her summer, because though summers are usually a time to relax, she argues, she is doing the job of an actual engineer through her internship.

**44.** Which choice most accurately and effectively represents the information in the graph and the passage?
A) NO CHANGE
B) 32 internships per 1,000 hires.
C) 35 internships per 60 hires.
D) 32 internships per 60 hires.

# MATH TEST

### 25 Minutes—20 Questions

## NO-CALCULATOR SECTION

Turn to Section 3 of your answer sheet to answer the questions in this section.

**Directions:** For this section, solve each problem and decide which is the best of the choices given. Fill in the corresponding oval on the answer sheet. You may use any available space for scratch work.

Notes:

1. Calculator use is NOT permitted.
2. All numbers used are real numbers.
3. All figures used are necessary to solving the problems that they accompany. All figures are drawn to scale EXCEPT when it is stated that a specific figure is not drawn to scale.
4. Unless stated otherwise, the domain of any function $f$ is assumed to be the set of all real numbers $x$, for which $f(x)$ is a real number.

Information:

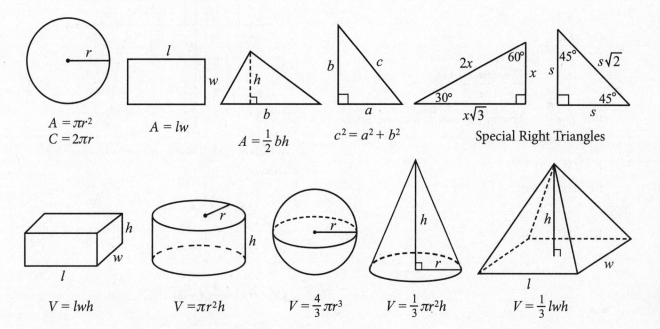

$A = \pi r^2$
$C = 2\pi r$

$A = lw$

$A = \frac{1}{2} bh$

$c^2 = a^2 + b^2$

Special Right Triangles

$V = lwh$

$V = \pi r^2 h$

$V = \frac{4}{3} \pi r^3$

$V = \frac{1}{3} \pi r^2 h$

$V = \frac{1}{3} lwh$

The sum of the degree measures of the angles in a triangle is 180.

The number of degrees of arc in a circle is 360.

The number of radians of arc in a circle is $2\pi$.

GO ON TO THE NEXT PAGE ⇨

**Fence Installation**

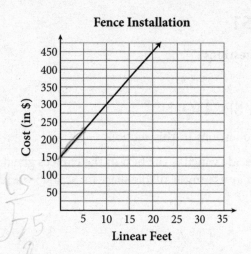

1. The graph shows the cost of installing a vinyl privacy fence. The company charges a flat installation fee plus a cost per linear foot of fencing. Based on the graph, how much does one linear foot of this particular vinyl fence cost?

   A)   $5

   B)   $15

   C)   $75

   D)   $150

$$\frac{24x^4 + 36x^3 - 12x^2}{12x^2}$$

2. Which of the following expressions is equivalent to the expression shown above?

   A)  $2x^2 + 3x$

   B)  $24x^4 + 36x^3$

   C)  $2x^2 + 3x - 1$

   D)  $24x^4 + 36x^3 - 1$

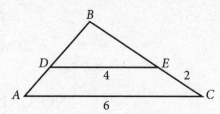

Note: Figure not drawn to scale.

3. In the figure shown, $\triangle ABC \sim \triangle DBE$. What is the length of $\overline{BE}$ ?

   A)   3.5

   B)   3.75

   C)   4

   D)   4.5

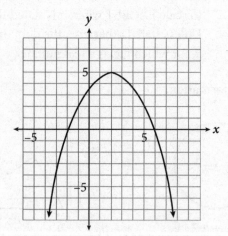

4. Which of the following represents the function shown?

   A)  $f(x) = -\frac{1}{3}(x-2)^2 + 5$

   B)  $f(x) = -\frac{1}{3}(x+2)^2 + 5$

   C)  $f(x) = \frac{1}{3}(x+2)^2 + 5$

   D)  $f(x) = 3(x-2)^2 + 5$

**GO ON TO THE NEXT PAGE**

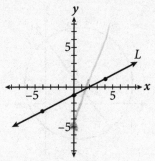

5. If line $L$ shown here is reflected over the $x$-axis, what is the slope of the new line?

A) $-2$

B) $-\dfrac{1}{2}$

C) $\dfrac{1}{2}$

D) $2$

6. If $p = 4x^3 + x - 2$, $q = x^2 - 1$, and $r = 3x - 5$, then what is $2p - (q + r)$ ?

A) $7x^3 - x + 2$

B) $8x^3 - x^2 - x + 2$

C) $8x^3 - x^2 - x - 10$

D) $8x^3 - x^2 + 5x - 8$

7. Which of the following are the roots of the equation $2x^2 + 4x - 3 = 0$ ?

A) $\dfrac{-2 \pm \sqrt{10}}{2}$

B) $-2 \pm \sqrt{5}$

C) $-1 \pm \sqrt{10}$

D) $-1 \pm 2\sqrt{10}$

8. If $g(x) = 3x - 5$ and $h(x) = \dfrac{7x + 10}{4}$, at what point does the graph of $g(x)$ intersect the graph of $h(x)$ ?

A) $(-2, -11)$

B) $(-2, 1)$

C) $(3, 4)$

D) $(6, 13)$

9. If $x = k^{-\frac{1}{3}}$, where $x > 0$ and $k > 0$, which of the following equations gives $k$ in terms of $x$ ?

A) $k = \dfrac{1}{x^3}$

B) $k = \dfrac{1}{\sqrt[3]{x}}$

C) $k = -\sqrt[3]{x}$

D) $k = -x^3$

$$4x - (10 - 2x) = c(3x - 5)$$

10. If the equation shown has infinitely many solutions, and $c$ is a constant, what is the value of $c$ ?

A) $-2$

B) $-\dfrac{2}{3}$

C) $\dfrac{2}{3}$

D) $2$

11. If $0 < 1 - \dfrac{a}{3} \le \dfrac{1}{2}$, which of the following is not a possible value of $a$ ?

A) $1.5$

B) $2$

C) $2.5$

D) $3$

GO ON TO THE NEXT PAGE

$$\begin{cases} y - \dfrac{2}{k}x \le 0 \\ \dfrac{1}{k}x - \dfrac{1}{2}y \le -1 \end{cases}$$

12. If the system of inequalities shown has no solution, what is the value of $k$ ?

A) 1

B) 2

C) There is no value of $k$ that results in no solution.

D) There are infinitely many values of $k$ that result in no solution.

$$\frac{4x}{x-7} + \frac{2x}{2x-14} = \frac{70}{2(x-7)}$$

13. What value(s) of $x$ satisfy the equation above?

A) 0

B) 7

C) No solution

D) Any value such that $x \ne 7$

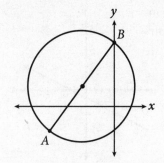

14. The circle shown is given by the equation $x^2 + y^2 + 6x - 4y = 12$. What is the shortest distance from $A$ to $B$ ?

A)    5

B)    10

C)  $4\sqrt{3}$

D)    24

15. If $g$ is a function defined over the set of all real numbers and $g(x-1) = 3x^2 + 5x - 7$, then which of the following defines $g(x)$ ?

A)  $g(x) = 3x^2 - x - 9$

B)  $g(x) = 3x^2 + 5x + 1$

C)  $g(x) = 3x^2 + 11x + 1$

D)  $g(x) = 3x^2 + 11x - 6$

GO ON TO THE NEXT PAGE

**Directions:** For questions 16-20, solve the problem and enter your answer in the grid, as described below, on the answer sheet.

1. Although not required, it is suggested that you write your answer in the boxes at the top of the columns to help you fill in the circles accurately. You will receive credit only if the circles are filled in correctly.

2. Mark no more than one circle in any column.

3. No question has a negative answer.

4. Some problems may have more than one correct answer. In such cases, grid only one answer.

5. **Mixed numbers** such as $3\frac{1}{2}$ must be gridded as 3.5 or $\frac{7}{2}$.

   (If $3\frac{1}{2}$ is entered into the grid as $\boxed{3\,|\,1\,|\,/\,|\,2}$, it will be interpreted as $\frac{31}{2}$, not $3\frac{1}{2}$.)

6. **Decimal answers:** If you obtain a decimal answer with more digits than the grid can accommodate, it may be either rounded or truncated, but it must fill the entire grid.

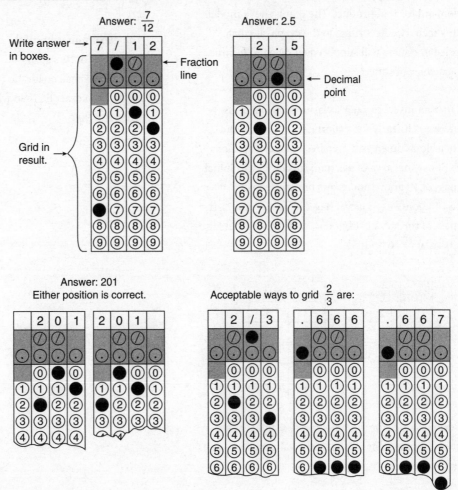

GO ON TO THE NEXT PAGE

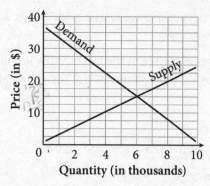

**Quantity (in thousands)**

16. Retail businesses strive to price their products so that they sell as many as possible without losing money. Economic equilibrium is the price point at which the supply for a product is equal to the demand for that product. The graph above models this scenario. According to the graph, at what price in dollars will supply equal demand for this particular product?

$15

17. Once an insect reaches its larval stage, its mass increases linearly for a short period of time and then slows down as it prepares to enter pupation. Suppose the larva of a certain species has an initial mass of 10 grams and grows linearly from $t = 0$ to $t = 48$ hours of its larval stage. If after 48 hours, the mass of the larva is 14 grams, what was its mass in grams at $t = 6$ hours ?

10.5

| $x$ | $f(x)$ |
|----|----|
| −1 | −2 |
| 0 | 0 |
| 1 | 2 |
| 2 | 4 |
| 3 | 6 |

| $x$ | $g(x)$ |
|----|----|
| −2 | 3 |
| −1 | 2 |
| 0 | 1 |
| 1 | −1 |
| 2 | −2 |

18. Several values for the functions $f(x)$ and $g(x)$ are shown in the tables. What is the value of $f(g(-1))$ ?

19. If $(4 + 3i)(1 - 2i) = a + bi$, then what is the value of $a$ ? (Note that $i = \sqrt{-1}$ .)

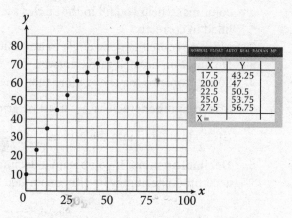

20. The maximum value of the data shown in the scatterplot occurs at $x = 56.25$. If the data is modeled using a quadratic regression and the model is an exact fit, then what is the $y$-value when $x = 90$ ?

# MATH TEST

**55 Minutes—38 Questions**

## CALCULATOR SECTION

Turn to Section 4 of your answer sheet to answer the questions in this section.

**Directions:** For this section, solve each problem and decide which is the best of the choices given. Fill in the corresponding oval on the answer sheet. You may use any available space for scratch work.

Notes:

1. Calculator use is permitted.
2. All numbers used are real numbers.
3. All figures used are necessary to solving the problems that they accompany. All figures are drawn to scale EXCEPT when it is stated that a specific figure is not drawn to scale.
4. Unless stated otherwise, the domain of any function $f$ is assumed to be the set of all real numbers $x$, for which $f(x)$ is a real number.

Information:

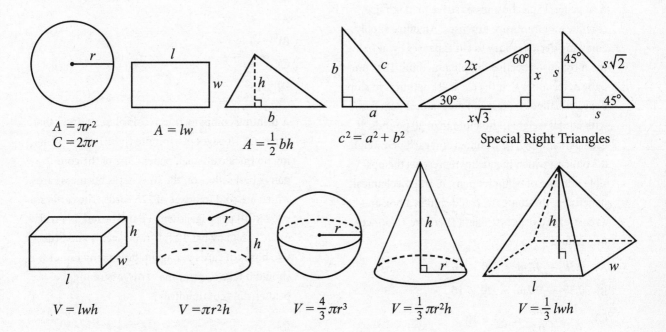

$A = \pi r^2$
$C = 2\pi r$

$A = lw$

$A = \frac{1}{2} bh$

$c^2 = a^2 + b^2$

Special Right Triangles

$V = lwh$

$V = \pi r^2 h$

$V = \frac{4}{3} \pi r^3$

$V = \frac{1}{3} \pi r^2 h$

$V = \frac{1}{3} lwh$

The sum of the degree measures of the angles in a triangle is 180.

The number of degrees of arc in a circle is 360.

The number of radians of arc in a circle is $2\pi$.

GO ON TO THE NEXT PAGE ⟹

1. The U.S. Centers for Disease Control recommends that adults engage in 2.5 hours per week of vigorous exercise. A local health society conducts a survey to see if people are meeting this goal. They ask 100 people with gym memberships how many minutes of exercise they engage in per week. After analyzing the data, the health society finds that the average respondent exercises 142 minutes per week, but the margin of error was approximately 36 minutes. The society wants to lower this margin of error. Using which of the following samples instead would do so?

   A) 50 people with gym memberships

   B) 50 people randomly selected from the entire adult population

   C) 100 people with gym memberships, but from a variety of gyms

   D) 200 people randomly selected from the entire adult population

2. As a general rule, businesses strive to maximize revenue and minimize expenses. An office supply company decides to try to cut expenses by utilizing the most cost-effective shipping method. The company determines that the cheapest option is to ship boxes of ballpoint pens and mechanical pencils with a total weight of no more than 20 pounds. If each pencil weighs 0.2 ounces and each pen weighs 0.3 ounces, which inequality represents the possible number of ballpoint pens, $b$, and mechanical pencils, $m$, the company could ship in a box and be as cost-effective as possible? (There are 16 ounces in 1 pound.)

   A) $0.3b + 0.2m < 20 \times 16$

   B) $0.3b + 0.2m \leq 20 \times 16$

   C) $\dfrac{b}{0.3} + \dfrac{m}{0.2} < 20 \times 16$

   D) $\dfrac{b}{0.3} + \dfrac{m}{0.2} \leq 20 \times 16$

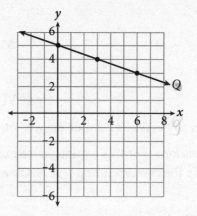

3. Where will line $Q$ shown in the graph intersect the $x$-axis?

   A) 13

   B) 14

   C) 15

   D) 16

4. The function $f(x)$ is defined as $f(x) = 2g(x)$, where $g(x) = x + 5$. What is the value of $f(3)$?

   A) $-4$

   B) 6

   C) 8

   D) 16

5. A printing company uses a color laser printer that can print 18 pages per minute (ppm) when printing on thick cardstock paper. One of the company's best sellers on the Internet is business cards, which are sold in boxes of 225 cards. The cards are printed 10 per page, then cut and boxed. If a real estate company has 12 full-time agents and orders two boxes of cards per agent, how many minutes should it take to print the cards, assuming the printer runs continuously?

   A) 15

   B) 20

   C) 30

   D) 45

GO ON TO THE NEXT PAGE ⟹

6.  If $0.002 \le x \le 0.2$ and $5 \le y \le 25$, what is the maximum value of $\dfrac{x}{y}$ ?

    A)  0.04

    B)  0.4

    C)  4

    D)  40

7.  Following a study of children in the United States under three years old, the American Academy of Pediatrics stated that there is a positive correlation between the amount of time spent watching television and the likelihood of developing an attention deficit disorder. Which of the following is an appropriate conclusion to draw from this statement?

    A)  There is an association between television time and attention disorders for American children under three years old.

    B)  There is an association between television time and attention disorders for all children under three years old.

    C)  An increase in attention disorders is caused by an increase in television time for American children under three years old.

    D)  An increase in attention disorders is caused by an increase in television time for all children under three years old.

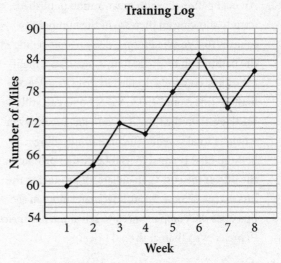

**Training Log**

8.  A bicyclist is training for the Liège-Bastogne-Liège, one of Europe's oldest road bicycle races. The line graph above shows the number of miles she biked each week for eight weeks. According to the graph, what was the greatest change (in absolute value) in the weekly number of miles she biked between two consecutive weeks?

    A)  7

    B)  8

    C)  9

    D)  10

9.  If a line that passes through the coordinates $(a - 1, 2a)$ and $(a, 6)$ has a slope of 5, what is the value of $a$ ?

    A)  $-2$

    B)  $-\dfrac{1}{2}$

    C)  $\dfrac{1}{2}$

    D)  2

10. An occupational health organization published a study showing an increase in the number of injuries that resulted from elderly people falling in the bathtub. In response to this increase, a medical supply company decided to drop its price on bathtub lifts from $450 to $375, hoping to still break even on the lifts. The company breaks even when its total revenue (income from selling $n$ bathtub lifts) is equal to its total cost of producing the lifts. If the cost $C$, in dollars, of producing the lifts is $C = 225n + 3{,}150$, how many more of the lifts does the company need to sell at the new price to break even than at the old price?

A)   7

B)   12

C)   14

D)   21

**Questions 11 and 12 refer to the following information.**

A zoo is building a penguin exhibit. It will consist of an underwater area and a land area. The land area is made of thick sheets of ice. An outline of the total space covered by the ice is shown below. A pipe 2 feet in diameter runs the full length of the exhibit under the ice. A substance known as ice-cold glycol continuously runs through the pipe to keep the ice frozen.

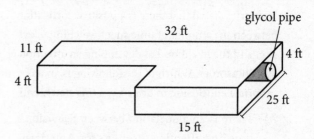

11. About how many cubic feet of water are needed to create the ice portion of the exhibit?

A)   1,850

B)   2,150

C)   2,450

D)   3,100

12. The zoo is planning to hire a company to fill the space with water. The company plans to use two 4-inch hoses that can each pump 60 gallons of water per minute. About how long should it take to fill the space? (There are 7.48 gallons of water in 1 cubic foot of ice.)

A)   1 hour

B)   1 hour, 30 minutes

C)   1 hour, 55 minutes

D)   2 hours, 15 minutes

GO ON TO THE NEXT PAGE ⟹

13. Which of the following quadratic equations has no solution?

    A) $0 = -2(x - 5)^2 + 3$

    B) $0 = -2(x - 5)(x + 3)$

    C) $0 = 2(x - 5)^2 + 3$

    D) $0 = 2(x + 5)(x + 3)$

/ **Questions 14 and 15 refer to the following information.**

Three airplanes depart from three different airports at 8:30 AM, all travelling to Chicago O'Hare International Airport (ORD). The distances the planes must travel are recorded in the following table.

| From | Distance to Chicago (ORD) |
| --- | --- |
| Kansas City (MCI) | 402 |
| Boston (BOS) | 864 |
| Miami (MIA) | 1,200 |

14. The plane traveling from Boston traveled at an average speed of 360 mph. The plane traveling from Kansas City arrived at 10:34 AM. How many minutes before the plane from Boston arrived did the plane from Kansas City arrive?

    A) 20

    B) 28

    C) 42

    D) 144

15. For the first $\frac{1}{4}$ of the trip, the plane from Miami flew through heavy winds and dense cloud cover at an average speed of 200 mph. For the remaining portion of the trip, the weather was ideal, and the plane flew at an average speed of 450 mph. Due to a backlog of planes at ORD, it was forced to circle overhead in a holding pattern for 25 minutes before landing. At what time did the plane from Miami land in Chicago?

    A) 12:00 PM

    B) 12:25 PM

    C) 12:50 PM

    D) 1:15 PM

16. If $h(t) = \sqrt{t^2 + 9}$ for all real values of $t$, which of the following is not in the range of $h(t)$?

    A) 1

    B) 3

    C) 9

    D) 10

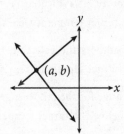

17. If $(a, b)$ represents the solution to the system of equations shown in the graph and $a = -3b$, then which of the following could be the value of $a + b$?

    A) −9

    B) 0

    C) 3

    D) 6

GO ON TO THE NEXT PAGE ▷

**Thermostat A**

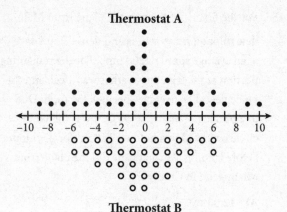

**Thermostat B**

18. A car manufacturer tested two types of thermostats to determine which one it wanted to use in a new model of car. The more consistently the thermostat engages the engine's cooling fan, the better the cooling system performs over the long run. The double dot plot above shows the test results, given the following conditions:

- Zero indicates that the cooling fan engaged at exactly the temperature at which the thermostat was set (the target temperature).

- Negative numbers indicate that the fan engaged below the target temperature.

- Positive numbers indicate that the fan engaged above the target temperature.

- The safe range for the fan to engage is 10 degrees above or below the target temperature.

Which of the following best states which thermostat the car manufacturer is likely to choose and why?

A) Thermostat A because the median of the data is 0, and the range is greater than that of Thermostat B

B) Thermostat B because the median of the data is 0, and the range is less than that of Thermostat A

C) Thermostat A because the mode of the data is 0, which indicates a more consistent thermostat

D) Thermostat B because the data is bimodal (has two modes), which indicates a more consistent thermostat

19. If $p$ and $q$ represent the zeros of a quadratic function and $p + q = -3$, which of the following could be the factored form of the function?

A) $f(x) = (x - 3)(x + 3)$

B) $f(x) = (x - 4)(x + 1)$

C) $f(x) = (x - 1)(x + 4)$

D) $f(x) = (x - 6)(x + 3)$

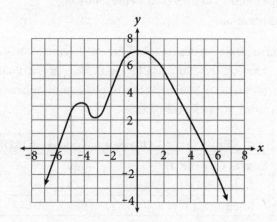

20. The figure above shows the graph of $p(x) - 4$. What is the value of $p(0)$ ?

A) 3

B) 4

C) 7

D) 11

GO ON TO THE NEXT PAGE

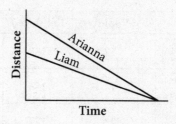

**Time**

21. Geraldine is making a simple AC electric generator for a science project using copper wire, cardboard, a nail, and magnets. The first step in building the generator is wrapping the wire around and around a rectangular prism made from the cardboard and connecting it to a small lightbulb, as shown in the figure. If Geraldine has 18 feet of wire and needs to leave 3 inches on each end to connect to the lightbulb, how many times can she wrap the wire around the cardboard prism?

A) 21
B) 28
C) 35
D) 42

**Organic Vegetable Harvest**

22. The bar graph above shows the vegetable harvest, in tons, at an organic produce farm during July and August. Of the following, which best approximates the percent increase in the harvest of squash at this farm from July to August?

A) 67%
B) 60%
C) 53%
D) 40%

23. Arianna and her brother Liam both walk home from school each day, but they go to different schools. The figure shows their trip home on Monday. Based on the graph, which of the following statements is true?

A) It took Liam longer to walk home because his school is farther away.

B) It took Arianna longer to walk home because her school is farther away.

C) Arianna and Liam walked home at the same rate.

D) Arianna walked home at a faster rate than Liam.

24. If line $L$ passes through the points $(-4, -8)$ and $(8, 1)$, which of the following points does line $L$ not pass through?

A) $(0, -5)$
B) $(4, -1)$
C) $(12, 4)$
D) $(16, 7)$

GO ON TO THE NEXT PAGE

| | Unemployed | Employed | Totals |
|---|---|---|---|
| **Female Degree** | 12 | 188 | 200 |
| **Female No Degree** | 44 | 156 | 200 |
| **Male Degree** | 23 | 177 | 200 |
| **Male No Degree** | 41 | 159 | 200 |
| **Totals** | 120 | 680 | 800 |

25. The table above shows the results of a sociological study identifying the number of males and females with and without college degrees who were unemployed or employed at the time of the study. If one person from the study is chosen at random, what is the probability that that person is an employed person with a college degree?

A) $\dfrac{73}{160}$

B) $\dfrac{10}{17}$

C) $\dfrac{17}{20}$

D) $\dfrac{73}{80}$

**Infected Patient**

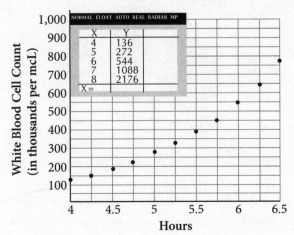

26. Typically, when people contract an infectious disease, their immune system immediately begins to produce extra white blood cells to fight the disease. The scatterplot shows the white blood cells reproducing in an infected patient, along with several values found when modeling the data using a graphing calculator. According to this model, how many white blood cells per microliter of blood did the patient have before he contracted the disease?

A) 3,400

B) 8,500

C) 10,000

D) 13,600

GO ON TO THE NEXT PAGE

27. A rodeo is building a circular arena. The arena will have a total area of $64\pi$ square yards and can either be left open for rodeo competitions or divided into 12 equal sections through the center for auctions. When holding auctions, the rodeo has an average of 4 bulls and 8 horses for sale. A bull cannot be placed in a section directly beside another section containing a bull, and all edges of these sections must be reinforced with strong steel to keep the bulls from getting out. Which of the following represents how much steel in yards the rodeo will need to reinforce the four bull sections?

A)  $32\pi$

B)  $64\pi$

C)  $32 + \dfrac{16\pi}{3}$

D)  $64 + \dfrac{16\pi}{3}$

28. Lena bought a saltwater fish tank that holds 400 gallons of water. She started filling the tank on Friday, but then stopped after putting only 70 gallons of water in the tank. On Saturday, she bought a bigger hose and began filling the tank again. It took her 1 hour and 50 minutes on Saturday to completely fill the tank. Which equation represents the number of gallons of water in the fish tank on Saturday, given the amount of time in minutes that Lena spent filling the tank?

A)  $y = 3x + 70$

B)  $y = 3x + 330$

C)  $y = 70x + 330$

D)  $y = 110x + 70$

29. A self-storage company has three sizes of storage units. The ratio of small to medium units is 3:5. The ratio of medium to large units is 3:2. The company analyzes its business model and current consumer demand and determines that it can benefit from utilizing larger economies of scale. In other words, it decides to grow its business based on current economic conditions and plans to build a second, larger self-storage building. The company's research indicates that the new market would benefit from having only two sizes of storage units, small and large, in the same ratio as its current facility. What ratio of small to large units should it use?

A)  1:1

B)  3:2

C)  5:3

D)  9:10

$$\frac{1}{x} + \frac{3}{x} = \frac{1}{7}$$

30. The equation shown above represents the following scenario: A chemical laboratory uses two air purifiers to clean the air of contaminants emitted while working with hazardous materials. One is an older model, and the other is a new model that is considerably more energy efficient. The new model can clean the air of contaminants three times as quickly as the older model. Working together, the two air purifiers can clean the air in the lab in 7 hours. Which of the following describes what the term $\dfrac{1}{x}$ in the equation represents?

A)  The portion of the air the older model can clean in 1 hour

B)  The portion of the air the new model can clean in 1 hour

C)  The time it takes the older model to clean the air by itself

D)  The time it takes the older model to clean $\dfrac{1}{7}$ of the air by itself

**GO ON TO THE NEXT PAGE** ⇒

**Directions:** For questions 31-38, solve the problem and enter your answer in the grid, as described below, on the answer sheet.

1.  Although not required, it is suggested that you write your answer in the boxes at the top of the columns to help you fill in the circles accurately. You will receive credit only if the circles are filled in correctly.

2.  Mark no more than one circle in any column.

3.  No question has a negative answer.

4.  Some problems may have more than one correct answer. In such cases, grid only one answer.

5.  **Mixed numbers** such as $3\frac{1}{2}$ must be gridded as 3.5 or $\frac{7}{2}$.

    (If $3\frac{1}{2}$ is entered into the grid as $\boxed{3\ 1\ /\ 2}$, it will be interpreted as $\frac{31}{2}$, not $3\frac{1}{2}$.)

6.  **Decimal answers:** If you obtain a decimal answer with more digits than the grid can accommodate, it may be either rounded or truncated, but it must fill the entire grid.

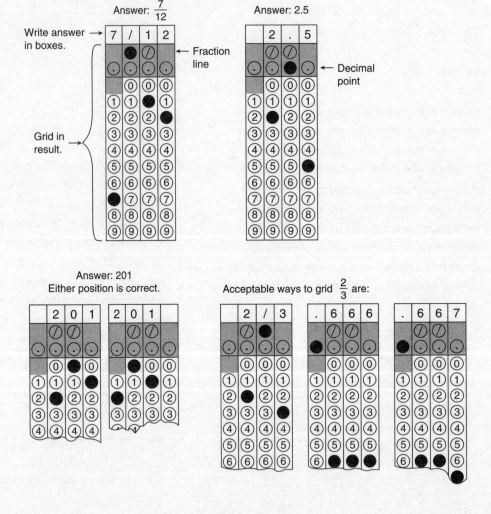

$$\frac{1}{3}(90x - 12) = \frac{1}{2}(8x + 10)$$

30x - 4 = 4x + 5

**31.** What is the solution to the equation shown?

24 x = 9    3/8

**32.** If $n^{\frac{5}{2}} = 32$, what is the value of $n$ ?

**33.** When a thrift store gets used furniture in good condition to sell, it researches the original price and then marks the used piece down by 40% of that price. On the first day of each of the following months, the price is marked down an additional 15% until it is sold or it reaches 30% of its original price. Suppose the store gets a piece of used furniture on January 15th. If the piece of furniture costs $1,848 new, and it is sold on March 10th of the same year, what is the final selling price, not including tax? Round your answer to the nearest whole dollar.

942

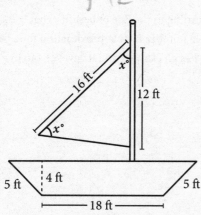

Note: Figure not drawn to scale.

**34.** Many sailboat manufacturers sell kits that include instructions and all the materials needed to build a simple sailboat. The figure shows the finished dimensions of a sailboat from such a kit. The instructions indicate that $\cos x° = b$, but do not give the value of $b$. What is the value of $b$ ?

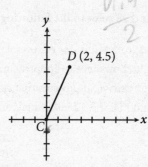

**35.** In the figure shown, line $B$ (not shown) is parallel to $\overline{CD}$ and passes through the point $(0, -1)$. If line $B$ also passes through the point $(2, y)$, what is the value of $y$ ?

3.5

**36.** Recycling of certain metals has been a common practice dating back to preindustrial times. For example, there is evidence of scrap bronze and silver being collected and melted down for reuse in a number of European countries. Today, there are recycling companies and even curbside collection bins for recycling. As a general rule, recycling companies pay for metals by weight. Suppose a person brings in 3 pounds of copper and receives $8.64, and 24 ounces of nickel and receives $10.08. If another person brings in equal weights of copper and nickel, what fractional portion of the money would he receive from the copper? (There are 16 ounces in 1 pound.)

**Questions 37 and 38 refer to the following information.**

Body mass index, or BMI, is one of several measures used by doctors to determine a person's health as indicated by weight and height. Low-density lipoprotein, or LDL cholesterol, known as the "bad" cholesterol, is another health indicator and consists of fat proteins that clog arteries. Following are the results of a study showing the relationship between BMI and LDL for 12 individuals and the line of best fit for the data.

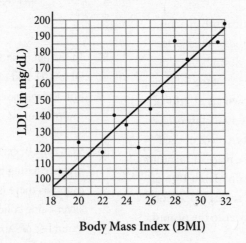

37. How many of the 12 people have an actual LDL that differs by 10 or more mg/dL from the LDL predicted by the line of best fit?

38. According to the line of best fit, what is the closest whole number BMI approximation for a person that has an estimated LDL level of 140 mg/dL ?

# ESSAY TEST

### 50 Minutes

The essay gives you an opportunity to show how effectively you can read and comprehend a passage and write an essay analyzing the passage. In your essay, you should demonstrate that you have read the passage carefully, present a clear and logical analysis, and use language precisely.

Your essay must be written on the lines provided in your answer booklet; except for the planning page of the answer booklet, you will receive no other paper on which to write. You will have enough space if you write on every line, avoid wide margins, and keep your handwriting to a reasonable size. Remember that people who are not familiar with your handwriting will read what you write. Try to write or print so that what you are writing is legible to those readers.

You have 50 minutes to read the passage and write an essay in response to the prompt provided inside this booklet.

1.   Do not write your essay in this booklet. Only what you write on the lined pages of your answer booklet will be evaluated.

2.   An off-topic essay will not be evaluated.

---

As you read the passage below, consider how the author uses

- evidence, such as facts or examples, to support claims.

- reasoning to develop ideas and to connect claims and evidence.

- stylistic or persuasive elements, such as word choice or appeals to emotion, to add power to the ideas expressed.

---

**This passage deals with the issue of compensation for college athletes.**

1    In the world of college sports, there is growing debate about whether student athletes should be awarded monetary compensation for their contribution to teams that garner millions of dollars for universities. Presently, the National Collegiate Athletics Association (NCAA), the governing body of college sports, doesn't allow it. Some hold this law as sacrosanct, saying it keeps college sports from becoming commercial and corrupting the experience of student athletes, who are in school, after all, for an education. But the reality is that we are past that point: college sports are big business, and the system that caps student salaries at zero is tantamount to wage fixing and collusion. If such practices happened in the investment market, universities would be fined by the FTC. In a labor market, they'd be shut down. Student athletes are being defrauded and taken advantage of.

2    So how much money is at stake? Basketball and football are the two main sports in question. Every year, the month of March becomes synonymous with a weeks-long basketball bracket that winnows down 64 teams to the single best. In football, a season of stadium-filling regular season games culminates in half a dozen lucrative "bowl games" sponsored by some of the biggest corporations in the world: FedEx, AT&T, and Mobil Oil.

3    For television networks, advertisers, universities, and local businesses where the events are held, these games are every bit as big as the NFL's Super Bowl and the NBA playoffs. In 2011, ESPN and Fox signed television rights deals worth $3 billion to the Pacific-12 conference. *Forbes* magazine reported that CBS and Turner Broadcasting

GO ON TO THE NEXT PAGE

make more than one billion dollars off the March Madness broadcasts, "thanks in part to a $700,000 advertising rate for a 30-second spot during the Final Four." One study put the value of a Texas A&M home game at $86 million for businesses in Brazos County, where A&M is located.

4    The dollar figures are indeed vast, and universities get their share. Here are two examples from schools with top football teams. According to the most recent federal data, the University of Texas football team netted a profit of $77.9 million in 2011-2012. Michigan made $61.6 million from football and $85.2 million in revenue.

5    Coaches, too, are a big part of the equation. Average salaries for major college football coaches have jumped more than 70 percent since 2006, to $1.64 million, according to *USA Today*. Nick Saban, head coach for Alabama, makes $7.3 million a year.

6    And yet, players take home no money. None. How can this be? Because, like unscrupulous tycoons from a Dickens novel, college presidents, athletic directors, and conference commissioners set their players' wages as low as they can get them—zero.

7    According to a recent study, if college football operated under the same revenue-sharing model as the NFL, each player on the Texas A&M squad would see a paycheck of about $225,000 per year.

8    All this talk of money might have you thinking that we should go back to square one and take the money out of college sports. But money is in college sports' DNA. It was conceived that way. It all grew out of the Morrill Land-Grant College Act of 1862. "As large public institutions spread into sparsely populated states, the competition for students grew fierce," says Allen Sack, a business professor at the University of New Haven. Football happened to be invented around that time, and schools took it up as a tool to draw students, and spectators, to campuses. The 1894 Harvard-Yale football game, for example, generated $119,000, according to the *New York Times*. That's nearly $3 million in today's dollars.

9    The historic justification for not paying players is that they are amateur student-athletes, and the value of their scholarships is payment enough. But the NCAA's own study shows that its scholarship limit leaves so-called "full" scholarship athletes with $3,000 to $5,000 in out-of-pocket expenses each year. The average shortfall is $3,200. Furthermore, most scholarships are revocable, so if an athlete doesn't perform well on the field, or is injured, he can, in a sense, lose that compensation. A student athlete devotes 40 hours a week on average towards sport; that's equivalent to a full-time job. Zero pay and immediate termination with no recourse? Those are labor conditions that any sensible workforce would unionize to change. But students are powerless to change. They are up against the NCAA, the Big 10 commission, university boards, and the almighty corporate dollar. Someone needs to become their advocate and get student athletes the compensation they deserve.

---

Write an essay in which you explain how the author builds an argument to persuade his audience that student athletes deserve fair compensation. In your essay, analyze how the author uses one or more of the features listed in the box that precedes the passage (or features of your own choice) to strengthen the logic and persuasiveness of his argument. Be sure that your analysis focuses on the most relevant features of the passage.

Your essay should not explain whether you agree with the author's claims, but rather explain how the author builds an argument to persuade his audience.

# SAT®
## Practice Test 2

# READING TEST

## 65 Minutes—52 Questions

Turn to Section 1 of your answer sheet to answer the questions in this section.

Each passage or pair of passages below is followed by a number of questions. After reading each passage or pair, choose the best answer to each question based on what is stated or implied in the passage or passages and in any accompanying graphics (such as a table or graph).

**Questions 1-10 are based on the following passage.**

The following passage is adapted from the nineteenth-century novel *Three Men in a Boat*. In this scene, George, William Samuel, Harris, Jerome, and a dog named Montmorency take a typical boating holiday of the time on a Thames River camping skiff. Jerome, the narrator, shares the story of how the journey with his friends began.

George had towed us up to Staines, and we had taken the boat from there, and it seemed that we were dragging fifty tons after us, and were walking
Line forty miles. It was half-past seven when we were
(5) through, and we all got in, and sculled up close to the left bank, looking out for a spot to haul up in.

We had originally intended to go on to Magna Carta Island, a sweetly pretty part of the river, where it winds through a soft, green valley, and to
(10) camp in one of the many picturesque inlets to be found round that tiny shore. But, somehow, we did not feel that we yearned for the picturesque nearly so much now as we had earlier in the day. A bit of water between a coal-barge and a gas-works would
(15) have quite satisfied us for that night. We did not want scenery. We wanted to have our supper and go to bed. However, we did pull up to the point—"Picnic Point," it is called—and dropped into a very pleasant nook under a great elm-tree, to the
(20) spreading roots of which we fastened the boat.

Then we thought we were going to have supper (we had dispensed with tea, so as to save time), but George said no; that we had better get the canvas up first, before it got quite dark, and while we could

(25) see what we were doing. Then, he said, all our work would be done, and we could sit down to eat with an easy mind.

That canvas wanted more putting up than I think any of us had bargained for. It looked so
(30) simple in the abstract. You took five iron arches, like gigantic croquet hoops, and fitted them up over the boat, and then stretched the canvas over them, and fastened it down: it would take quite ten minutes, we thought.

(35) That was an under-estimate.

We took up the hoops, and began to drop them into the sockets placed for them. You would not imagine this to be dangerous work; but, looking back now, the wonder to me is that any of us are
(40) alive to tell the tale. They were not hoops, they were demons. First they would not fit into their sockets at all, and we had to jump on them, and kick them, and hammer at them with the boat-hook; and, when they were in, it turned out that they were the
(45) wrong hoops for those particular sockets, and they had to come out again.

But they would not come out, until two of us had gone and struggled with them for five minutes, when they would jump up suddenly, and try and
(50) throw us into the water and drown us. They had hinges in the middle, and, when we were not look-ing, they nipped us with these hinges in delicate parts of the body; and, while we were wrestling with one side of the hoop, and endeavouring to
(55) persuade it to do its duty, the other side would come behind us in a cowardly manner, and hit us over the head.

GO ON TO THE NEXT PAGE

We got them fixed at last, and then all that was to be done was to arrange the covering over them.
(60) George unrolled it, and fastened one end over the nose of the boat. Harris stood in the middle to take it from George and roll it on to me, and I kept by the stern to receive it. It was a long time coming down to me. George did his part all right, but it was
(65) new work to Harris, and he bungled it.

How he managed it I do not know, he could not explain himself; but by some mysterious process or other he succeeded, after ten minutes of superhuman effort, in getting himself completely rolled up
(70) in it. He was so firmly wrapped round and tucked in and folded over, that he could not get out. He, of course, made frantic struggles for freedom . . . and, in doing so, knocked over George. . . .

1. According to the passage, the men change their minds about their destination because

   A) the weather is turning bad.

   B) they fear the location will be too crowded.

   C) they have lost interest in scenery.

   D) the supplies are running low.

2. As used in line 22, "dispensed with" most nearly means

   A) administered.

   B) distributed.

   C) served.

   D) skipped.

3. Based on paragraphs 1-3, it can reasonably be inferred that the men are

   A) thirsty and sore.

   B) tired and hungry.

   C) panicked and frantic.

   D) curious and content.

4. Which choice provides the best evidence for the answer to the previous question?

   A) Lines 1-4 ("George had . . . forty miles")

   B) Lines 13-15 ("A bit of water . . . for that night")

   C) Lines 16-17 ("We wanted . . . to bed")

   D) Lines 25-27 ("Then, he said, . . . easy mind")

5. What theme does the passage communicate through the experiences of its characters?

   A) It is important to plan in advance.

   B) Conflicts among friends should be avoided.

   C) False confidence can lead to difficulties.

   D) Every group benefits from a leader.

6. Based on information in the passage, it can reasonably be inferred that

   A) none of the men were experienced camper-boaters.

   B) the majority of the men were experienced camper-boaters.

   C) the narrator is the only one with camping-boating experience.

   D) George is the only one with camping-boating experience.

7. Which choice provides the best evidence for the answer to the previous question?

   A) Lines 23-25 ("we had better . . . doing")

   B) Lines 28-29 ("That canvas . . . bargained for")

   C) Lines 58-59 ("We got . . . over them")

   D) Lines 70-71 ("He was so . . . get out")

8. As used in line 30, "in the abstract" most nearly means

   A) in summary.

   B) in the directions.

   C) in the ideal.

   D) in theory.

**GO ON TO THE NEXT PAGE**

9. The author's main purpose of including the description of the hoops in paragraph 7 is to

A) convey anger through the use of hyperbole.

B) convey humor through the use of personification.

C) convey severity through the use of understatement.

D) convey confidence through the use of active verbs.

10. The tone of the passage is primarily one of

A) fear and panic.

B) comic reflection.

C) arrogant frustration.

D) mockery and disgust.

**Questions 11-20 are based on the following passage.**

The following passage is adapted from President John F. Kennedy's 1962 speech, which has come to be called "We Choose to Go to the Moon." Kennedy delivered the speech at Rice University in Texas.

We meet at a college noted for knowledge, in a city noted for progress, in a State noted for strength, and we stand in need of all three, for we
Line meet in an hour of change and challenge, in a dec-
(5) ade of hope and fear, in an age of both knowledge and ignorance. The greater our knowledge increases, the greater our ignorance unfolds. . . .

No man can fully grasp how far and how fast we have come, but condense, if you will, the 50,000
(10) years of man's recorded history in a time span of but a half-century. Stated in these terms, we know very little about the first forty years, except at the end of them advanced man had learned to use the skins of animals to cover them. Then about ten
(15) years ago, under this standard, man emerged from his caves to construct other kinds of shelter. Only five years ago man learned to write and use a cart with wheels. Christianity began less than two years ago. The printing press came this year, and then less
(20) than two months ago, during this whole fifty-year

span of human history, the steam engine provided a new source of power.

Newton explored the meaning of gravity. Last month electric lights and telephones and auto-
(25) mobiles and airplanes became available. Only last week did we develop penicillin and television and nuclear power, and now if America's new spacecraft succeeds in reaching Venus, we will have literally reached the stars before midnight tonight.

(30) This is a breathtaking pace, and such a pace cannot help but create new ills as it dispels old, new ignorance, new problems, new dangers. Surely the opening vistas of space promise high costs and hardships, as well as high reward.

(35) So it is not surprising that some would have us stay where we are a little longer to rest, to wait. But this city of Houston, this State of Texas, this country of the United States was not built by those who waited and rested and wished to look behind them.
(40) This country was conquered by those who moved forward—and so will space.

William Bradford, speaking in 1630 of the founding of the Plymouth Bay Colony, said that all great and honorable actions are accompanied with
(45) great difficulties, and both must be enterprised and overcome with answerable courage.

If this capsule history of our progress teaches us anything, it is that man, in his quest for knowledge and progress, is determined and cannot be
(50) deterred. The exploration of space will go ahead, whether we join in it or not, and it is one of the great adventures of all time. . . .

This generation does not intend to founder in the backwash of the coming age of space. We mean
(55) to be a part of it—we mean to lead it. For the eyes of the world now look into space, to the moon and to the planets beyond, and we have vowed that we shall not see it governed by a hostile flag of conquest, but by a banner of freedom and peace. We
(60) have vowed that we shall not see space filled with weapons of mass destruction, but with instruments of knowledge and understanding.

Yet the vows of this nation can only be fulfilled if we in this nation are first. . . . In short, our leader-

**GO ON TO THE NEXT PAGE**

(65) ship in science and in industry, our hopes for peace and security, our obligations to ourselves as well as others, all require us to make this effort . . . to become the world's leading space-faring nation.

(70) We set sail on this new sea because there is new knowledge to be gained, and new rights to be won, and they must be won and used for the progress of all people . . . .

There is no strife, no prejudice, no national conflict in outer space as yet. Its hazards are hostile to us (75) all. Its conquest deserves the best of all mankind, and its opportunity for peaceful cooperation may never come again. But why, some say, the moon? Why choose this as our goal? And they may well ask why climb the highest mountain? Why, thirty-five years (80) ago, fly the Atlantic? Why does Rice play Texas?[1]

We choose to go to the moon. We choose to go to the moon in this decade and do the other things, not because they are easy, but because they are hard, because that goal will serve to organize and (85) measure the best of our energies and skills. . . .

[1]This is a college sports reference. Kennedy's audience (at Rice University) would have understood the University of Texas at Austin to be the challenging athletic opponent of Rice.

11. Which statement best describes Kennedy's purpose for giving this speech?

A) To present a chronology of human achievements

B) To explain the threat that other countries pose to the United States

C) To encourage students to support the United States in the race to reach the moon

D) To promote increased funding for NASA and space exploration

12. Which choice provides the best evidence for the answer to the previous question?

A) Lines 8-11 ("No man . . . half-century")

B) Lines 47-50 ("If this . . . deterred")

C) Lines 50-52 ("The exploration . . . all time")

D) Lines 81-85 ("We choose . . . skills")

13. As used in line 45, "enterprised" most nearly means

A) undertaken.

B) funded.

C) promoted.

D) determined.

14. What does Kennedy suggest about the motivations of other countries attempting to reach the moon?

A) They wish to embarrass the United States by reaching the moon first.

B) They are trying to advance technology for the good of humanity.

C) They want to use the moon for hostile military actions.

D) They lack the scientific knowledge to accomplish their goals.

15. Which choice provides the best evidence for the answer to the previous question?

A) Lines 25-29 ("Only last . . . tonight")

B) Lines 30-32 ("This is . . . new dangers")

C) Lines 59-62 ("We have . . . understanding")

D) Lines 69-72 ("We set . . . all people")

16. As used in line 53, "founder" most nearly means

A) begin.

B) innovate.

C) dissolve.

D) sink.

17. According to the passage, what does Kennedy say is true of progress?

A) It creates new problems as it solves old ones.

B) It was minimal until the invention of written language.

C) It must be accomplished cooperatively with other countries.

D) It leads to an increase in global hostilities.

GO ON TO THE NEXT PAGE

18. The statement in lines 64-68 ("In short, . . . space-faring nation") supports the overall argument of the passage in its suggestion that

    A) the monetary rewards for space exploration are too great to pass up.

    B) the U.S. military will never use space for strategic operations.

    C) the United States is better equipped than other nations to ensure that space remains a peaceful frontier.

    D) the space race is an opportunity to solidify the position of the United States as a military superpower.

19. Based on the information in the passage, to what group can Kennedy's audience best be compared?

    A) Soldiers who were drafted for service and bravely served their country

    B) Farmers who have worked in the field for months and now see their harvest

    C) Students who are studying and preparing for graduation

    D) Pioneers who are about to embark on a difficult but important journey

20. Kennedy's main purpose of including paragraphs 2 and 3 was to

    A) persuade the audience to fund the race to the moon.

    B) frame space exploration as a logical next step in human progress.

    C) warn of the potential hazards of technological advances.

    D) encourage audience members to be leaders of their generation.

**Questions 21-31 are based on the following passages and supplementary material.**

The following passages discuss the success of the Vikings, skilled sailors from modern Scandinavia who traveled throughout northern and central Europe in the 8th to 11th centuries.

**Passage 1**

At the end of the eighth century, the Scandinavians known as the Vikings took to the seas, traveling to areas including Iceland, Greenland, England,
*Line* Ireland, France, and Russia, and even reaching the
(5) shores of America some 500 years before Columbus. The Vikings' innovations in shipbuilding were central to constructing their empire. They relied on the superior ships conjured in the minds of master shipwrights for travel and exploration. Us-
(10) ing vessels such as the longboat, these fascinating seafarers opened up new foreign connections. The great longboat itself attests to their outstanding maritime skills.

Viking travel was a mystery before archaeolo-
(15) gists discovered ships buried in the muck of Danish fjords, but now ship reconstruction has provided some answers. Viking ships were designed and built with uncommon ingenuity to serve the Vikings' purposes. The secret of the signature
(20) Viking ship is found in its unique construction. The invention of the longboat meant Vikings could travel vast distances over treacherous open water. In contrast to modern sailboats, the longboat was riveted together with enough spacing so that the
(25) boat was flexible. It could bend as it rode over waves instead of taking the full impact of a swell. Incredibly, simple tools such as axes, hammers, and scrapers were all that carpenters used to frame a ship.

Additionally, the sleek longboat was an exceed-
(30) ingly streamlined vessel. One kind of longboat could ride high by skimming the waves to swiftly transport a crew of about 30. This fast ship had a draft of as little as 20 inches, allowing navigation in extremely shallow water.

(35) While its shallow draft and ease of construction made the Viking longboat a superior seafaring vessel, the seamanship of the Norsemen was the most decisive factor in the success of their boats. For

GO ON TO THE NEXT PAGE ▷

example, Vikings navigated by looking at the sky
(40) through a crystal, which was known as a sunstone.
The composition of the crystal was recently identified as a transparent calcite common in Iceland.

The Vikings' outstanding talents in ship
construction, coupled with their superlative skills
(45) as navigators, greatly impacted Scandinavia. In
turn, through their explorations, the Vikings
influenced the rest of the world.

**Passage 2**

The Gokstad ship was excavated in 1880 and
dates to around AD 890; discovery of this Viking
(50) ship revealed innovations in construction. Aptly
named "longboats," such ships were long and narrow and could travel on the open sea as well as
along rivers. The Gokstad ship is considered the
best preserved of the Viking longboats. It reveals
(55) the technical achievements of the Vikings because
the shape was different from the norm.

The Gokstad ship owes nothing to earlier boat
designs, including those of the Egyptians and
Romans. The longboat was developed specifically
(60) for Arctic waters. Its shallow draft, plus its ability to
change direction quickly, was a tremendous asset to
the Vikings. The Gokstad ship is 78 feet long with
two high, pointed ends. Constructed out of sturdy
oak, it features a low freeboard[1] and is therefore
(65) fast, the kind of ship used to carry Vikings on raids
across the North Sea.

The ship has been restored to reveal the
Gokstad's original shape. With holes for 16 oars
along each side of the ship, the crew would have
(70) numbered about 34, counting 32 oarsmen plus a
steerman and lookout. Oars were typically 17 to
19 feet long, constructed of pine with a narrow
blade that made each oar both efficient and light-
weight. In addition, the Gokstad features a mast
(75) near the center that carried a large rectangular sail.

The Gokstad is different from earlier boat
designs in its planking, or framing out, as well; its
carvel planking made the ship watertight. Carvel
planking involves attaching wooden planks to a
(80) frame and having the planks butt up edge to edge,
providing support from the frame and forming a
smooth surface.

Contrary to popular belief, the Vikings were not
just warriors; they were also coastal farmers, fish-
(85) ers, hunters, and craftsmen. Their lands were harsh,
however, and increases in their population forced
some men to search for other opportunities. Vikings,
therefore, turned to trade and sea raiding. Their swift
sailing ships, already perfect for coastal fishing, ena-
(90) bled Vikings to attack ports and towns, making these
seamen effective as both raiders and traders.

Truly, the Gokstad ship is representative of a
great leap in seafaring, for this finest expression of
technical achievement could serve many purposes.
(95) In 1982, its swiftness and seaworthiness was proven
when a copy, the *Hjemkomst,* journeyed from the
United States to Norway.

[1]freeboard: the distance between the level of the water and the
upper edge of the side of a boat

### Partial Timeline of Viking History

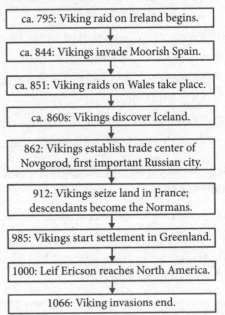

| ca. 795: Viking raid on Ireland begins. |
| ca. 844: Vikings invade Moorish Spain. |
| ca. 851: Viking raids on Wales take place. |
| ca. 860s: Vikings discover Iceland. |
| 862: Vikings establish trade center of Novgorod, first important Russian city. |
| 912: Vikings seize land in France; descendants become the Normans. |
| 985: Vikings start settlement in Greenland. |
| 1000: Leif Ericson reaches North America. |
| 1066: Viking invasions end. |

GO ON TO THE NEXT PAGE ⟶

21. The central idea of Passage 1 is that Vikings

    A) excelled at shipbuilding and navigation.

    B) had a passion for global exploration.

    C) helped map the known world of their time.

    D) led European peoples in technological innovation.

22. The first paragraph of Passage 1 most strongly suggests that which of the following is true?

    A) The Vikings depended on sea trade and fishing to survive.

    B) The Vikings expanded cultural interactions through seafaring.

    C) The Vikings relied on colonization to support a growing population.

    D) The Vikings sustained their economic development through sea raids.

23. Which choice provides the best evidence for the answer to the previous question?

    A) Lines 1-2 ("At the end . . . to the seas")

    B) Lines 7-9 ("They relied . . . exploration")

    C) Lines 9-11 ("Using vessels . . . connections")

    D) Lines 11-13 ("The great longboat . . . skills")

24. As used in line 30, "streamlined" most nearly means

    A) contoured.

    B) efficient.

    C) simplistic.

    D) slight.

25. The author of Passage 2 most likely chose to write about the Gokstad ship because it

    A) contradicts prevailing beliefs about modern shipbuilding.

    B) gives insight into various seafaring economic activities.

    C) stands out as a unique example of early shipbuilding.

    D) was a recent maritime archaeological discovery.

26. Passage 2 most strongly suggests that the Vikings

    A) adapted to their geography by moving often.

    B) became seafarers to spread their civilization.

    C) learned shipbuilding from other peoples.

    D) used raiding as a means of livelihood.

27. Which choice provides the best evidence for the answer to the previous question?

    A) Lines 57-59 ("The Gokstad . . . Romans")

    B) Lines 83-85 ("Contrary to . . . craftsmen")

    C) Lines 85-87 ("Their lands . . . opportunities")

    D) Lines 95-97 ("In 1982 . . . Norway")

28. As used in line 93, "expression" most nearly means

    A) adaptation.

    B) embodiment.

    C) sentiment.

    D) simplification.

29. The author of Passage 2 uses the phrase "a great leap" (lines 92-93) to emphasize

    A) the technological progress that Vikings made.

    B) the distance that Vikings traveled.

    C) the strong faith and traditions on which Vikings relied.

    D) the widespread influence of Viking culture.

30. Both passages support which generalization about the Vikings?

    A) Devoted to warfare, the Vikings built an empire that reshaped the map of Europe.

    B) Innovations in shipbuilding and navigation saved the Vikings from decline and extinction.

    C) The Vikings were noble warriors and farmers who sought to better understand the world.

    D) Through their seafaring skills and abilities, the Vikings expanded and changed the world.

GO ON TO THE NEXT PAGE ▷

31. Which inference from the two passages is supported by the information in the timeline?

    A) The Vikings endeavored to relocate surplus population through colonization.

    B) The Vikings hoped to expand their cultural influence through economic exchange.

    C) The Vikings traveled extensively to launch sea raids and conduct trade.

    D) The Vikings were compelled to abandon their homelands because of scarcity.

**Questions 32-42 are based on the following passage.**

The following passage describes what scientists are learning from the discovery of specimens encased in amber from the carnivorous Roridulaceae plant family.

Fossil tree resin, commonly known as amber, has the ability to encase and preserve things for extensive periods of time. Researchers in Kaliningrad, Russia,
Line have recently discovered fossilized carnivorous
(5) plants for the first time. Encased in the variety of amber commonly found in the Baltic region, leaves from these rare and interesting plants have been preserved for what scientists estimate to be between 35 and 47 million years.
(10) Amber is often confused with sap because of its sticky, liquid form. It is chemically different, though, and hardens to such an extent that it can immaculately preserve what it encases. As a result, researchers often encounter insects and other
(15) animals preserved in amber for long periods of time. Considered a type of fossil, these findings are incredibly useful, as the animals found in amber are not usually found elsewhere in the fossil record. Plants, on the other hand, are rarely seen preserved
(20) this way. This new discovery, along with amber-encased animals, provides scientists with a more comprehensive view of life in earlier times.

The newly discovered plant fossils are also groundbreaking for two more specific reasons: They
(25) are the only fossilized carnivorous plant traps ever found, as well as the only fossilized evidence of the plant family Roridulaceae. The Roridulaceae plant has been seen only in seed form until now. While the seeds did offer scientists valuable information,
(30) the trapping mechanism of the plant's leaves was left to conjecture. In these newly discovered fossils, the leaves of the plants are fully intact and contain organic animal matter that had been captured in the leaves' tentacles when the plant was living.
(35) Geologists and botanists in Germany published these findings in the *Proceedings of the National Academy of Sciences*, noting that the leaves look similar to a genus of carnivorous plants called *Roridula,* which, until now, were considered
(40) endemic to Africa, where they still thrive. Unlike Venus flytraps, which are known to catch and dissolve insects using a digestive mechanism, all *Roridula* plants (and their newly discovered ancestor) absorb nutrients secondhand through
(45) a symbiotic relationship with an insect known as *Pameridea*. The *Pameridea* insect generates a greasy film, which allows it to live on *Roridula*'s leaves without being ensnared in the plant's tentacles. The insect then captures and digests its prey while still
(50) on the leaves of the plant, and then passes nutrients to the plant through its feces. This way of ingesting nutrients is the major link between this insect and the Roridulaceae family of plants.

The new fossil discovery in Russia completely
(55) challenges the conclusions that scientists had previously drawn about the paleobiogeography of the species. Roridulaceae was previously thought to originate from the prehistoric Pangaean supercontinent called Gondwana, which included
(60) modern- day Africa, South America, India, Antarctica, and Australia. However, recent findings suggest that the shared ancestors of these plant species had a much wider distribution. Researchers will need to continue to search for plant matter preserved in
(65) amber to fill in more of the blanks in the fossil record.

GO ON TO THE NEXT PAGE

32. The primary purpose of this passage is to

    A) explain how scientists use new technology to explore old findings.

    B) contrast the differences among various types of fossil tree resin.

    C) inform the reader about new plant fossils discovered in amber.

    D) encourage the reader to learn more about the plant fossil record.

33. Based on the information in the passage, the reader can infer that the author

    A) was part of the research team that discovered the new fossils.

    B) considers the discovery of the plant fossils in amber scientifically valuable.

    C) thinks the conclusions drawn by the scientists in Germany are flawed.

    D) does not expect scientists to find many more fossils in amber.

34. The author claims that animal fossils found in amber are important to scientists because they

    A) are samples of rare ancient life forms, though poorly preserved.

    B) contain remains of life forms not typically found in the fossil record.

    C) are easier to study than fossils found buried in rock formations.

    D) contain DNA that resembles various types of animals living today.

35. Which choice provides the best support for the answer to the previous question?

    A) Lines 5-9 ("Encased . . . million years")

    B) Lines 11-13 ("It is chemically . . . encases")

    C) Lines 16-18 ("Considered . . . record")

    D) Lines 23-27 ("The newly discovered . . . Roridulaceae")

36. As used in line 13, "immaculately" most nearly means

    A) correctly.

    B) innocently.

    C) perfectly.

    D) purely.

37. The author uses the phrase "rare and interesting" (line 7) to emphasize the importance of

    A) the discovery of the fossilized carnivorous plants.

    B) the study of paleontology and geology.

    C) the preservation of the existing fossil record.

    D) the continued exploration in the Baltic region.

38. It can most reasonably be inferred from the passage that

    A) scientists will begin to find *Roridula* plants in warm regions outside of Africa.

    B) future discoveries could change current theories about plant evolution.

    C) plants fossilized in amber can only be found in the Baltic region of Russia.

    D) the Venus flytrap is the only plant with a symbiotic relationship with insects.

39. Which choice provides the best evidence for the answer to the previous question?

    A) Lines 35-40 ("Geologists . . . thrive")

    B) Lines 43-46 ("all *Roridula* . . . *Pameridea*")

    C) Lines 54-57 ("The new fossil . . . species")

    D) Lines 57-63 ("Roridulaceae was . . . distribution")

GO ON TO THE NEXT PAGE ▷

40. According to the passage, the *Pameridea* insect is able to live on *Roridula*'s leaves without being eaten by the plant because

   A) the insect secretes a substance that prevents it from getting caught in the plant's tentacles.

   B) the plant does not need to eat the insect because it gets its energy from photosynthesis.

   C) the insect does not stay on the plant's leaves long enough to get caught in its sticky leaves.

   D) the plant only ingests insects that have already died and begun to decompose.

41. As used in line 40, "thrive" most nearly means

   A) advance.

   B) develop.

   C) flourish.

   D) succeed.

42. Which choice best describes how the discovery of the ancestor of the Roridulaceae plant changed scientists' thinking?

   A) They realized that the fossilized plants are more closely related to the Venus flytrap than previously thought.

   B) They realized that the fossilized plants did not have a symbiotic relationship with the *Pameridea* insect.

   C) They realized that the fossilized plants ingested insects directly rather than secondhand like modern *Roridula* plants.

   D) They realized that the Roridulaceae plant family was more widely distributed than previously believed.

**Questions 43-52 are based on the following passage and supplementary material.**

The following passage explains the cycles of sunspots that can be observed on the sun's surface, as well as how sunspots' resultant solar flares can impact the earth.

Sunspots are relatively cool areas on the surface of the sun, formed by changes in the sun's magnetic field. The sun's surface is very hot, approximately
*Line* 10,000°F, while the center of a sunspot is
(5) comparatively cool at about 6,000°F. Scientists do not know exactly what causes sunspots, but the magnetic field within a sunspot is about 100 times stronger than it is on the rest of the sun's surface. Normally, hot gases flow from the interior of the sun
(10) to the surface, maintaining the high temperature. Within a sunspot, however, the concentrated magnetic field inhibits the movement of the gases, causing the surface of the sunspot to cool.

Galileo and other astronomers started recording
(15) the sunspots they viewed through telescopes in the early 1600s, although sunspots had been observed and recorded without telescopes for over 2,000 years. When another astronomer, Samuel Schwabe, plotted the number of sunspots recorded each year,
(20) he found that the number increased and decreased in a cyclic pattern. Approximately every 11 years, the number of sunspots reaches a maximum. A graph of sunspots over the years has a fairly regular pattern of peaks and valleys, with about 11 years
(25) between peaks. Most recently, the sunspot cycle peaked around the middle of 2013, and it will reach its nadir around 2020.

Scientists use the 11-year cycle to predict solar flares, which cause changes in Earth's atmosphere.
(30) When two or more sunspots having magnetic fields with opposite directions are near each other, the magnetic fields can interact with plasma on the surface between the sunspots. The interaction between the fields sends a burst of plasma away
(35) from the surface, forming the solar flare. The flares quickly heat to several million degrees and release as much energy as several hundred million atomic bombs. Strong magnetic fields and x-rays travel from the flares to Earth, resulting in geomagnetic

GO ON TO THE NEXT PAGE ⟶

(40) storms. If these storms are strong enough, they have the potential to disrupt power and radio communications on Earth. Satellites are particularly susceptible to disruption by solar flares, thus causing interference with GPS, weather prediction,
(45) and mobile phone communication. A positive effect of these storms is that the increased energy and plasma particles interact with Earth's atmosphere, enhancing the auroras, also known as the Northern (and Southern) Lights.

(50)     Sunspots do not always follow the 11-year solar cycle; there was almost no sunspot activity between around 1645 and 1715. This minimum, which was named the Maunder Minimum after the husband and wife team who discovered patterns in the
(55) location of sunspots during the 11-year solar cycle, occurred during a period of lower-than-normal global temperatures known as the Little Ice Age. Scientists mostly agree that the lack of sunspot activity did not contribute very much, if at all, to
(60) the lowered temperatures.

    Sunspot activity has been decreasing during the last few cycles, and it is possible we will see another minimum in the next 20 years. The strength of the magnetic field in the sunspots also seems to
(65) be diminishing, which could be another sign of a minimum in our future. If we do experience a minimum, scientists will be able to learn more about the effect of sunspots on Earth's climate, in addition to learning more about the sun, its surface,
(70) and its magnetic fields.

**Solar Cycle**

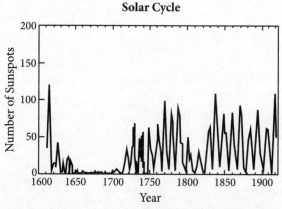

Adapted from NASA's Solar Science website
(http://solarscience.msfc.nasa.gov/images/ssn_yearly.jpg)

43.  The passage is primarily concerned with

A)  how solar activity can affect the climate on Earth.

B)  the history of methods used by astronomers to study the sun.

C)  scientists' current understanding of sunspots and solar flares.

D)  the 11-year cycle of solar flare activity.

44.  Which choice provides the best evidence for the answer to the previous question?

A)  Lines 5-10 ("Scientists . . . high temperature")

B)  Lines 14-18 ("Galileo . . . years")

C)  Lines 50-52 ("Sunspots do not . . . 1715")

D)  Lines 58-60 ("Scientists mostly agree . . . temperatures")

45.  The author refers to the enhanced auroras resulting from solar flares mainly to

A)  provide contrast with the negative effects of solar flares described.

B)  illustrate the powerful effects of solar flares on Earth's atmosphere.

C)  suggest that solar flares might cause more damage than previously believed.

D)  give an example of how the solar flares affect Earth's climate.

46.  According to the passage, which choice best describes what scientists currently understand about how solar flare activity affects the Earth?

A)  Low solar flare activity can cause lower temperatures on Earth.

B)  High solar flare activity can lead to disruptions of communication on Earth.

C)  Low solar flare activity can cause an enhancement of the auroras on Earth.

D)  High solar flare activity can lead to increased severe weather on Earth.

GO ON TO THE NEXT PAGE ⟩

47. Which of the following pieces of evidence would most strengthen the author's line of reasoning in the paragraph?

    A) Details added to paragraph 1 about features other than sunspots on the sun's surface and how they affect Earth

    B) Information added to paragraph 2 about how astronomers Galileo and Schwabe made their observations

    C) Examples in paragraph 3 of problems caused by disruption to communication caused by solar flares

    D) Examples in paragraph 5 of other periods in history during which the sun exhibited a decrease in observed sunspot activity

48. As used in line 34, "burst" most nearly means

    A) breach.

    B) eruption.

    C) force.

    D) fracture.

49. The passage most strongly suggests that which of the following statements is accurate?

    A) Although scientists have observed patterns in sunspot activity, it is not always possible to predict when sunspot activity will occur.

    B) Scientists will not be able to solve the mystery of what causes sunspots until technology allows astronauts to travel to the sun.

    C) Unless scientists find a way to control sunspot activity, radio and satellite communication on Earth will continue to be interrupted.

    D) The next minimum could interfere with weather prediction and cause drastic changes in the climate on Earth.

50. Which choice provides the best evidence for the answer to the previous question?

    A) Lines 18-21 ("When another . . . pattern")

    B) Lines 33-35 ("The interaction . . . flare")

    C) Lines 50-51 ("Sunspots . . . cycle")

    D) Lines 66-70 ("If we . . . fields")

51. As used in line 48, "enhancing" most nearly means

    A) developing.

    B) enlarging.

    C) improving.

    D) intensifying.

52. Which lines from the passage are best supported by the data presented in the graphic?

    A) Lines 14-16 ("Galileo . . . early 1600s")

    B) Lines 25-27 ("Most recently . . . 2020")

    C) Lines 51-52 ("there was . . . 1715")

    D) Lines 61-63 ("Sunspot activity . . . 20 years")

IF YOU FINISH BEFORE TIME IS CALLED, YOU MAY CHECK YOUR WORK ON THIS SECTION ONLY. DO NOT TURN TO ANY OTHER SECTION IN THE TEST.   **STOP**

# WRITING AND LANGUAGE TEST

### 35 Minutes—44 Questions

Turn to Section 2 of your answer sheet to answer the questions in this section.

Each passage below is accompanied by a number of questions. For some questions, you will consider how the passage might be revised to improve the expression of ideas. For other questions, you will consider how the passage might be edited to correct errors in sentence structure, usage, or punctuation. A passage or a question may be accompanied by one or more graphics (such as a table or graph) that you will consider as you make revising and editing decisions.

Some questions will direct you to an underlined portion of a passage. Other questions will direct you to a location in a passage or ask you to think about the passage as a whole.

After reading each passage, choose the answer to each question that most effectively improves the quality of writing in the passage or that makes the passage conform to the conventions of standard written English. Many questions include a "NO CHANGE" option. Choose that option if you think the best choice is to leave the relevant portion of the passage as it is.

**Questions 1-11 are based on the following passage.**

## In Defense of *Don Quixote*

Before the holiday, the World Literature professor assigned the **1** classes' next novel, *Don Quixote*.

"Miguel de Cervantes Saavedra wrote *Quixote* in Spanish," he boomed over the end-of-class shuffle of notebooks and bags. "Find a good translation, start reading—and class?" **2** All motion stopped he had their attention. "Do more than read it; prepare to defend why you spent your holiday break reading a thousand pages of turn-of-the-seventeenth-century Spanish literature. Read the experts, check the data: Why does the book still matter?"

1. A) NO CHANGE
   B) class'
   C) class's
   D) classes

2. A) NO CHANGE
   B) All motion stopped: he had
   C) All motion stopped, and had
   D) All motion stopped. Had

GO ON TO THE NEXT PAGE ⟶

Class dismissed, the students entered break feeling uneasy at the prospect of this hefty early-modern novel, but each soon found in its pages a captivating story, beautiful and strange. **3** Clarified with paradoxes of sane and insane, tragic and comic, ideal and real, the novel surprised its newest set of readers with intellectual complexity as well as deeply human—and charmingly **4** adverse—characters.

As the students gradually finished their copies of *Quixote*, most felt the defense the professor had requested was somewhat unnecessary—it was a literary masterpiece. But research **5** will have been required, so they dutifully opened laptops and visited libraries.

For Monday's post-holiday class, students presented **6** its short defenses of *Quixote*. Most began with their personal appreciation of the novel and the enduring **7** triviality of questions it raised. Several students then mentioned scholars' praise for *Quixote*'s ideological impact on culture, challenging worldviews and highlighting ambiguities between reality and perception. *Quixote*, some noted, not only changed the literary imagination by expanding the possibilities of what a novel could intellectually accomplish, but also offered important early contributions to emerging discussions regarding psychology and women's rights.

3. A) NO CHANGE
   B) Deprived
   C) Peppered
   D) Littered

4. A) NO CHANGE
   B) averse
   C) bazaar
   D) bizarre

5. A) NO CHANGE
   B) is
   C) was
   D) will be

6. A) NO CHANGE
   B) it's
   C) their
   D) they're

7. A) NO CHANGE
   B) pertinence
   C) irrelevance
   D) inertia

**GO ON TO THE NEXT PAGE**

To illustrate the book's importance, many students cited a famous 2002 survey of authors worldwide and the ensuing compilation of the world's "100 Best Books." This survey, students found, listed every qualifying "best" book at equal ranking, isolating only one as undeniably first: *Don Quixote*. **8**

After the last presentation was completed, the professor explained that **9** the university curriculum required students to read *Quixote* for World Literature. "Some call it the first great novel; many call it the greatest novel of all time, but superlatives aside, the true reason it's worth reading is somewhat indescribable, isn't it? **10** It changed you it moved you you were drawn to its beauty its ugliness or some confusion of the two. So it goes with great literature: The defense for its permanence is hidden in the piece itself."

8. Which sentence provides information that best supports the paragraph?

A) Most students also discovered that *Quixote* was second only to the Bible in its number of translations and publications across history, signifying its paramount global influence.

B) Students learned that around 100 well-known authors participated in the survey to identify the "most meaningful book of all time," organized by editors in Oslo, Norway.

C) Authors noted in the survey were few and far between but included Doris Lessing, Salman Rushdie, Chinua Achebe, and Toni Morrison.

D) The survey, although often cited by literary critics, has not been repeated since 2002.

9. Which choice most effectively establishes the main topic of the paragraph?

A) NO CHANGE

B) *Quixote* has touched the far reaches of the literary world.

C) he disagreed with experts regarding the literary value of *Quixote*.

D) he was pleased with the students' performance.

10. A) NO CHANGE

B) It changed you it moved you, you were drawn to its beauty, or its ugliness or some combination of the two.

C) It changed you it moved you, you were drawn to its beauty or its ugliness or some combination of the two.

D) It changed you; it moved you; you were drawn to its beauty, its ugliness, or some combination of the two.

GO ON TO THE NEXT PAGE ▷

Opening **11** their books with a fondness like old friendship, the class began to discuss *Quixote* together.

**Questions 12-22 are based on the following passage and supplementary material.**

## Women's Ingenuity

Until about 1840, only twenty-one patents for inventions were issued to women in the United States. **12** Yet by 1870, the number of patents granted to women had more than doubled. What spurred this increase of women as inventors?

[1]The secret lies partly in the stories of individual female inventors. [2] Some inventors—men and women—worked in teams, but many worked alone. [3] The most famous nineteenth-century female inventor became part of this patentee explosion. [4] She wasn't the first, but over her lifetime, Margaret Knight earned some twenty-six patents. [5] Her machine that made flat-bottomed paper bags is still in use. **13**

Knight spent her life working and inventing. As a child, she worked in the cotton mills and **14** many years later in her life, she was employed by the Columbia Paper Bag Company. While at the paper bag company, Knight perfected an idea for an automated machine that would cut, fold, and paste paper bags. **15** However,

11.  A) NO CHANGE
     B) there
     C) it's
     D) our

12.  Which choice most accurately and effectively represents the information in the graph?
     A) NO CHANGE
     B) Yet by 1865, the number of patents granted to women had more than doubled.
     C) Yet by 1870, the number of patents granted to women had surpassed those granted to men.
     D) Yet by 1866, the number of patents granted to women had fallen short of the 1840 count.

13.  Which sentence should be eliminated to improve the paragraph's focus?
     A) Sentence 1
     B) Sentence 2
     C) Sentence 3
     D) Sentence 5

14.  A) NO CHANGE
     B) many years later on,
     C) years later,
     D) later on in her life,

15.  A) NO CHANGE
     B) Furthermore,
     C) Also,
     D) Although

**GO ON TO THE NEXT PAGE**

when a man stole her idea, Knight fought for her rights. In the *Knight v. Annan* dispute of 1871, she won **16** an odd victory for women. The Patent Office eventually issued the patent to her. Knight's **17** alternate inventions included a rotary engine and a shoe-cutting machine.

In Knight's case, her profession helped her perceive the demand for an invention. **18** Knight's first invention was for a device that would stop machinery from injuring workers. Plus, she acquired the skills to become a trailblazer. During the Industrial Age, many women, like Knight, were able to secure jobs in **19** factories, this resulted in their higher labor market participation.

**20** The progress of feminism in the twentieth century that improved women's rights and provided greater

16. A) NO CHANGE
    B) an inconceivable
    C) a trivial
    D) a rare

17. A) NO CHANGE
    B) subsequent
    C) former
    D) ultimate

18. Which choice most effectively supports the claim made in paragraph?
    A) NO CHANGE
    B) At least some of this can be attributed to her own qualities rather than social conditions.
    C) This is obvious when one considers the impressive rate of her creations.
    D) This was a quality few women had at the time, as it was considered unfeminine.

19. A) NO CHANGE
    B) factories, because this resulted
    C) factories; this resulted
    D) factories, but resulted

20. A) NO CHANGE
    B) The progress of feminism in the twentieth century, which
    C) The progress of feminism in the twentieth century,
    D) The progress of feminism in the twentieth century, it

**GO ON TO THE NEXT PAGE** ⟶

access to education, also contributed to women's ingenuity. By 1998, some ten percent of all patents issued were to American women. [21] Nevertheless, Dr. Carol B. Muller founder of a nonprofit that promotes women in science states, "Until women are fully represented in the fields of science and engineering, society is losing out on the talents of a vast number of potential contributors."

In the future, if women can attain more university research positions, graduate-level degrees in science and engineering, and leadership positions in high-tech companies, the result may well be more participation as patentees. [22]

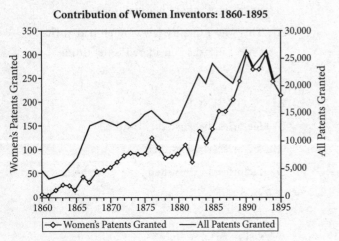

**Contribution of Women Inventors: 1860-1895**

Adapted from *The Democratization of Invention: Patents and Copyrights in American Economic Development, 1790-1920*, by B. Zorina Khan. Cambridge University Press, 2005.

21. A) NO CHANGE

B) Nevertheless, Dr. Carol B. Muller, founder of a nonprofit that promotes women in science states

C) Nevertheless Dr. Carol B. Muller, founder of a nonprofit that promotes women in science, states,

D) Nevertheless, Dr. Carol B. Muller, founder of a nonprofit that promotes women in science, states,

22. Which choice most effectively concludes the paragraph?

A) Given that we all benefit from new inventions that improve the quality of our lives, let us hope this becomes reality.

B) Recent social changes have had a positive impact on today's women inventors.

C) Unfortunately, women today are barely doing better than in Knight's day.

D) The patent system is alive and well in the twenty-first century, thanks to women trailblazers such as Margaret Knight.

**Questions 23-33 are based on the following passage.**

## Working from Home: Too Good to Be True?

It can be hard to break into your desired field, whether that's advertising, medicine, or technology. New graduates usually have to start at entry-level positions, where salaries are low. Meanwhile, the cost of rent can be 23 high, and if you live with your parents to save on rent, perhaps in the suburbs, then you might have a costly commute.

It may be tempting to take a position that promises high income for working at home. But don't be tempted. Many of these advertised "work-from-home" positions are outright scams. Of the 8,192 24 compliants filed with Federal Trade Commission (FTC) in 2010 involving work-at-home business opportunities, the FTC estimates that only 1 in every 55 cases involved any real business. 25

The scams come in many forms, but one thing they have in common is the promise of thousands of dollars per week, with no skills, experience, or degree required. That sounds too good to be true—precisely because it is. The other thing 26 it has in common is that they require a fee for the materials to get you started, everything from lists of phone numbers to registration with bogus agencies.

23. A) NO CHANGE
    B) high
    C) high:
    D) high—

24. A) NO CHANGE
    B) complaints
    C) compliments
    D) complements

25. At this point, the writer wants to add specific information that supports the main topic of the paragraph. Which choice provides the most relevant detail?

    A) Victims of scams should contact their local or state consumer affairs agency.
    B) Sadly, most cases are not covered by fraud protection policies offered by banks.
    C) Therefore, work-from-home opportunities have increased over the last decade.
    D) That means that 98 percent of the time, these "opportunities" are traps set to steal your cash.

26. A) NO CHANGE
    B) they have
    C) one has
    D) it has

GO ON TO THE NEXT PAGE

[27] Victims often find the paperwork difficult to complete. The [28] certification fee is supposed to get you marketing materials, software, and a training session. But once the company has your money, the training sessions are postponed indefinitely, and the materials never arrive. You don't earn a cent.

[29] Stuffing envelopes, assembling crafts, and entering data are all schemes that promise easy dollars for performing simple work. In each case, the company collects your setup fee and never provides any work. There is no service [30] department (with which to lodge complaints), and there are no refunds.

The lure of money is very powerful, but people entering the job market for the first time need to understand that earning a substantial income is something that comes from skill, education, and hard work. [31] They're are no shortcuts in life or in business, and anyone who thrills at the thought of getting something for nothing, or who loves the idea of working in pajamas, should learn that fast tracks to wealth are [32] a distortion.

27. Which choice provides the most effective topic sentence for this paragraph?

A) NO CHANGE

B) Training sessions are often long and tedious.

C) One scam involves a fee to process insurance claims for doctors.

D) Many people are naive enough to believe that fraud can't happen to them.

28. A) NO CHANGE

B) registration

C) conclusion

D) termination

29. A) NO CHANGE

B) Envelope stuffing, assembling crafts, and data entry

C) Envelope stuffing, craft assembly, and entering data

D) Stuffing envelopes, craft assembly, and entering data

30. A) NO CHANGE

B) department—with which to lodge complaints,

C) department with which to lodge complaints,

D) department, with which to lodge complaints,

31. A) NO CHANGE

B) They

C) Their

D) There

32. A) NO CHANGE

B) an impression

C) an illusion

D) an apparition

GO ON TO THE NEXT PAGE

Besides, you'll get more satisfaction out of performing real work that uses real skills than you would stuffing envelopes. **33** Starting in a career field, building your experience and skills will earn you bigger dividends in the future. That's a guarantee that no work-from-home scam can match.

**Questions 34-44 are based on the following passage and supplementary material.**

## Is Gluten-Free the Way to Be?

**34** A lot of people suffer from celiac disease and find it hard to control the symptoms. Most of these people, however, are not doing so because of medical necessity. Gluten is not **35** an absolutely essential nutrient, so no one is harmed by following a gluten-free diet. In fact, it may be a good idea to try going gluten-free, as it may reveal some health issues that might have gone undiagnosed.

Studies indicate that about 1 percent of Americans have celiac disease, meaning that eating even **36** standard amounts of gluten will make them ill. Gluten is a protein composite found in **37** wheat, barley, rye—and a few other related grains, and it contains amino acid sequences that trigger immune responses in people with celiac disease. Tissues in the small intestine

33. A) NO CHANGE
B) Just starting in a career field, building experience
C) If starting in a career field, building your experience
D) When starting in a career field, building your experience

34. Which choice provides the most appropriate introduction to the main topic of the paragraph?
A) NO CHANGE
B) Today, many people try different diets to see which ones they like the best.
C) Gluten can cause gastric trouble if people who eat it are allergic to it.
D) More and more people are trying to remove gluten from their diet.

35. A) NO CHANGE
B) the very most essential,
C) an essential nutrient,
D) a very essential nutrient,

36. A) NO CHANGE
B) nonexistent
C) strong
D) trace

37. A) NO CHANGE
B) wheat, barley, rye, and a few other related grains,
C) wheat barley, rye and a few other related grains,
D) wheat, barley, rye, and, a few other related grains,

**GO ON TO THE NEXT PAGE**

react as if the protein belonged to a harmful virus or [38] bacteria. They become inflamed. This inflammation prevents nutrients from being properly absorbed in the small intestine, resulting in a variety of serious conditions. It also causes gas and bloating, cramps, and diarrhea or constipation.

Although a small percentage of Americans have celiac disease, a much higher percentage report that they try to eat a gluten-free diet or are trying to eat less gluten. [39] According to one survey, some 20 percent of people are trying to avoid or cut back on gluten. Why are so many people following, or trying to follow, a gluten-free diet if they have not been diagnosed with celiac disease? In some cases, they might feel better on the diet because they have celiac disease but have never been diagnosed. People who suspect they have celiac disease because a gluten-free diet made them feel better still need to get diagnosed, but they might never have suspected they had the disease if going gluten-free had not become so popular. [40] A recent study estimates that many Americans with celiac disease do not know they have it.

A lot of people who have been found not to have celiac disease still feel better when they follow a gluten-free diet. Researchers have carefully tested groups of these people, giving them a diet that omitted gluten and then adding gluten back into their diet in [41] pill form, some felt no difference when gluten was added back

38. Which choice most effectively combines the sentences at the underlined portion?

A) bacteria as they become inflamed.

B) bacteria and become inflamed.

C) bacteria, however they become inflamed.

D) bacteria; become inflamed.

39. Which choice offers an accurate interpretation of the data in the graph?

A) NO CHANGE

B) According to data gathered in 2012, a greater percentage of people were trying to cut back or avoid gluten than in previous years.

C) According to data gathered in 2011, about 25 percent of people were trying to cut back or avoid gluten in 2011.

D) According to one survey, just under 29 percent of people are trying to cut back or avoid gluten.

40. Which choice best supports the claim made in the previous sentence?

A) NO CHANGE

B) A recent study estimates that Americans do not always know they have celiac disease.

C) A recent study estimates that about 5 out of every 6 Americans with celiac disease do not know they have it.

D) A recent study estimates that a high percentage of Americans with celiac disease do not know they have it.

41. A) NO CHANGE

B) pill form. Some felt

C) pill form some felt

D) pill form consequently some felt

GO ON TO THE NEXT PAGE ⟩

into their diets. Some, **42** moreover, were affected by gluten, which suggests that there might be other health conditions related to gluten besides celiac disease. These conditions affect only a small percentage of people, so the conditions might not have been noticed and studied if gluten-free diets had not become so popular.

Although it will not necessarily improve the health of everyone who tries it, a gluten-free diet does no harm and definitely **43** benefiting more people than doctors and researchers originally **44** studied.

42. A) NO CHANGE
    B) in addition,
    C) however,
    D) besides,

43. A) NO CHANGE
    B) benefits
    C) is benefiting
    D) did benefit

44. A) NO CHANGE
    B) wanted
    C) tested
    D) suspected

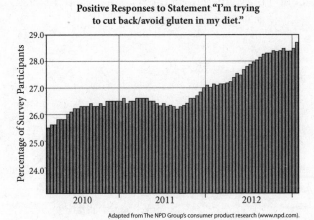

**Positive Responses to Statement "I'm trying to cut back/avoid gluten in my diet."**

Adapted from The NPD Group's consumer product research (www.npd.com).

# MATH TEST

### 25 Minutes—20 Questions

## NO-CALCULATOR SECTION

Turn to Section 3 of your answer sheet to answer the questions in this section.

**Directions:** For this section, solve each problem and decide which is the best of the choices given. Fill in the corresponding oval on the answer sheet. You may use any available space for scratch work.

Notes:

1. Calculator use is NOT permitted.
2. All numbers used are real numbers.
3. All figures used are necessary to solving the problems that they accompany. All figures are drawn to scale EXCEPT when it is stated that a specific figure is not drawn to scale.
4. Unless stated otherwise, the domain of any function $f$ is assumed to be the set of all real numbers $x$, for which $f(x)$ is a real number.

Information:

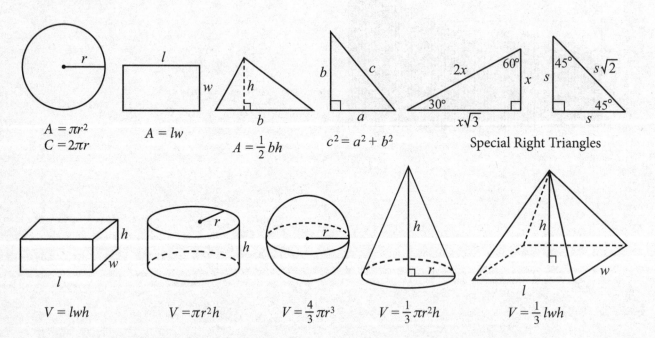

$A = \pi r^2$
$C = 2\pi r$

$A = lw$

$A = \frac{1}{2}bh$

$c^2 = a^2 + b^2$

Special Right Triangles

$V = lwh$

$V = \pi r^2 h$

$V = \frac{4}{3}\pi r^3$

$V = \frac{1}{3}\pi r^2 h$

$V = \frac{1}{3}lwh$

The sum of the degree measures of the angles in a triangle is 180.

The number of degrees of arc in a circle is 360.

The number of radians of arc in a circle is $2\pi$.

GO ON TO THE NEXT PAGE ⟶

| Number of Runs | Total Number of People Who Have Ridden the Swings |
|:---:|:---:|
| 2 | 28 |
| 3 | 42 |
| 5 | 70 |

1.  The giant swings in an amusement park are run only when completely full to maintain a fairly even distribution of weight. The number of times the swings have been run, along with a cumulative rider count, is recorded in the table above. Based on the information, how many people will have ridden the giant swings when they have been run eight times?

    A) 98
    B) 112
    C) 140
    D) 224

2.  Which of the following expressions is equivalent to $a^{\frac{2}{6}}$ ?

    A) $\sqrt[3]{a}$

    B) $\sqrt{3a}$

    C) $\dfrac{a}{3}$

    D) $\dfrac{2}{a^6}$

3.  A publishing company ships books to schools, some of which are hardback textbooks and some of which are paperback workbooks. Each shipping box can hold a maximum of 20 textbooks or 64 workbooks. Each textbook takes up 192 cubic inches of space, and each workbook takes up 60 cubic inches of space. One box can hold a maximum of 3,840 cubic inches. The shipping department is packing a box containing both types of books. Which of the following systems of inequalities can the department use to determine how many textbooks, $t$, and workbooks, $w$, can be shipped in one box?

    A) $\begin{cases} t \le 20 \\ w \le 64 \\ 60t + 192w \le 3{,}840 \end{cases}$

    B) $\begin{cases} t \ge 20 \\ w \ge 64 \\ 192t + 60w \ge 3{,}840 \end{cases}$

    C) $\begin{cases} t \le 20 \\ w \le 64 \\ 192t + 60w \le 3{,}840 \end{cases}$

    D) $\begin{cases} t \le 192 \\ w \le 60 \\ 20t + 64w \le 3{,}840 \end{cases}$

4.  A nutritionist is studying the effects of nutritional supplements on athletes. She uses the function $P_i(a)$ to represent the results of her study, where $a$ represents the number of athletes who participated in the study, and $P_i$ represents the number of athletes who experienced increased performance while using the supplements over a given period of time. Which of the following lists could represent a portion of the domain for the nutritionist's function?

    A) $\{\dots -100, -75, -50, -25, 0, 25, 50, 75, 100\dots\}$
    B) $\{-100, -75, -50, -25, 0, 25, 50, 75, 100\}$
    C) $\{0, 2.5, 5, 7.5, 10, 12.5, 15\dots\}$
    D) $\{0, 15, 30, 45, 60, 75\dots\}$

**GO ON TO THE NEXT PAGE**

5. Which of the following does not represent a linear relationship?

A)

| x | −1 | −4 | −7 | −10 | −13 |
|---|----|----|----|-----|-----|
| y | 8  | 6  | 4  | 2   | 0   |

B)

| x | −3 | −1 | 1 | 3  | 5  |
|---|----|----|----|----|----|
| y | 5  | 3  | 1 | −1 | −3 |

C)

| x | 1  | 2  | 3  | 4  | 5  |
|---|----|----|----|----|----|
| y | −5 | −5 | −5 | −5 | −5 |

D)

| x | −2 | −1 | 0 | 1 | 2 |
|---|----|----|----|----|----|
| y | 4  | 1  | 0 | 1 | 4 |

$$\begin{cases} Ax - 2y = 18 \\ Bx + 6y = 26 \end{cases}$$

6. If the graphs of the lines in the system of equations above intersect at $(4, -1)$, what is the value of $\dfrac{B}{A}$?

A) $-3$

B) $-\dfrac{1}{3}$

C) $\dfrac{1}{2}$

D) $2$

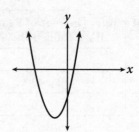

7. Which of the following equations could represent the graph in the figure shown above?

A) $y = x^2 - 4x - 4$

B) $y = x^2 + 4x - 4$

C) $y = x^2 - 8x + 16$

D) $y = x^2 + 8x + 16$

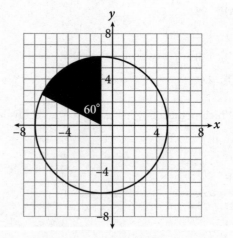

8. What is the area of the shaded sector of the circle shown in the figure above?

A) $2\pi$

B) $6\pi$

C) $12\pi$

D) $36\pi$

GO ON TO THE NEXT PAGE

9. Which of the following expressions has the same value as $\sqrt{0.25} \times \sqrt{2}$ ?

A) $\dfrac{\sqrt{2}}{4}$

B) $\dfrac{1}{2}$

C) $\dfrac{\sqrt[4]{2}}{2}$

D) $\dfrac{\sqrt{2}}{2}$

11. Given the polynomial $6x^4 + 2x^2 - 8x - c$, where $c$ is a constant, for what value of $c$ will $\dfrac{6x^4 + 2x^2 - 8x - c}{x + 2}$ have no remainder?

A) $-120$

B) $-60$

C) $60$

D) $120$

**Wool-Polyester Blend Production**

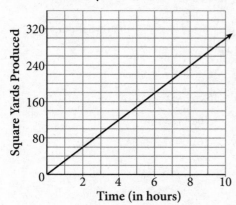

10. The figure above shows the rate at which a textile machine can produce a wool-polyester blend fabric. To produce a 100% polyester fabric, the same machine can produce 40 square yards per hour. Given that the company needs to fill an order for 2,400 square yards of each type of fabric, which of the following statements is true?

A) It will take half as long to make the blended fabric as the 100% polyester fabric.

B) It will take twice as long to make the blended fabric as the 100% polyester fabric.

C) It will take 20 more hours to make the blended fabric than the 100% polyester fabric.

D) It will take 20 fewer hours to make the blended fabric than the 100% polyester fabric.

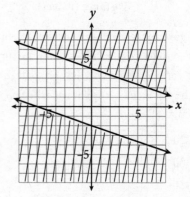

12. Which of the following systems of inequalities could be represented by the graph shown above?

A) $\begin{cases} 3x - y \geq 4 \\ 3x - y \leq -2 \end{cases}$

B) $\begin{cases} 3x + y \geq 4 \\ 3x + y \leq -2 \end{cases}$

C) $\begin{cases} x - 3y \geq 12 \\ x - 3y \leq -6 \end{cases}$

D) $\begin{cases} x + 3y \geq 12 \\ x + 3y \leq -6 \end{cases}$

GO ON TO THE NEXT PAGE ▷

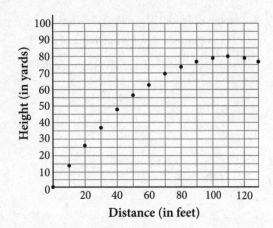

13. The figure above shows part of the path of a planned roller coaster hill. What is the sum, in feet, of the vertical height and the horizontal distance that the roller coaster will travel while on this particular hill?

A) 220

B) 300

C) 460

D) 900

14. Which of the following expressions is equivalent to the complex number $\dfrac{2}{i+6} + (2+5i)$? (Note that $\sqrt{-1} = i$.)

A) $\dfrac{32i+9}{i+6}$

B) $\dfrac{34i+7}{i+6}$

C) $\dfrac{32i+19}{i+6}$

D) $\dfrac{37i+14}{i+6}$

15. If $g(x) = 4x^2 - x + 5$, then what does $g(-2x)$ equal?

A) $16x^2 + 2x + 5$

B) $16x^2 - 2x + 5$

C) $-16x^2 + 2x + 5$

D) $-16x^2 - 2x + 5$

**GO ON TO THE NEXT PAGE**

**Directions:** For questions 16-20, solve the problem and enter your answer in the grid, as described below, on the answer sheet.

1. Although not required, it is suggested that you write your answer in the boxes at the top of the columns to help you fill in the circles accurately. You will receive credit only if the circles are filled in correctly.

2. Mark no more than one circle in any column.

3. No question has a negative answer.

4. Some problems may have more than one correct answer. In such cases, grid only one answer.

5. **Mixed numbers** such as $3\frac{1}{2}$ must be gridded as 3.5 or $\frac{7}{2}$.

   (If $3\frac{1}{2}$ is entered into the grid as $\boxed{3\ 1\ /\ 2}$, it will be interpreted as $\frac{31}{2}$, not $3\frac{1}{2}$.)

6. **Decimal answers:** If you obtain a decimal answer with more digits than the grid can accommodate, it may be either rounded or truncated, but it must fill the entire grid.

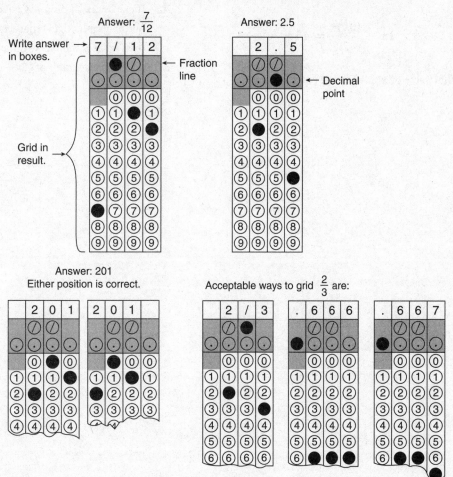

16. If $0.2x + 1.8 = 3 - 0.6x$, what is the value of $x$ ?

| Equation 1 | |
|---|---|
| $x$ | $y$ |
| 5 | $-8$ |
| 4 | $-5$ |
| 3 | $-2$ |
| 2 | 1 |

| Equation 2 | |
|---|---|
| $x$ | $y$ |
| $-8$ | 3 |
| $-6$ | 4 |
| $-4$ | 5 |
| $-2$ | 6 |

17. The tables above represent data points for two linear equations. If the two equations form a system, what is the $x$-coordinate of the solution to that system?

$$18 - \frac{(3x)^{\frac{1}{2}}}{2} = 15$$

18. What value of $x$ satisfies the equation above?

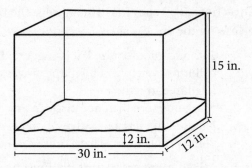

15 in.

2 in.

30 in.

12 in.

19. The figure above shows a fish tank with sand in the bottom. If the water level is to be 3 inches below the top, how many cubic inches of water are needed to fill the tank?

20. If $g(x) = 2x^3 - 5x^2 + 4x + 6$, and $P$ is the point on the graph of $g(x)$ that has an $x$-coordinate of 1, then what is the $y$-coordinate of the corresponding point on the graph of $g(x - 3) + 4$ ?

# MATH TEST

### 55 Minutes—38 Questions

## CALCULATOR SECTION

Turn to Section 4 of your answer sheet to answer the questions in this section.

**Directions:** For this section, solve each problem and decide which is the best of the choices given. Fill in the corresponding oval on the answer sheet. You may use any available space for scratch work.

Notes:

1. Calculator use is permitted.
2. All numbers used are real numbers.
3. All figures used are necessary to solving the problems that they accompany. All figures are drawn to scale EXCEPT when it is stated that a specific figure is not drawn to scale.
4. Unless stated otherwise, the domain of any function $f$ is assumed to be the set of all real numbers $x$, for which $f(x)$ is a real number.

Information:

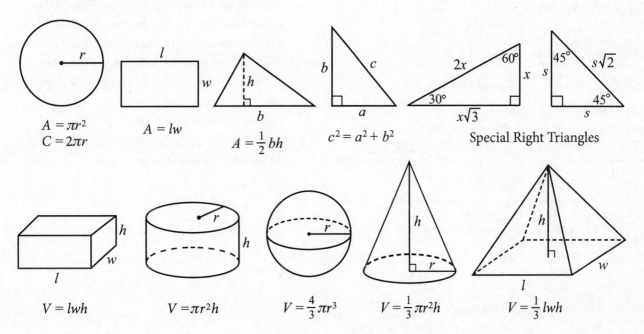

$A = \pi r^2$
$C = 2\pi r$

$A = lw$

$A = \frac{1}{2}bh$

$c^2 = a^2 + b^2$

Special Right Triangles

$V = lwh$

$V = \pi r^2 h$

$V = \frac{4}{3}\pi r^3$

$V = \frac{1}{3}\pi r^2 h$

$V = \frac{1}{3}lwh$

The sum of the degree measures of the angles in a triangle is 180.

The number of degrees of arc in a circle is 360.

The number of radians of arc in a circle is $2\pi$.

GO ON TO THE NEXT PAGE

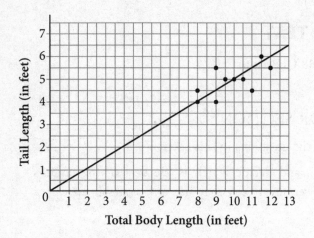

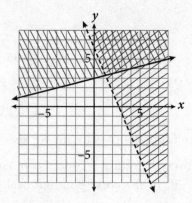

1. The Florida Department of Wildlife caught and tagged 10 adult female alligators as part of an effort to protect this endangered species. They took various measurements and readings related to body size and health. The total body length is plotted against the tail length in the scatterplot shown above, along with a line of best fit. Which of the following equations best models the data?

   A) $y = 0.5x$

   B) $y = 2x$

   C) $y = 0.4x + 1$

   D) $y = 0.6x - 1$

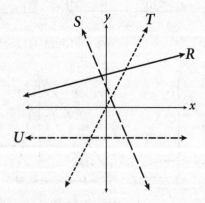

2. Which of the following lists correctly orders the lines in the figure above according to their slopes, from least to greatest?

   A) $R, T, S, U$

   B) $S, U, R, T$

   C) $S, R, U, T$

   D) $U, S, R, T$

3. Which of the following is a solution to the system of inequalities shown in the figure above?

   A) $(-5, 2)$

   B) $(-2, 5)$

   C) $(2, 5)$

   D) $(5, 2)$

4. The American political system is largely a two-party system. In fact, only six candidates who were not associated with either the Republican or the Democratic Party have been elected governor in any state since 1990. In one such election, the ratio of votes received for the Independent candidate to the Democratic candidate to the Republican candidate was approximately 19:18:13. If 510,000 votes were cast in the election, how many more votes were cast for the Independent candidate than for the Republican candidate?

   A)   6,000

   B)   10,200

   C)   61,200

   D)   193,800

**GO ON TO THE NEXT PAGE**

| Selection Method | Number of States |
|---|---|
| Election | 22 |
| Gubernatorial appointment | 11 |
| Legislative appointment | 2 |
| Missouri Plan | 15 |

5.  There are four ways in which state judges are selected for their positions. One is by election, another is appointment by the governor (usually with the confirmation by the state legislature), and a third is appointment by the state legislature. The final way is a hybrid of the last two, called the Missouri Plan, in which a nonpartisan legislative committee recommends a list of candidates and the governor chooses from this list. The table above shows the number of states that engage in each process for the highest court of the state, usually called the state Supreme Court. What percent of states select judges using the Missouri Plan?

    A)  17%

    B)  30%

    C)  33%

    D)  43%

6.  A botanist collects and models some data and is able to determine that the number of germinated seeds of a certain plant is linearly correlated to the amount of rainfall during the previous month, according to the equation $s = 28.5r + 83$. In this equation, $s$ is the number of seeds germinated, and $r$ is the amount of rainfall in inches. In a certain geographic region that the botanist is studying, 197 seeds germinated. Approximately how many inches of rainfall did that area receive during the previous month?

    A)  3.1

    B)  4

    C)  7

    D)  9.8

7.  A dendrologist (a botanist who studies trees exclusively) is examining the way in which a certain tree sheds its leaves. He tracks the number of leaves shed each day over the period of a month, starting when the first leaf is shed. He organizes the data in a scatterplot and sees that the data can be modeled using an exponential function. He determines the exponential model to be $f(x) = 6(1.92)^x$, where $x$ is the number of days after the tree began to shed its leaves. What does the value 1.92 in the function tell the dendrologist?

    A)  The number of leaves shed almost doubles each day.

    B)  The number of leaves shed almost doubles every six days.

    C)  The number of leaves left on the tree is reduced by about 92% each day.

    D)  The number of leaves left on the tree is reduced by about 92% every six days.

**GO ON TO THE NEXT PAGE**

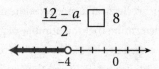

$$\frac{12 - a}{2} \; \boxed{\phantom{x}} \; 8$$

8. Which inequality symbol would make the above statement true?

A) $\leq$

B) $\geq$

C) $<$

D) $>$

| Price per Pencil | Projected Number of Units Sold |
|---|---|
| $0.20 | 150,000 |
| $0.25 | 135,000 |
| $0.30 | 120,000 |
| $0.35 | 105,000 |
| $0.40 | 90,000 |
| $0.45 | 75,000 |

9. Generally, the price of an item is a good indicator of how many units of that item will be sold. The lower the price, the more units will be sold. A marketing department develops a table showing various price points and the projected number of units sold at that price point. Which of the following represents the linear relationship shown in the table, where $x$ is the price and $y$ is the number of units sold?

A) $y = 0.03x + 150,000$

B) $y = 300,000x + 75,000$

C) $y = -300,000x + 90,000$

D) $y = -300,000x + 210,000$

10. A mailing supply store sells small shipping boxes in packs of 8 or 20. If the store has 61 packs in stock totaling 800 small shipping boxes, how many packs have 20 boxes in them, assuming all the packs are full?

A) 26

B) 32

C) 35

D) 40

11. Given that $\sqrt{-1} = i$, which of the following is equivalent to the sum $i^{125} + i^{125}$?

A) $i^{14}$

B) $i^{250}$

C) $2i^{45}$

D) $2i^{250}$

$$-\frac{9}{2}x^{10} - \frac{3}{2}x^9 + \frac{15}{2}x^8$$

12. Which of the following is equivalent to the expression above?

A) $-\frac{3}{2}x^8(3x^2 + x - 5)$

B) $-\frac{1}{2}x^8(9x^2 + 3x - 5)$

C) $\frac{3}{2}x^8(-3x^2 + x + 5)$

D) $3x^8(-3x^2 - x + 5)$

**GO ON TO THE NEXT PAGE**

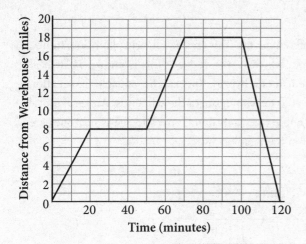

13. The graph above shows a delivery truck's distance from the company's warehouse over a two-hour period, during which time the delivery people made two deliveries and then returned to the warehouse. Based on the graph, which of the following statements could be true?

A) Each delivery took 30 minutes to complete, not including driving time.

B) The location of the second delivery was about 70 miles from the warehouse.

C) The truck traveled about 18 miles from the time it left the warehouse until it returned.

D) The second delivery was about 18 miles farther from the warehouse than the first delivery.

GO ON TO THE NEXT PAGE

**Questions 14 and 15 refer to the following information.**

Plants are capable of cross-pollinating with related but different plants. This creates a hybrid plant. Sometimes, a hybrid plant is superior to the two different plants from which it was derived. This is known as "hybrid vigor." Scientists can examine the DNA of a plant to see if it is a hybrid. This can be valuable information because if the plant appears superior, it would be beneficial to develop more of these hybrids. An agricultural scientist examines an orchard that has several types of apple trees and orange trees to see which ones are hybrids. Some of the information she collected is shown in the table below.

|  | Apple Trees | Orange Trees | Total |
|---|---|---|---|
| **Hybrid** | | | 402 |
| **Non-hybrid** | | 118 | |
| **Total** | | | 628 |

14. Based on the data, if 45% of the apple trees are not hybrids, how many apple trees are hybrids?

    A)  50

    B)  132

    C)  226

    D)  240

15. The scientist wants to study the orange trees to check for hybrid vigor. If she chooses one orange tree at random, what is the probability that it will be a hybrid?

    A)  $\dfrac{59}{194}$

    B)  $\dfrac{135}{314}$

    C)  $\dfrac{97}{157}$

    D)  $\dfrac{135}{194}$

GO ON TO THE NEXT PAGE

$$(5x^4 - \frac{1}{4}x^3 + 3x) \div \frac{1}{2}x$$

16. What is the result of dividing the two expressions above?

A) $\frac{5}{2}x^3 - \frac{1}{8}x^2 + \frac{3}{2}$

B) $\frac{5}{2}x^3 - 2x^2 + \frac{3}{2}x$

C) $10x^3 - \frac{1}{2}x^2 + 6$

D) $10x^3 - \frac{1}{8}x^2 + 6x$

| $x$ | $y$ |
|---|---|
| $-1$ | 7 |
| 0 | 5 |
| 1 | 3 |
| 2 | 1 |

17. If graphed, the ordered pairs in the table above would form a line. Where would this line intersect the $x$-axis?

A) $-2\frac{1}{2}$

B) $-\frac{1}{2}$

C) $2\frac{1}{2}$

D) 5

18. Mount Fuji in Japan was first climbed by a monk in 663 AD and subsequently became a Japanese religious site for hundreds of years. It is now a popular tourist site. When ascending the mountain, tourists drive part of the distance and climb the rest of the way. Suppose a tourist drove to an elevation of 2,390 meters and from that point climbed to the top of the mountain, and then descended back to the car taking the same route. If it took her a total of 7 hours to climb up and back down, and she climbed at an average rate of 264 vertical meters per hour going up and twice that going down, approximately how tall is Mount Fuji?

A) 1,386 meters

B) 2,772 meters

C) 3,776 meters

D) 5,172 meters

$$\begin{cases} y = 3x \\ -3x^2 + 2y^2 = 180 \end{cases}$$

19. If $(x, y)$ is a solution to the system of equations above, what is the value of $x^2$?

A) 12

B) 20

C) 60

D) 144

20. If $M = 3x^2 + 9x - 4$ and $N = 5x^2 - 12$, then what is $2(M - N)$?

A) $-2x^2 + 9x + 8$

B) $-4x^2 + 18x - 32$

C) $-4x^2 + 18x + 16$

D) $8x^2 + 9x - 16$

GO ON TO THE NEXT PAGE

**U.S. Bridges**

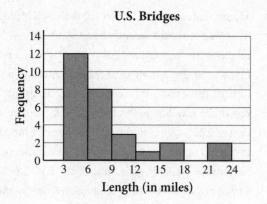

21. The Lake Pontchartrain Causeway Bridge in Louisiana is the longest bridge in the United States, at 23.83 miles long. The histogram above shows the distribution of the lengths, in miles, of 28 of the longest bridges in the United States, including Lake Pontchartrain Causeway Bridge. Which of the following could be the median length of the 28 bridges represented in the histogram?

A) 5.9

B) 7.9

C) 9.2

D) 9.9

22. In the United States, the original full retirement age was 65. The retirement age has since been pushed to 66 and will soon move to 67, as life expectancies go up. The Social Security Administration periodically conducts studies regarding retirement age. One such study focused on whether or not retiring early lowers a person's life expectancy. The study found a weak positive correlation between retirement age and life expectancy. If data from the study were graphed in a scatterplot, which of the following statements would be true?

A) The slope of the line of best fit would be a large positive number.

B) The slope of the line of best fit would be a negative number close to 0.

C) The data points would follow, but not closely, an increasing line of best fit.

D) The data points would be closely gathered around an increasing line of best fit.

23. A student is doing a scale drawing of a woolly mammoth on a piece of poster board for her presentation on the last ice age. She was surprised to find that the woolly mammoth, reaching a height of only about 10 feet, 6 inches, was actually smaller than today's African elephant. Even more surprising is the fact that the woolly mammoth's tusks averaged 11.5 feet in length. If the student draws the mammoth 14 inches tall on her poster, approximately how many inches long should she make the tusks? (There are 12 inches in 1 foot.)

A) 12.78

B) 15.0

C) 15.33

D) 16.1

24. Johanna picked 3 pounds of strawberries at a "pick-your-own" patch. At this particular patch, the cost is $1.50 for the pail and $3.99 per pound of strawberries picked. If a linear equation is created to represent the situation and written in the form $y = mx + b$, which piece of the equation would the value 13.47 in this scenario most likely represent?

A) $b$

B) $m$

C) $x$

D) $y$

GO ON TO THE NEXT PAGE

25. In an effort to decrease reliance on fossil fuels, some energy producers have started to utilize renewable resources. One such power plant uses solar panels to create solar energy during the day and then shifts to natural gas at night or when there is cloud cover. One particularly bright morning, the company increases the amount of its power typically generated by solar panels by 60%. During a cloudy spell, it decreases the amount by 30%, and then when the sun comes back out, it increases the amount again by 75% before shutting the panels down for the night. What is the net percent increase of this company's reliance on solar panels during that day?

    A)  75%

    B)  96%

    C)  105%

    D)  165%

26. Zoos use various methods for determining how to feed different animals. Sometimes they use age, weight, or, usually in the case of snakes, length. If a snake that is 2 feet, 6 inches long receives 12 grams of frog mash per feeding, how many grams should a snake that is 1 meter in length get? (Use the approximate conversion 1 foot = 0.3 meters.)

    A)  5

    B)  13

    C)  14.5

    D)  16

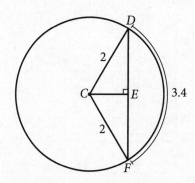

27. Which of the following gives the length of chord *DF* in the figure above?

    A)  2 cos(1.7)

    B)  2 sin(1.7)

    C)  4 cos(0.85)

    D)  4 sin(0.85)

28. If $y = 12 - x$ and $\dfrac{3y}{4} + 11 = \dfrac{-x}{2}$, what is the value of $\dfrac{x}{5} + \dfrac{y}{4}$?

    A)  −1

    B)  $\dfrac{19}{4}$

    C)  $\dfrac{75}{4}$

    D)  33

GO ON TO THE NEXT PAGE

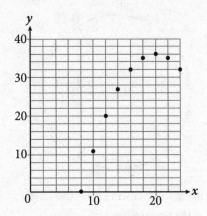

29. If a quadratic equation is used to model the data shown in the scatterplot above, and the model fits the data exactly, which of the following is a solution to the quadratic equation?

   A) 28

   B) 32

   C) 34

   D) 36

30. If $h$ is a function defined over the set of all real numbers and $h(x - 4) = 6x^2 + 2x + 10$, then which of the following defines $h(x)$ ?

   A) $h(x) = 6x^2 - 2x + 114$

   B) $h(x) = 6x^2 - 46x + 98$

   C) $h(x) = 6x^2 + 2x + 98$

   D) $h(x) = 6x^2 + 50x + 114$

**GO ON TO THE NEXT PAGE**

**Directions:** For questions 31-38, solve the problem and enter your answer in the grid, as described below, on the answer sheet.

1. Although not required, it is suggested that you write your answer in the boxes at the top of the columns to help you fill in the circles accurately. You will receive credit only if the circles are filled in correctly.

2. Mark no more than one circle in any column.

3. No question has a negative answer.

4. Some problems may have more than one correct answer. In such cases, grid only one answer.

5. **Mixed numbers** such as $3\frac{1}{2}$ must be gridded as 3.5 or $\frac{7}{2}$.

    (If $3\frac{1}{2}$ is entered into the grid as [3 1 / 2], it will be interpreted as $\frac{31}{2}$, not $3\frac{1}{2}$.)

6. **Decimal answers:** If you obtain a decimal answer with more digits than the grid can accommodate, it may be either rounded or truncated, but it must fill the entire grid.

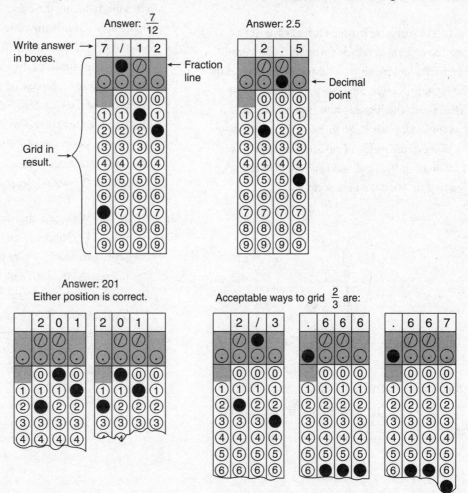

GO ON TO THE NEXT PAGE

31. The Bar Exam is a test given in each state to determine whether or not a law school graduate is competent to practice law. The American Bar Association surveyed 3,000 law school graduates across the country who passed the bar exam in 2000. Of those surveyed, 720 were not practicing law in 2012. If 55,200 graduates passed the bar in 2000, about how many of them were practicing law in 2012, assuming the sample was a good representation of the population of law school graduates who passed the bar in 2000? Round to the nearest thousand and enter your answer in terms of thousands. (For example, enter 18,000 as 18.)

32. In recent years, car manufacturers have started producing hybrid vehicles, which run on both electricity and gasoline, resulting in a significantly higher gas mileage. Suppose the odometer of a hybrid car, which shows how many miles the car has traveled, reads 4,386 miles. If the car averages 48 miles to the gallon of gas and currently has 12 gallons in the tank, what should the odometer reading be when the tank is empty?

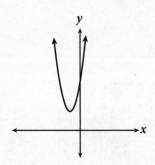

33. If the equation of the graph shown above is $y = 2(x + 3)^2 + 10$, what is the $y$-intercept of the graph?

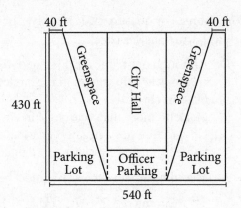

34. Many cities try to work "greenspaces" into their city planning because living plants help filter the city's air, reducing the effects of pollution. The figure above shows the plans for a new greenspace around City Hall, which will be created by converting portions of the existing parking lots. If the width of each parking lot is the same as the width of the City Hall building, how many thousands of square feet of greenspace will there be after the conversion? Round to the nearest thousand and enter your answer in terms of thousands. (For example, enter 14,000 as 14.)

35. Rasha volunteers at a charity that helps feed the homeless. He collects donations and then uses the money to buy food for care packages. This week, he collected $145. Each care package will include canned vegetables and bags of rice in the ratio 3:1. The cans cost $0.89 each, and the bags of rice cost $3.49 each. Using the given ratio, what is the maximum number of complete vegetable/rice care packages Rasha can make?

GO ON TO THE NEXT PAGE ⟶

36. A subway car on the New York City subway travels at an average speed of 17.4 miles per hour. Train cars on the Chicago L travel at an average speed that is 30% faster than that of the NYC subway. The DC Metro travels at an average speed that is 30% faster than that of the Chicago L. Marc rode the NYC subway from one stop to another and it took 6 minutes; Lizzie rode the Chicago L from one stop to another and it took 4.8 minutes; and Darius rode the DC Metro, which took 3.6 minutes between stops. How many miles did the person who traveled the shortest distance between stops travel? Round to the nearest tenth of a mile.

**Questions 37 and 38 refer to the following information.**

Mercury is a naturally occurring metal that can be harmful to humans. The current recommendation is for humans to take in no more than 0.1 microgram for every kilogram of their weight per day. Fish generally carry high levels of mercury, although certain fish have higher mercury content than others. Fish, however, are healthy sources of many other nutrients, so nutritionists recommend keeping them in the human diet. The figure shown here shows the average mercury content of several types of fish.

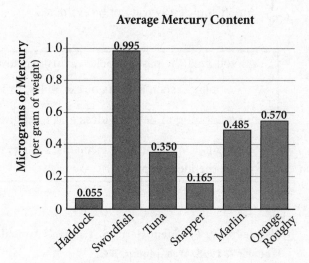

**Average Mercury Content**

37. If a person weighs 82 kilograms, how many grams of snapper can he safely consume per day? Round your answer to the nearest gram.

38. Suppose in a week, a person regularly eats one portion of each type of the fish shown in the bar graph, except the fish with the highest mercury content. What is this person's average daily mercury consumption, in micrograms, assuming a portion size of 100 grams? Round your answer to the nearest microgram.

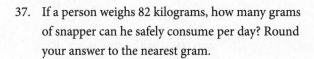

# ESSAY TEST

### 50 Minutes

The essay gives you an opportunity to show how effectively you can read and comprehend a passage and write an essay analyzing the passage. In your essay, you should demonstrate that you have read the passage carefully, present a clear and logical analysis, and use language precisely.

Your essay must be written on the lines provided in your answer booklet; except for the planning page of the answer booklet, you will receive no other paper on which to write. You will have enough space if you write on every line, avoid wide margins, and keep your handwriting to a reasonable size. Remember that people who are not familiar with your handwriting will read what you write. Try to write or print so that what you are writing is legible to those readers.

You have 50 minutes to read the passage and write an essay in response to the prompt provided inside this booklet.

1.  Do not write your essay in this booklet. Only what you write on the lined pages of your answer booklet will be evaluated.
2.  An off-topic essay will not be evaluated.

---

As you read the passage below, consider how President Truman uses

- evidence, such as facts or examples, to support claims.

- reasoning to develop ideas and to connect claims and evidence.

- stylistic or persuasive elements, such as word choice or appeals to emotion, to add power to the ideas expressed.

---

**Adapted from President Harry S. Truman's Annual Message to the Congress on the State of the Union, January 7, 1948, Washington, DC.**

1   We are here today to consider the state of the Union.

2   On this occasion, above all others, the Congress and the President should concentrate their attention, not upon party but upon the country; not upon things which divide us but upon those which bind us together—the enduring principles of our American system, and our common aspirations for the future welfare and security of the people of the United States.

3   The United States has become great because we, as a people, have been able to work together for great objectives even while differing about details....

4   The United States has always had a deep concern for human rights. Religious freedom, free speech, and freedom of thought are cherished realities in our land. Any denial of human rights is a denial of the basic beliefs of democracy and of our regard for the worth of each individual.

**GO ON TO THE NEXT PAGE** ▷

5    Today, however, some of our citizens are still denied equal opportunity for education, for jobs and economic advancement, and for the expression of their views at the polls. Most serious of all, some are denied equal protection under laws. Whether discrimination is based on race, or creed, or color, or land of origin, it is utterly contrary to American ideals of democracy.

6    The recent report of the President's Committee on Civil Rights points the way to corrective action by the federal government and by state and local governments. Because of the need for effective federal action, I shall send a special message to the Congress on this important subject....

7    Our second goal is to protect and develop our human resources.

8    The safeguarding of the rights of our citizens must be accompanied by an equal regard for their opportunities for development and their protection from economic insecurity. In this Nation the ideals of freedom and equality can be given specific meaning in terms of health, education, social security, and housing.

9    Over the past twelve years we have erected a sound framework of Social Security legislation. Many millions of our citizens are now protected against the loss of income which can come with unemployment, old age, or the death of wage earners. Yet our system has gaps and inconsistencies; it is only half finished.

10    We should now extend unemployment compensation, old age benefits, and survivors' benefits to millions who are not now protected. We should also raise the level of benefits.

11    The greatest gap in our Social Security structure is the lack of adequate provision for the Nation's health. We are rightly proud of the high standards of medical care we know how to provide in the United States. The fact is, however, that most of our people cannot afford to pay for the care they need....

12    Another fundamental aim of our democracy is to provide an adequate education for every person.

13    Our educational systems face a financial crisis. It is deplorable that in a Nation as rich as ours there are millions of children who do not have adequate schoolhouses or enough teachers for a good elementary or secondary education. If there are educational inadequacies in any State, the whole Nation suffers. The Federal Government has a responsibility for providing financial aid to meet this crisis.

14    In addition, we must make possible greater equality of opportunity to all our citizens for education. Only by so doing can we insure that our citizens will be capable of understanding and sharing the responsibilities of democracy.

15    The Government's programs for health, education, and security are of such great importance to our democracy that we should now establish an executive department for their administration....

16    Our third goal is to conserve and use our natural resources so that they can contribute most effectively to the welfare of our people.

17    The resources given by nature to this country are rich and extensive. The material foundations of our growth and economic development are the bounty of our fields, the wealth of our mines and forests, and the energy of our waters. As a Nation, we are coming to appreciate more each day the close relationship between the conservation of these resources and the preservation of our national strength.

18    We are doing far less than we know how to do to make use of our resources without destroying them. Both the public and private use of these resources must have the primary objective of maintaining and increasing these basic supports for an expanding future.

GO ON TO THE NEXT PAGE

Write an essay in which you explain how President Truman builds an argument to persuade his audience that continued investment in the nation's collective welfare is based on the ideals of American democracy. In your essay, analyze how he uses one or more of the features listed in the box that precedes the passage (or features of your own choice) to strengthen the logic and persuasiveness of his argument. Be sure that your analysis focuses on the most relevant features of the passage.

Your essay should not explain whether you agree with Truman's claims, but rather explain how he builds an argument to persuade his audience.

## KAPLAN

### TEST PREP AND ADMISSIONS

# SAT®
## Practice Test 3

# READING TEST

## 65 Minutes—52 Questions

Turn to Section 1 of your answer sheet to answer the questions in this section.

**Directions:** Each passage or pair of passages below is followed by a number of questions. After reading each passage or pair, choose the best answer to each question based on what is stated or implied in the passage or passages and in any accompanying graphics (such as a table or graph).

**Questions 1-10 are based on the following passage.**

The following passage is adapted from the short story "Village Opera," by early 20th-century Chinese writer Lu Hsun. The narrator recalls a childhood memory of being a guest, along with his mother, in his grandmother's home in Pingchao Village.

It was the custom in Luchen where we lived
for married women who were not yet in charge of
the household to go back to their parents' home
Line for the summer. Although my father's mother was
(5) then still quite strong, my mother had quite a few
household duties. She could not spend many days
at her own home during the summer. She could
take a few days only after visiting the ancestral
graves. At such times I always went with her to
(10) stay in her parents' house. It was in a place called
Pingchao Village, not far from the sea, a very out-
of-the-way little village on a river, with less than
thirty households, peasants, and fishermen, and
just one tiny grocery....
(15)     We spent most of our days digging up worms,
putting them on little hooks made of copper wire,
and lying on the river bank to catch shrimps.
Shrimps are the silliest water creatures: they willingly
use their own pincers to push the point of the hook
(20) into their mouths; so in a few hours we could catch
a big bowlful. It became the custom to give these
shrimps to me. Another thing we did was to take
the buffaloes out together, but, maybe because they
are animals of a higher species, oxen and buffaloes
(25) are hostile to strangers, and they treated me with
contempt so that I never dared get too close to them.
I could only follow at a distance and stand there....
    What I looked forward to most was going to
Chaochuang to see the opera. Chaochuang was
(30) a slightly larger village about two miles away. Since

Pingchiao was too small to afford to put on operas, every year it contributed some money for a
performance at Chaochuang. At the time, I wasn't
curious why they should have operas every year.
(35) Thinking about it now, I dare say it may have been
for the late spring festival or for the village sacrifice.
    That year when I was eleven or twelve, the
long-awaited day arrived. But as ill luck would
have it, there was no boat for hire that morning.
(40) Pingchiao Village had only one sailing boat,
which left in the morning and came back in the
evening. This was a large boat which it was out of
the question to hire; and all the other boats were
unsuitable because they were too small. Someone
(45) was sent round to the neighbouring villages to ask
if they had boats, but no—they had all been hired
already. My grandmother was very upset, blamed
my cousins for not hiring one earlier, and began to
complain. Mother tried to comfort her by saying
(50) the operas at Luchen were much better than in
these little villages, and there were several every
year, so there was no need to go today. But I was
nearly in tears from disappointment, and mother
did her best to impress on me that no matter what,
(55) I must not make a scene, because it would upset my
grandmother; and I mustn't go with other people
either, for then grandmother would be worried.
    In a word, it had fallen through. After lunch,
when all my friends had left and the opera had
(60) started, I imagined I could hear the sound of gongs
and drums, and saw them, with my mind's eye, in
front of the stage buying soya-bean milk.
    I didn't catch shrimps that day, and didn't eat
much either. Mother was very upset, but there was
(65) nothing she could do. By supper time grandmother

GO ON TO THE NEXT PAGE

realized how I felt, and said I was quite right to be angry, they had been too negligent, and never before had guests been treated so badly. After the meal, youngsters who had come back from the

(70) opera gathered round and gaily described it all for us. I was the only one silent; they all sighed and said how sorry they were for me. Suddenly one of the brightest, called Shuang-hsi, had an inspiration, and said: "A big boat—hasn't Eighth Grand-uncle's

(75) boat come back?" A dozen other boys picked up the idea in a flash, and at once started agitating to take the boat and go with me. I cheered up. But grandmother was nervous, thinking we were all children and undependable. And mother said that

(80) since the grown-ups all had to work the next day, it wouldn't be fair to ask them to go with us and stay up all night. While our fate hung in the balance, Shuang-hsi went to the root of the question and declared loudly: "I give my word it'll be all right! It's

(85) a big boat, Brother Hsun never jumps around, and we can all swim!"

It was true. There wasn't one boy in the dozen who wasn't a fish in water, and two or three of them were first-rate swimmers.

(90) Grandmother and mother were convinced and did not raise any more objections. They both smiled, and we immediately rushed out to the evening performance of the opera.

1. According to the passage, why does the narrator spend time in his mother's parents' home?

   A) He always goes with his mother when she visits there.

   B) His grandmother insists that he come with his mother.

   C) He lives with his grandmother most of the year.

   D) His grandmother needs extra help.

2. As used in line 54, "impress on me" most nearly means

   A) infer.

   B) emphasize.

   C) mark.

   D) understand.

3. The passage most strongly suggests that which of the following is true?

   A) The narrator's grandmother lets the narrator do whatever he wants.

   B) The narrator's mother does not enjoy visiting her mother's home.

   C) The narrator's mother is not head of her household.

   D) The narrator's grandmother thinks his mother is too strict with him.

4. Which choice provides the best evidence for the answer to the previous question?

   A) Lines 1-4 ("It was the . . . summer")

   B) Lines 9-10 ("At such times . . . parents' house")

   C) Lines 15-17 ("We spent . . . to catch shrimps")

   D) Lines 35-36 ("Thinking about it . . . the village sacrifice")

5. What theme does the passage communicate through the experiences of the narrator?

   A) Traditions are meant to be changed.

   B) Hope is hard to maintain.

   C) Hardship is a part of life.

   D) Problems can sometimes be solved.

6. Based on the passage, why do the narrator's mother and grandmother change their minds about letting him go to the opera?

   A) They decide they could trust the person who owns the boat.

   B) They want to please the narrator since he was so sad.

   C) They are assured that the boys would not be in danger.

   D) They realize that the boat is not that small.

7. Which choice provides the best evidence for the answer to the previous question?

   A) Lines 42-44 ("This was . . . too small")

   B) Lines 58-62 ("After lunch . . . soya-bean milk")

   C) Lines 79-82 ("And mother . . . all night")

   D) Lines 87-89 ("It was . . . swimmers")

8. The author's use of the phrase "with my mind's eye" (line 61) implies that the narrator

   A) sees visions.

   B) has poor eyesight.

   C) wants to go to sleep.

   D) has a good imagination.

9. As used in line 76, "agitating" most nearly means

   A) campaigning.

   B) shaking.

   C) disturbing.

   D) stirring.

10. Based on the tone of this passage, what emotion does the author want the reader to feel toward the narrator?

    A) Sympathy

    B) Criticism

    C) Indifference

    D) Hostility

**Questions 11-20 are based on the following passage.**

The following passage is adapted from a pivotal 1964 speech by South Africa's Nelson Mandela, called "An Ideal for Which I Am Prepared to Die." Mandela, later elected first president of democratic South Africa, gave this speech before his trial and imprisonment for activism against apartheid, a now-obsolete system of racial segregation in South Africa.

The lack of human dignity experienced by Africans is the direct result of the policy of white supremacy. . . . Menial tasks in South Africa are
*Line* invariably performed by Africans. When anything
(5) has to be carried or cleaned the white man will look around for an African to do it for him, whether the African is employed by him or not. Because of this sort of attitude, whites . . . do not look upon them as people with families of their own; they do not
(10) realise that they have emotions—that they fall in love like white people do; that they want to be with their wives and children like white people want to be with theirs; that they want to earn enough money to support their families properly, to feed
(15) and clothe them and send them to school. . . .

   Pass laws[1], which to the Africans are among the most hated bits of legislation in South Africa, render any African liable to police surveillance at any time. I doubt whether there is a single African
(20) male in South Africa who has not at some stage had a brush with the police over his pass. Hundreds and thousands of Africans are thrown into jail each year under pass laws. Even worse than this is the fact that pass laws keep husband and wife apart and
(25) lead to the breakdown of family life.

   Poverty and the breakdown of family life have secondary effects. Children wander about the streets of the townships because they have no schools to go to, or no money to enable them to go
(30) to school, or no parents at home to see that they go to school, because both parents (if there be two) have to work to keep the family alive. This leads to a breakdown in moral standards . . . and to growing

[1]Pass laws: Black South Africans were legally required to carry pass books, which were like internal passports with the purpose of restricting where Africans could go, thus maintaining racial segregation.

**GO ON TO THE NEXT PAGE**

*everything goes Bat shit crazy*

violence which erupts not only politically, but
(35) everywhere. . . .

*life out*

Africans want to perform work which they
are capable of doing, and not work which the
government declares them to be capable of.
Africans want to be allowed to live where they
(40) obtain work, and not be endorsed out of an area
because they were not born there. Africans want to
be allowed to own land in places where they work,
and not to be obliged to live in rented houses which
they can never call their own. Africans want to be
(45) part of the general population, and not confined
to living in their own ghettoes. African men want
to have their wives and children to live with them
where they work. . . . Africans want to be allowed
out after eleven o'clock at night and not to be
(50) confined to their rooms like little children. Africans
want to be allowed to travel in their own country
and to seek work where they want to and not where
the labour bureau tells them to. Africans want a
just share in the whole of South Africa; they want
(55) security and a stake in society.

*Political rights*

Above all, we want equal political rights, because
without them our disabilities will be permanent. I
know this sounds revolutionary to the whites in this
country, because the majority of voters will be
(60) Africans. This makes the white man fear democracy.

But this fear cannot be allowed to stand in the
way of the only solution which will guarantee racial
harmony and freedom for all. It is not true that the
enfranchisement of all will result in racial domina-
(65) tion. Political division, based on colour, is entirely
artificial and, when it disappears, so will the domination of one colour group by another. The ANC[2] has
spent half a century fighting against racialism. When
it triumphs it will not change that policy.

(70)    This then is what the ANC is fighting. Their
struggle is a truly national one. It is a struggle of
the African people, inspired by their own suffering
and their own experience. It is a struggle for the
right to live.

(75)    During my lifetime I have dedicated myself to
this struggle of the African people. I have fought
against white domination, and I have fought

---

[2]ANC: African National Congress, the political organization that
spearheaded the movement for equal rights in South Africa.

against black domination. I have cherished the
ideal of a democratic and free society in which all
(80) persons live together in harmony and with equal
opportunities. It is an ideal which I hope to live
for and to achieve. But if needs be, it is an ideal for
which I am prepared to die.

11. The most likely intended purpose of this speech is to

A) explain the political goals of the ANC.

B) explain why Mandela is not guilty of the
crime of which he is accused.

C) argue that the laws passed under apartheid
are illegal.

D) explain to white South Africans why the
apartheid system must be abolished.

12. Which choice provides the best evidence for the
answer to the previous question?

A) Lines 1-3 ("The lack of . . . supremacy")

B) Lines 36-37 ("Africans want . . . of doing")

C) Lines 67-68 ("The ANC . . . racialism")

D) Lines 75-76 ("During . . . African people")

13. As used in line 40, the phrase "endorsed out of"
most nearly means

A) supported by.

B) restricted from.

C) authorized for.

D) approved to be in.

14. It can most reasonably be inferred that pass laws

A) led to the criminal behavior they were
designed to prevent.

B) were fundamentally European and incom-
patible with African life.

C) led to the passage of additional apartheid
laws.

D) were a necessary part of South Africa's
transition to democracy.

GO ON TO THE NEXT PAGE

15. Which choice provides the best evidence for the answer to the previous question?

    A) Lines 19-21 ("I doubt . . . his pass")

    B) Lines 21-23 ("Hundreds . . . pass laws")

    C) Lines 26-27 ("Poverty . . . effects")

    D) Lines 32-35 ("This leads to . . . but everywhere")

16. As used in line 66, "artificial" most nearly means

    A) simulated.

    B) not genuine.

    C) imitative.

    D) human-made.

17. According to Mandela's claims, what is true of democracy?

    A) It is fundamentally incompatible with white rule.

    B) It existed in South Africa before apartheid.

    C) It is a goal of white South Africans.

    D) It would lead to increased crime at all levels.

18. The statement in lines 67-69 ("The ANC . . . policy") is important to the overall argument in its suggestion that

    A) black South Africans will initiate steps to curb violence without pass laws.

    B) black South Africans will be happier once there are equal political rights.

    C) black South Africans will not retaliate once there are equal political rights.

    D) black South Africans will continue to endorse a separate but equal system.

19. It can most reasonably be inferred that Mandela would most likely support which of the following future policies?

    A) Reduction of domestic employment

    B) Job training for untrained workers

    C) Pass laws for all whites and blacks

    D) Investment in overseas business

20. The sixth paragraph of Mandela's speech can best be described as

    A) a promise that the changes he proposes will be good for all people.

    B) a contrast between his former beliefs and those he currently holds.

    C) an acknowledgment that he knows there is no perfect system.

    D) a thank-you for people's continued support in a difficult situation.

**Questions 21-31 are based on the following passage and supplementary material.**

The following passage discusses the surprisingly complex endeavor of keeping dictionaries up-to-date.

If you've ever played Scrabble, you know who the ultimate arbiter in that word game is: You challenge a word your opponent makes by reaching
*Line* for that infallible judge, the dictionary. After all,
(5) a dictionary is a definitive collection of words, spellings, and meanings, right?

Actually, that isn't quite so, because while we regard dictionaries as catalogs of correctness, the truth is that dictionaries do not tell the whole story.
(10) We can think of them as horses pulling tidy carts of our cluttered language, but in fact, as David Skinner wrote in the *New York Times* (May 17, 2013), "in following *Webster*'s you're following the followers."

That's because language is an ever-changing
(15) thing in which new words are invented all the time and old words are put to new use. Keeping up with this is daunting task, as the writers of the *Oxford English Dictionary*, or *OED*, found out over 100 years ago.

GO ON TO THE NEXT PAGE ▷

(20)  In 1879, members of the Philological Society of London began working with James Murray of Oxford University Press to produce a more complete dictionary than what was available at the time. In ten years, they estimated, they would (25) publish a four-volume, 6,400-page dictionary covering all English language vocabulary from the Early Middle English period (c. AD 1150) onward. However, five years along they were only as far as the word "ant"! The task of tracking new words and (30) new meanings of existing words while examining the previous seven centuries of the language's development proved monumental.

It turned out that their work required ten volumes, included over 400,000 words, and was not (35) fully published until 1924. Even then, the editors' first job after completion of the monstrous *OED* was to print an addendum, which came out a mere nine years later.

As Skinner says, "There is always much more to (40) know about a word than what a dictionary can tell you."

According to Global Language Monitor, a new word is created every 98 minutes; this results in an average of about 14 words per day. They (45) come from regular people; from writers; from specialized, often scientific fields; and from the Internet.

A short list of the words spawned by the Internet and its technologies includes "blog," "avatar," "spam," (50) and "webisode." Every year, Merriam-Webster's, publisher of America's premier dictionary, adds a jumble of words that have been coined by Web users and promulgated across the Internet's multitudinous channels: websites, chat rooms, forums, blogs, and, (55) of course, social media platforms.

Just like other professional and social realms, the Internet produces both new words and new definitions of old words. The word "troll," for example, dates back to 1616 as a name for "a (60) dwarf or giant in Scandinavian folklore inhabiting caves or hills." In the last decade, however, "troll" emerged as a term for someone who participates in Internet discussions, not to contribute meaningfully, but for the sole purpose of making

(65) harsh rebuttals and insults.

Dictionary makers are faced with tough decisions. Any dictionary that doesn't include Internet-produced words would be seen as being behind the times, although many feel that (70) dictionaries go too far in their role as recorders of what gets said rather than rule-makers of correct usage. One of the most controversial new entries happened in 2013, when several major dictionaries added a definition for "literally" that literally (75) means the literal opposite of its meaning! To some it seemed to erode the very purpose of a dictionary, but consensus prevailed, and Merriam-Webster's now lists "in effect; virtually" as one meaning of literally. In response to criticism it (80) received, Merriam-Webster's wrote, "the use is pure hyperbole intended to gain emphasis." Seemingly as a concession to those who call the definition incorrect, it added, "but it often appears in contexts where no additional emphasis is necessary."

(85)  For those who grumble about the imprecision that this entry enjoins, perhaps the best attitude to have is that expressed on the *Oxford English Dictionary*'s website: "An exhilarating aspect of a living language is that it continually changes."

### Internet Words Added to Merriam-Webster's Dictionary

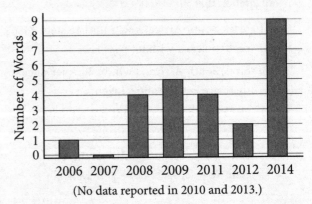

(No data reported in 2010 and 2013.)

Data from merriam-webster.com.

GO ON TO THE NEXT PAGE

21. The stance the author takes in the passage is best described as that of

    A) a columnist discussing a topic of interest.

    B) a pundit advocating support for a position.

    C) a reporter investigating a current event.

    D) a researcher cataloguing historical data.

22. According to the first two paragraphs, what claim does the author seek to refute?

    A) The assertion that Merriam-Webster's is the best authority to follow

    B) The assumption that Scrabble users rely on dictionaries for aid

    C) The notion that dictionaries are absolute and undeniable authorities

    D) The prediction that dictionaries will become cluttered over time

23. Which choice provides the best evidence for the answer to the previous question?

    A) Lines 1-2 ("If you've . . . game is")

    B) Lines 2-4 ("You challenge . . . dictionary")

    C) Lines 4-6 ("After all, . . . right")

    D) Lines 11-13 ("David Skinner . . . followers")

24. As used in line 32, "monumental" most nearly means

    A) important.

    B) impossible.

    C) tremendous.

    D) ungainly.

25. What idea does the author convey in lines 45-46 through the use of the succession of phrases "from regular people; from writers; from specialized, often scientific fields"?

    A) Definitions of words reflect usage for varied purposes among different people.

    B) Dictionaries must be accessible to users from all walks of life.

    C) People from several professional fields contributed to the development of the *OED*.

    D) Words come from many sources, including nonphilological ones.

26. What conclusion can most reasonably be inferred from lines 50-55 ("Every year . . . social media platforms")?

    A) Dictionaries are easily updated through online and other digital tools.

    B) Navigating the Web requires adopting new meanings for existing words.

    C) The Internet is the most prolific source of new words today.

    D) Words gain not only meaning but also legitimacy through usage.

27. Which choice provides the best evidence for the answer to the previous question?

    A) Lines 42-44 ("According to . . . per day")

    B) Lines 58-61 ("The word . . . or hills")

    C) Lines 61-65 ("In the last . . . insults")

    D) Lines 75-77 ("To some . . . a dictionary")

GO ON TO THE NEXT PAGE

28. What statement is best supported by the data presented in the graphic?

    A) Before 2014, fewer than five words from the Internet were added.

    B) Fewer words from the Internet were added from 2006-2008 than during 2009.

    C) More words from the Internet were added in the years after 2010 than before 2010.

    D) So far, in the 21st century, twenty-six words from the Internet have been added.

29. As used in line 76, "erode" most nearly means

    A) diminish.

    B) dissolve.

    C) consume.

    D) wear.

30. As presented in the passage, the relationship between language and dictionaries is

    A) dictionaries reflect the flaws and inconsistencies of language.

    B) dictionaries attempt to address the idea that language changes over time.

    C) dictionaries establish definite meanings for new words.

    D) dictionaries support the opinion that the study of language is exhilarating.

31. Data in the graphic most directly support which conclusion from the passage?

    A) Dictionaries are imperfect records of the English language.

    B) Language changes in response to the needs of those who use it.

    C) Many new words originate from evolving technologies.

    D) Online usage constantly adapts the meaning of existing words.

**Questions 32-42 are based on the following passages.**

Passage 2 describes the unique wildlife habitat found in the Sargasso Sea. Passage 1 focuses on new techniques for tracking newborn loggerhead sea turtles, one species found in the Sargasso Sea.

**Passage 1**

A baby loggerhead sea turtle hatches in its nest buried deep in the sand. Soon, it emerges onto the beach with its siblings. The palm-sized creatures
Line venture across the sand and into the waves of
(5) the Atlantic Ocean. The tiny turtles must vanish quickly to avoid the many predators looming on the dunes or near the water. Seagulls, raccoons, and other animals are eager to make a meal out of the brand-new hatchlings.
(10) Until now, scientists have been unable to track where baby sea turtles go once they reach the water. Small satellite transmitters have allowed older loggerheads to be tracked and studied from afar, giving researchers a window into their migration
(15) patterns, their social behaviors, and other patterns that can be difficult to track in the ocean. But the travels of a newly hatched sea turtle have remained a mystery.
Scientists on the island of Boa Vista, off the coast
(20) of West Africa, have successfully tagged eleven hatchlings with nanoacoustic tags. This has allowed scientists to follow the baby turtles for their first eight hours in the ocean. The tags, which send a ping that the researchers can then plot, are glued
(25) to the shells of the baby loggerheads. The glue was specifically designed to dissolve completely within a few days. The tags are small enough to avoid interfering with the turtles' swimming.
The hatchlings surprised scientists with their
(30) speed. Once the turtles found the ocean currents that would transport them, they could travel at a speed of nearly 200 feet per minute. In the first eight hours of their journeys, some traveled more than nine miles. Tagged turtles released in various
(35) locations all eventually made their way to the Sargasso Sea in the Northern Atlantic Ocean. Here, they become part of the floating ecosystem, eating bite-sized prey and using the sargassum seaweed as rafts. They can sometimes spend up to a decade

GO ON TO THE NEXT PAGE

(40) here before returning to the shores where they hatched. The use of nanoacoustic tags should help protect this endangered species by giving scientists more information about these turtles and when they are most vulnerable.

**Passage 2**

(45)     A great number of species make their home in the vast waters of the Atlantic Ocean. Although the entire ocean makes up an ecosystem, many smaller habitats are found within, including an open-water habitat off the coast of the Northern Atlantic Ocean
(50) known as the Sargasso Sea. Sargassum is an algae that floats in masses that can continue for miles. The waters of the Gulf Stream push the water in a northward motion into this area. This constant motion and varying temperatures support the
(55) accumulation of the brown-colored seaweed.

    The Sargasso Sea is so immense that one method of information collection has not been enough for scientists to obtain an accurate picture of what takes place within this ecosystem. Researchers
(60) have needed to employ several methods of sampling. Methods such as dragging mesh nets over the surface of the water and videotaping beneath areas of sargassum have served scientists well. Information collected has shown that the Gulf
(65) Stream pushes brown algae from open water into the Sargasso Sea area, creating a diverse floating habitat in an area that would otherwise not support that wildlife.

    In the most recent study of the sargassum
(70) community off the shores of North Carolina, eighty-one fish species were documented as using the area as a microhabitat. This is an increase from previous studies. The types of fish found here are both commercially and environmentally important.
(75) Also found here are juvenile loggerhead sea turtles. The South Atlantic Fishery Management Council is working to regulate the harvesting of sargassum. The Council hopes to have the area classified as an Essential Fish Habitat, which would afford it
(80) certain protections.

    Further research needs to be done before scientists understand how best to protect the

Sargasso Sea as well as understand how it goes about supporting so many important types of
(85) wildlife.

32.  The central idea of Passage 1 is that

A)  the island of Boa Vista, off the coast of Africa, has become a key research center for monitoring baby loggerhead sea turtles.

B)  the number of baby loggerhead sea turtles decreases every year, which concerns scientists around the world.

C)  scientists are using new technology to track the movements of newborn loggerhead sea turtles, and the results have surprised them.

D)  scientists are interested in how long loggerhead sea turtles remain in the Sargasso Sea before returning to where they hatched.

33.  Passage 1 most strongly suggests that which of the following is true of the scientists' usage of nanoacoustic tags?

A)  The size of the tags is appropriate for baby turtles and will thus offer the most accurate readings.

B)  The low cost of the tags is greatly preferable to the expensive satellite technology previously used.

C)  The tags protect baby loggerhead turtles from the predators they are likely to meet in the first eight hours of their journey.

D)  Scientists prefer gluing the tags because they believe it is more humane than clipping older satellite tags to flippers.

GO ON TO THE NEXT PAGE ⟶

34. Which choice provides the best evidence for the answer to the previous question?

    A) Lines 21-23 ("This has . . . ocean")

    B) Lines 23-25 ("The tags, which . . . loggerheads")

    C) Lines 27-28 ("The tags are . . . swimming")

    D) Lines 34-36 ("Tagged turtles . . . Ocean")

35. As used in line 44 of Passage 1, "vulnerable" most nearly means

    A) defenseless.

    B) inexperienced.

    C) naive.

    D) open.

36. Passage 2 most strongly suggests that which of the following is true of the importance of the Sargasso Sea research?

    A) The research is important in order to ensure that the Gulf Stream does not push the algae too far north.

    B) Data about the Sargasso ecosystem is valuable to conservationists and the fishing industry alike.

    C) The research is important for convincing politicians that fish species are disappearing from the ecosystem.

    D) Through these studies, scientists are able to eliminate predators from the North Carolina microhabitat.

37. Which choice provides the best evidence for the answer to the previous question?

    A) Lines 52-53 ("The waters of . . . area")

    B) Lines 53-55 ("This constant . . . seaweed")

    C) Lines 69-72 ("In the most . . . microhabitat")

    D) Lines 73-74 ("The types of fish . . . important")

38. As used in line 78 of Passage 2, "classified" most nearly means

    A) arranged.

    B) cataloged.

    C) categorized.

    D) pigeonholed.

39. It can most reasonably be inferred from the phrase "needs to be done" (line 81) that the author of Passage 2 thinks

    A) new methods for researching the ecosystem are required before funding continues.

    B) the Sargasso Sea is becoming a problem for shipping lanes and requires removal.

    C) the scientific community has ignored this complex and delicate ecosystem.

    D) the Sargasso ecosystem is worthy of our attention and requires intense study.

40. The author uses the words "great," "vast," and "immense" in Passage 2 in order to emphasize that

    A) the work researchers conduct is highly respected by a growing scientific community.

    B) the microhabitats are large despite their name and require extensive periods for study.

    C) the amount of funding required for Sargasso Sea research is commensurate with the large area that must be covered.

    D) the level of complexity for researchers is heightened by the large area that must be covered.

GO ON TO THE NEXT PAGE

41. Which statement best describes the difference between the purpose of Passage 1 and the purpose of Passage 2?

    A) The purpose of Passage 2 is to convince politicians to lend aid, while Passage 1 speaks to a general audience.

    B) Passage 1 aims to convince readers that these studies are futile, while Passage 2 has a more optimistic viewpoint of the research.

    C) Passage 2 discusses current research trends for an entire ecosystem, while Passage 1 focuses on a single species.

    D) The purpose of Passage 2 is to show that scientists cannot agree on a single research method, while they are able to do so in Passage 1.

42. Both passages support which generalization?

    A) The most dangerous period of time for young loggerhead turtles is the first eight hours of life.

    B) The technology used to research the ecosystem and its inhabitants continues to evolve.

    C) Recent studies show that the number of fish and turtle species in the Sargasso Sea is increasing.

    D) The ability of scientists to collect data on the Sargasso Sea properly depends on vital government grants.

**Questions 43-52 are based on the following passage and supplementary material.**

The following passage explains what causes colorblindness and why men are affected more often than women.

About eight percent of men of European descent are colorblind, but only about half a percent of women are affected by the same condition. Most of
*Line* these people are "red-green" colorblind, meaning
(5) they cannot see colors related to green or red. Not only are they unable to tell red and green apart, but yellows and oranges do not appear different, nor do blues and purples. Colorblindness is not "blindness" but is instead an inability to distinguish
(10) certain wavelengths of light. A red-green colorblind man looking at a red object can see the object and can see that it is not white; however, he is unable to tell whether the object is red or green, as they both appear similar to him.

(15) People with normal color vision see color because they have an array of three types of photosensitive cells, called cones, on the back of their retinas. Each type of cone has a different pigment that is sensitive to a certain part of the
(20) visible light spectrum. The visible light spectrum runs from smaller wavelengths at the blue end, through medium wavelengths in the green to yellow range, to long wavelengths at the red end.

The cones are often referred to as blue, green,
(25) and red cones, based on the wavelength of light they absorb most. The blue cones absorb the blue wavelengths of light most, although they also absorb a small amount of the green wavelengths. The green cones have their maximum absorption
(30) in the green wavelengths, but also absorb partially into the blue and up into the yellow wavelengths. The range that the red cones absorb significantly overlaps the range of the green cones; the red cone maximum absorption is in the yellow wave-
(35) lengths, but red cones also absorb a bit down into the green, through the yellow, and up into the red wavelengths.

Even though the green and red cones absorb much of the same part of the visible spectrum, a
(40) person who lacks the sensitive pigment in either red or green cones will have difficulty perceiving either color, because the brain compares the signals from both to determine exactly which region of light is being absorbed. With only one set of cones
(45) sending signals, the brain will perceive light from the green, yellow, and red wavelengths to be about the same.

A person will lack the pigment for either green or red cones if he or she lacks the gene necessary
(50) to make that pigment. Because genes are inherited

GO ON TO THE NEXT PAGE ➡

from our parents, half from each parent, we would expect men and women to have an equal chance of being colorblind. The actual ratio is about sixteen colorblind men for each colorblind woman. The
(55) reason for this inequality becomes clear once we know that the genes for making the cone pigments are on the X chromosome.

Women have two X chromosomes, one from each parent. Men only have one X chromosome, which
(60) they get from their mother. A woman can receive a colorblind gene on an X chromosome from one parent, but if the other X chromosome has a normal cone pigment gene, she will still make normal pigments and have normal color vision.
(65) The woman would need to receive the colorblind gene from each parent to be colorblind. Since a man only has the one X chromosome, receiving the colorblind gene from his mother will always cause colorblindness in a man.

(70) Women who have only one copy of the colorblind gene are referred to as carriers because they carry the gene but are not affected by it. By tracking the family members with colorblindness, we can create a chart, called a pedigree, to determine which
(75) women in the family are carriers. A colorblind daughter must have had a colorblind father and either a colorblind or carrier mother, as she must have received a copy of the colorblind gene from each parent. A colorblind son also must have had
(80) either a colorblind or carrier mother, but whether or not the father was colorblind will not affect the son.

43. The passage is primarily concerned with

A) how to determine whether a person is colorblind.

B) research being conducted about colorblindness.

C) how people who are colorblind perceive color.

D) the genetic and physiological causes of colorblindness.

44. Which choice provides the best evidence for the answer to the previous question?

A) Lines 1-3 ("About eight . . . condition")

B) Lines 15-18 ("People with . . . retinas")

C) Lines 24-26 ("The cones . . . absorb most")

D) Lines 48-50 ("A person . . . pigment")

45. In the sixth paragraph, the author mentions details about X chromosomes primarily to

A) give examples of other traits inherited from mothers.

B) explain why more men than women are colorblind.

C) illustrate how genes affect vision and colorblindness.

D) contrast colorblindness with other genetic disorders.

**Pedigree Chart of Color Blindness**
**Within One Family**

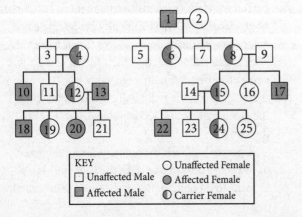

KEY
□ Unaffected Male
■ Affected Male
○ Unaffected Female
● Affected Female
◐ Carrier Female

GO ON TO THE NEXT PAGE

46. Based on the information in the passage, which choice best describes what causes red and green to be the two colors that a colorblind person often cannot perceive?

    A) A colorblind person is missing both red and green cones on the back of the retinas.

    B) Because blue wavelengths are brighter, they overpower both red and green wavelengths.

    C) Because red and green absorption ranges overlap greatly, the colorblind person's brain has trouble interpreting the difference between those two colors.

    D) Red and green are on opposite sides of the color wheel, so their absorption ranges are at the farthest, opposite ends of the visible light spectrum.

47. Which choice would best support the author's line of reasoning in the first paragraph?

    A) Details about other types of colorblindness

    B) A more detailed explanation of the light spectrum

    C) A list of other genetic disorders that affect men

    D) Information about how colorblindness is diagnosed

48. As used in line 19, "sensitive" most nearly means

    A) delicate.

    B) responsive.

    C) sympathetic.

    D) vulnerable.

49. Based on the information in the passage, it can most reasonably be inferred that which of the following statements is true?

    A) Colorblindness can be corrected with treatments designed to encourage the growth of the missing genes that make pigments.

    B) A person with normal color vision can become colorblind as he or she ages and the photosensitive cells degenerate.

    C) A person who is colorblind will experience the visual world in a way that is different from a person with normal color vision.

    D) Colorblindness cannot be diagnosed without invasive and expensive genetic testing of both a person and his or her parents.

50. Which choice provides the best evidence for the answer to the previous question?

    A) Lines 10-14 ("A red-green . . . him")

    B) Lines 26-27 ("The blue cones . . . wavelengths")

    C) Lines 42-44 ("the brain . . . absorbed")

    D) Lines 72-75 ("By tracking . . . carriers")

GO ON TO THE NEXT PAGE ⟹

51. As used in line 72, "affected" most nearly means

    A) changed.

    B) concerned.

    C) exaggerated.

    D) involved.

52. Based on the information in the passage and the graphic, which of the following statements is true?

    A) A male with a colorblind mother and a father who is not colorblind has a 100% chance of being a carrier for the colorblind gene, but not colorblind himself.

    B) A male with a colorblind father and a mother who is a carrier has a 100% chance of being colorblind.

    C) A female with a colorblind father and a mother who is not a carrier has a 100% chance of being a carrier for the colorblind gene.

    D) A female with a mother who is a carrier but not colorblind and a colorblind father has a 100% chance of being colorblind.

# WRITING AND LANGUAGE TEST

## 35 Minutes—44 Questions

Turn to Section 2 of your answer sheet to answer the questions in this section.

**Directions:** Each passage below is accompanied by a number of questions. For some questions, you will consider how the passage might be revised to improve the expression of ideas. For other questions, you will consider how the passage might be edited to correct errors in sentence structure, usage, or punctuation. A passage or a question may be accompanied by one or more graphics (such as a table or graph) that you will consider as you make revising and editing decisions.

Some questions will direct you to an underlined portion of a passage. Other questions will direct you to a location in a passage or ask you to think about the passage as a whole.

After reading each passage, choose the answer to each question that most effectively improves the quality of writing in the passage or that makes the passage conform to the conventions of standard written English. Many questions include a "NO CHANGE" option. Choose that option if you think the best choice is to leave the relevant portion of the passage as it is.

**Questions 1-11 are based on the following passage and supplementary material.**

## Antarctic Treaty System in Need of Reform

The Antarctic Treaty System (ATS) was established in 1959 to provide governance over an entire continent and the surrounding Southern Ocean. Twelve member **1** countries, including the United States currently manage the affairs of Antarctica. In the next fifty years, however, it is likely that existing conflicts will **2** accelerate over the sovereignty and resources of Antarctica, challenging the ATS. Some countries feel the ATS should be reformed, while other countries argue that Antarctica should be designated as the shared heritage of humankind and be placed under the watch of the United Nations.

1. A) NO CHANGE
   B) countries including the United States, currently manage
   C) countries: including the United States currently manage
   D) countries including the United States currently manage

2. A) NO CHANGE
   B) anticipate
   C) decelerate
   D) vacillate

GO ON TO THE NEXT PAGE

**3** Altogether, opponents of the ATS believe that politics should trump science in Antarctica. A main objective of the ATS was to establish international research on a continent considered a "perfect laboratory." But new technological advances have countries **4** interested in Antarctic minerals, although mineral extraction is currently banned to protect the environment. **5** New players in Antarctic affairs such as China are oil-poor states. They view Antarctica's mineral resources as one solution to their increasing oil demands.

3. A) NO CHANGE
   B) Mainly,
   C) Surprisingly,
   D) Selfishly,

4. A) NO CHANGE
   B) thinking about
   C) curious about
   D) uninterested in

5. Which choice most effectively combines the underlined sentences?

   A) New players in Antarctic affairs such as China are oil-poor states, and so they view Antarctica's mineral resources as one solution to their increasing oil demands.

   B) New players in Antarctic affairs such as China are oil-poor states, even though they view Antarctica's mineral resources as one solution to their increasing oil demands.

   C) New players in Antarctic affairs such as China are oil-poor states, viewing Antarctica's mineral resources as the solution to their increasing oil demands.

   D) New players in Antarctic affairs such as China are oil-poor states, despite their view that Antarctica's mineral resources are one solution to their increasing oil demands.

GO ON TO THE NEXT PAGE

**6** In the case of China, its future demand for energy from resources such as oil and coal is forecasted to surpass that of all other countries.

**7** Because of its many reserves such as coal, uranium, oil, and natural gas, Antarctica is indeed a rich continent. Yet, for environmental reasons, and because icebergs and weather have made mineral extraction expensive, there has never been commercial mining.

6. Which choice best supports the author's claim that China is an "oil-poor state" with accurate data based on the graphic?

   A) NO CHANGE

   B) In 2010, China's oil consumption exceeded production by approximately 10 million barrels per day.

   C) By 2015, China's oil consumption is forecasted to exceed production by approximately 7 million barrels per day.

   D) By 2015, China's oil production is forecasted to exceed consumption by approximately 7 million barrels per day.

7. A) NO CHANGE

   B) With reserves such as coal, uranium, oil, and natural gas,

   C) Because it has various reserves which include coal, uranium, oil, and natural gas,

   D) Due to its reserves like coal, uranium, and oil, and natural gas,

But non-member countries believe that easier methods of extracting oil will bring the ATS's mineral ban into review. **[8]** Right now, the ATS's superpowers choose to ignore the prediction that Antarctica may hold 200 billion barrels of oil. When the protocol banning extraction is re-examined in 2048, **[9]** it will be waiting to capitalize on mineral claims in Antarctic locations.

There is also the economic issue of the Southern Ocean, because management of the commercial exploitation of marine resources is part of the ATS. **[10]** Fishing

8. A) NO CHANGE
   B) At the current moment, the superpowers of the ATS fail to realize the prediction that Antarctica may hold 200 billion barrels of oil.
   C) Currently, the ATS's superpowers are not addressing the prediction that Antarctica may hold 200 billion barrels of oil.
   D) For now, the ATS's superpowers don't seem to mind the prediction that Antarctica may hold 200 billion barrels of oil.

9. A) NO CHANGE
   B) an energy-hungry world
   C) they
   D) this banning protocol

10. At this point, the writer wants to add specific information that connects the ideas of the first sentence with the rest of the paragraph. Which choice most effectively accomplishes this goal?

    A) Antarctica has a wide variety of fish.
    B) This is one of several areas of responsibility assigned to the ATS.
    C) Other areas of the world have been heavily overfished.
    D) Non-member nations want to utilize the fishing ground.

**GO ON TO THE NEXT PAGE** →

is a primary industry for many countries; 11 therefore, Chinese Russian and other officials argue that forming marine preserves in Antarctica's periphery will seal off future fishing possibilities as fish stocks in the world are being depleted. Such a challenge has people wondering if national economic incentives are overwhelming the ATS's competing science and conservation values for the Southern Ocean.

These examples illustrate that after two decades, Antarctica's current governance structure isn't addressing new global priorities such as fuel and food security. As has probably been said by others before, detractors already feel that the continent could be better governed by the United Nations instead of the ATS. Without concessions or reform, many doubt the system can accommodate a wider community and survive in its current form.

11. A) NO CHANGE
    B) therefore Chinese Russian and other officials
    C) therefore Chinese Russian, and other officials
    D) therefore, Chinese, Russian, and other officials

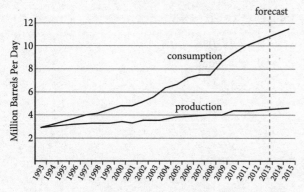

**China's Oil Production and Consumption, 1993-2015**

Adapted from U.S. Energy Information Administration, International Energy Statistics and Short-Term Energy Outlook, January 2014.

GO ON TO THE NEXT PAGE

**Questions 12-22 are based on the following passage.**

## Finding Pluto

Clyde Tombaugh sat down at an apparatus called a blink comparator, where he had spent hundreds of hours looking at photographic images of stars that appeared as [12] tiny little white specks on the black photographic plates. It was Thursday, February 13, 1930, and Tombaugh had been working at Lowell Observatory for about [13] thirteen months, he was looking for a planet that Percival Lowell had predicted would be at the far boundary of the solar system. [14] However, finding this elusive planet was not an easy task.

Tombaugh picked up the next set of photographic plates; weeks earlier, he had taken the photographs by pointing a telescope at a particular spot in the night sky, days apart but at the same time. If Lowell was right, one of the white specks would be in two different positions on the two plates. Tombaugh [15] loaded the images side by side in the blink comparator and looked through the eyepiece to compare the enlarged images.

12. A) NO CHANGE
    B) very tiny, little white specks
    C) tiny miniscule white specks
    D) tiny white specks

13. A) NO CHANGE
    B) thirteen months; he was looking
    C) thirteen months he was looking
    D) thirteen months, however, he was looking

14. Which choice most effectively concludes the paragraph?
    A) NO CHANGE
    B) The blink comparator is one of the most valuable tools astronomers have.
    C) Astronomy is among the oldest of the natural sciences.
    D) The Lowell Observatory is located in Flagstaff, Arizona.

15. A) NO CHANGE
    B) burdened
    C) changed
    D) led

Like Lowell, Tombaugh believed there was an additional planet in our solar system, farther away than Neptune. Neptune's orbit did not exactly match the one predicted by calculations, and the presence of another planet could have caused that difference. [16]

Tombaugh moved a mirror in the viewer. It allowed him to look at a small area in the image on the left. When he moved the mirror again, he saw the image on the right in exactly the same place; the image did not change as he flipped back and forth, so he moved the images slightly and began looking at the next area, slowly working his way around the plates.

Tombaugh knew he could [17] check between a planet in our solar system and the stars; the planet, being closer, would change location in the sky relative to the stars. [18] Although, the farther the planet is from Earth, the more slowly that change happens, making it difficult to observe.

[1] Tombaugh continued to work his way, inch by inch, over the images, flipping back and forth with [19] the mirror; he saw no difference between the two images at each location, indicating he had nothing but far-away stars in the images. [2] Once more, he moved the images and flipped the mirror back and forth while looking through the eyepiece. [3] This time, as he blinked from one image to another, a speck seemed to move. [4] He knew immediately that it was significant; checking more images convinced him that he had found

16. At this point, the writer wants to add specific information that supports the central idea of the paragraph. Which choice most effectively accomplishes this goal?

   A) Tombaugh wanted to find a new planet very badly.

   B) This is because the gravitational pull of planets can affect the orbit of nearby planets.

   C) Neptune is the eighth planet from the sun and has an elliptical orbit.

   D) Lowell and Tombaugh disagreed about whether the presence of another planet could affect Neptune's orbit.

17. A) NO CHANGE

    B) compliment

    C) further

    D) distinguish

18. A) NO CHANGE

    B) Despite,

    C) However,

    D) Moreover,

19. A) NO CHANGE

    B) the mirror, he saw no difference

    C) the mirror he saw no difference

    D) the mirror so he saw no difference

GO ON TO THE NEXT PAGE ▷

a planet, which was eventually named Pluto. [5] Pluto was named for the Roman god of the underworld, because it was cold and far from the sun. **20**

Since that time, scientists **21** has determined that Pluto is smaller than it initially appeared and is actually a dwarf planet. **22** Pluto is, however, still a part of our solar system, located by calculations, careful observations, and a lot of patience.

20. Which sentence in the paragraph is least important to the main topic of the paragraph?

A) Sentence 2

B) Sentence 3

C) Sentence 4

D) Sentence 5

21. A) NO CHANGE

B) was determined

C) were determining

D) have determined

22. A) NO CHANGE

B) Pluto is however,

C) Pluto is; however,

D) Pluto is however

GO ON TO THE NEXT PAGE

**Questions 23-33 are based on the following passage.**

## Public Relations: Build Your Brand While Building for Others

[23] Public relations is all about communicating—in print, in press interviews, in web content, and on social media. Public relations specialists are the people [24] behind, corporations, politicians, entertainers, and athletes. Practically anyone with a public image needs someone on his or her staff to maintain that image. With media expanding into every area of our lives, it is no surprise that U.S. government economists expect this field to experience [25] above-average growth through the year 2020!

As a public relations specialist for the Broome Corporation, a global pharmaceutical company, Janice Lin is responsible for drawing positive attention to the company and therefore enhancing its reputation. "A big part of my job is maintaining relationships with people in the media— [26] journalists, television personalities, online bloggers. I work with them to make sure the excellent work of the Broome Corporation is presented to the public accurately and often."

23. A) NO CHANGE
    B) Public relations is all about communicating. In print, in press interviews, in web content, and on social media.
    C) Public relations is all about communicating; in print, in press interviews, in web content, and on social media.
    D) Public relations is all about communicating; in print, in press interviews, in web content. And on social media.

24. A) NO CHANGE
    B) behind: corporations, politicians, entertainers, and athletes.
    C) behind—corporations, politicians, entertainers, athletes.
    D) behind corporations, politicians, entertainers, and athletes.

25. A) NO CHANGE
    B) above-average growth through the year 2020....
    C) above-average growth through the year 2020.
    D) above-average growth through the year 2020?

26. A) NO CHANGE
    B) journalists, a television personality, online bloggers.
    C) journalists, television personalities, an online blogger.
    D) a journalist, television personalities, online bloggers.

Public relations specialists like Lin are often tasked with creating materials for use in print and on the Web. The materials must match **27** its company's brand and message. "I **28** provide press releases on a regular basis, but I also write scripts for web-based videos that can be found on our corporate website. I conduct interviews and review speeches, as well." In a media-savvy world, corporations and public figures are expected to communicate with the public across multiple platforms.

Most people in the public relations field have earned a bachelor's degree in communications, marketing, journalism, or other fields with **29** immovable skills. An entry-level position in public relations can pay $30,000 per year. Public relations specialists who rise in the field can earn increasingly higher salaries. **30** Many employees in upper-level management positions boast about their generous salaries. The Bureau of Labor Statistics expects the public relations field to grow 12 percent before 2022, which means an additional 27,400 jobs will be opening in the field.

27. A) NO CHANGE
    B) it's
    C) their
    D) they're

28. A) NO CHANGE
    B) form
    C) craft
    D) invent

29. A) NO CHANGE
    B) ordinary
    C) immobile
    D) transferable

30. Which choice best supports the claim made in the previous sentence?

    A) NO CHANGE
    B) Upper-level management positions pay significantly more at approximately $100,000 per year.
    C) PR workers who have been in the field for 30 or more years often rise to upper-level management positions.
    D) However, some PR specialists never rise in their field and rarely make more than $40,000 per year.

GO ON TO THE NEXT PAGE

[31] Lin has some advice for people who are considering a career in public relations: she suggests looking for local specialists in your area on a social media platform. [32] Reach out to them, request a meeting. [33] That will give you the opportunity of talking with them about their daily tasks and to observe how they talk to you about their company. You can learn a lot by listening. Also, consider joining a publication at your school. You'll learn to write effectively while also learning how to ask and answer difficult questions. That's the kind of thing I do every day.

31. Which sentence best establishes the central idea of the paragraph?

A) NO CHANGE

B) Lin expects social media to be the best method for connecting with specialists in the future.

C) Lin began her career as a public relations specialist before it was a popular career choice.

D) Lin believes that the Bureau of Labor Statistics offers support for students who want to pursue public relations careers.

32. A) NO CHANGE

B) Reach out to them, and request a meeting.

C) Reach out to them; and request a meeting.

D) Reach out to them; and, request a meeting.

33. A) NO CHANGE

B) That will give you the opportunity to talk to them about their daily tasks and to observe how they talk to you about their company.

C) That will give you the opportunity to talk to them about their daily tasks, and observing how they talk to you about their company.

D) That will give you the opportunity to talk to them about their daily tasks, and of observing how they are talking to you about their company.

**Questions 34-44 are based on the following passage and supplementary material.**

## Film, Culture, and Globalization

Globalization, or the integration of cultures across nations, is a prominent yet controversial topic. The controversy arises over concern about what is often called "cultural imperialism," or the notion of one culture's overpowering influence on another's cultural identity. [34] Some defend globalization for its benefits. Greater creativity and appreciation of heritage. Others argue that globalization damages cultures, especially in developing nations. For better or worse, advancing technology enables new levels of cross-cultural interconnectedness. The modern world is culturally intertwined, and there is no force more [35] inactive for globalization in the 21st century than the film industry.

[36] Filmmakers throughout the world are allowed to showcase their movies in the United States only if American film producers approve the project ahead of time. With multi-billion-dollar extranational revenues, Hollywood has inspired a global culture of moviemakers and moviegoers. Now, many nations enjoy booming domestic film markets that compare with or surpass the United States in production and popularity.

34. A) NO CHANGE
    B) Some defend globalization for its benefits greater creativity and appreciation of heritage.
    C) Some defend globalization for its benefits; greater creativity and appreciation of heritage.
    D) Some defend globalization for its benefits, including greater creativity and appreciation of heritage.

35. A) NO CHANGE
    B) ineffectual
    C) fragile
    D) potent

36. Which topic sentence most effectively establishes the central idea of the paragraph?
    A) NO CHANGE
    B) The past century has seen the rise of film and its predominance over much of popular culture, in and beyond the United States.
    C) This past century has seen Hollywood filmmakers striving to maintain their presence in the global cultural environment.
    D) Global filmmakers are anxious to share their products with the United States so that they may obtain the notoriety of American film producers.

As more countries produce and distribute films worldwide, the global sense of shared understanding and cultural appreciation [37] grow.

[38] Sharing cultural artifacts is central to globalization, and cultural artifacts are physical renderings of cultural identity. Foods, music, languages, books, art, and trade goods are all cultural artifacts. But films are cultural artifacts with more impact than others because of their vivid ability to document and portray a population's ideals, values, and commonalities. There is [39] naive appeal in viewers witnessing the heartfelt stories of people worlds away. Through film, the cross-cultural sharing of ideas, stories, ethics, humor, and much more can happen quickly.

The extent to which the world watches foreign, cross-cultural films is staggering. [40] Even as more countries increase film production the trend of cross-cultural film popularity is expected to remain; the difference will be the greater variety of cultures represented in those

37. A) NO CHANGE
    B) grows
    C) have grown
    D) were growing

38. A) NO CHANGE
    B) Cultural artifacts are physical renderings of cultural identity and are central to globalization.
    C) The sharing of cultural artifacts, which are physical renderings of cultural identity, is central to globalization.
    D) The sharing of cultural artifacts is central to globalization and they are physical renderings of cultural identity.

39. A) NO CHANGE
    B) senseless
    C) obtuse
    D) acute

40. A) NO CHANGE
    B) Even as more countries increase film production; the trend of cross-cultural film popularity is expected to remain
    C) Even as more countries increase film production; the trend of cross-cultural film popularity is expected to remain,
    D) Even as more countries increase film production, the trend of cross-cultural film popularity is expected to remain;

GO ON TO THE NEXT PAGE ⟩

films. **41** <u>Only the production of video games exceeds the film-making industry in the world market.</u>

Certainly, many individuals prefer films that reflect their own cultural identities, but trends indicate rising popular interest, even in Hollywood, in multicultural and cross-cultural movies. Despite valid concerns over cultural imperialism, the international film industry in many ways **42** <u>enables</u> positive culture sharing.

**43** <u>Films are increasingly used to teach, treasuring, and to preserve cultures and peoples,</u> strengthening those groups' identities and raising worldwide awareness and appreciation of their stories.

41. Which choice provides the most relevant detail to the paragraph?

A) NO CHANGE

B) Cross-cultural experiences extend beyond the foreign film industry to cuisine in popular international restaurants.

C) Outside the few nations whose powerhouse filmmaking industries dominate their own markets, nearly every moviegoer's experience is markedly cross-cultural.

D) The cross-cultural concept of sharing ideas and stories through humor is the most popular type of filmmaking both in the United States and in the current international market.

42. A) NO CHANGE

B) enabled

C) will enable

D) was enabling

43. A) NO CHANGE

B) Films are increasingly used to teach, treasure, and preserve cultures and peoples,

C) Films are increasingly used to teach, treasure, and preserving cultures and peoples,

D) Films are increasingly used for teaching, to treasure, and preserve cultures and peoples,

Statistics indicate that the global population will continue to frequent films from a variety of origins. According to information from the UNESCO Institute for Statistics, while film production fluctuates in many nations, only **44** India demonstrated a consistent increase in the number of films produced from 2005 to 2011. Filmmakers have the opportunity both to protect cultures and to creatively pioneer the route to true, sustained intercultural appreciation. Understanding the industry's undeniable impact on cultural identities and globalization is crucial in the world's progression toward collective prosperity, protection, and peace.

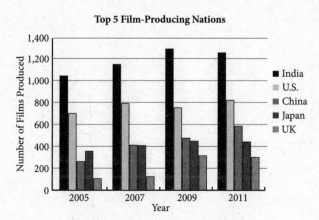

Top 5 Film-Producing Nations

Adapted from UNESCO Institute for Statistics, April 2013.

44. Which choice completes the sentence with accurate data based on the graphic?

A) NO CHANGE
B) China
C) the United States
D) the United Kingdom

# MATH TEST

### 25 Minutes—20 Questions

## NO-CALCULATOR SECTION

Turn to Section 3 of your answer sheet to answer the questions in this section.

**Directions:** For this section, solve each problem and decide which is the best of the choices given. Fill in the corresponding oval on the answer sheet. You may use any available space for scratch work.

Notes:

1. Calculator use is NOT permitted.
2. All numbers used are real numbers.
3. All figures used are necessary to solving the problems that they accompany. All figures are drawn to scale EXCEPT when it is stated that a specific figure is not drawn to scale.
4. Unless stated otherwise, the domain of any function $f$ is assumed to be the set of all real numbers $x$, for which $f(x)$ is a real number.

Information:

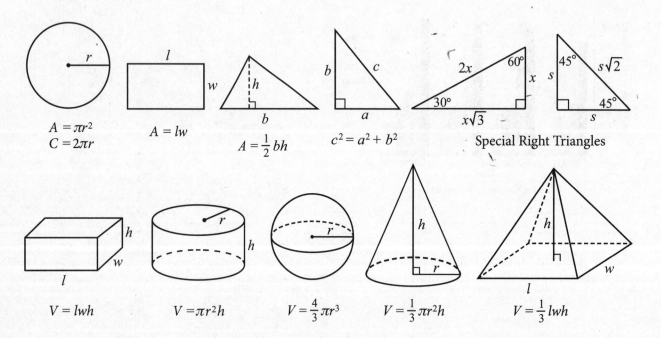

$A = \pi r^2$
$C = 2\pi r$

$A = lw$

$A = \frac{1}{2}bh$

$c^2 = a^2 + b^2$

Special Right Triangles

$V = lwh$

$V = \pi r^2 h$

$V = \frac{4}{3}\pi r^3$

$V = \frac{1}{3}\pi r^2 h$

$V = \frac{1}{3}lwh$

The sum of the degree measures of the angles in a triangle is 180.

The number of degrees of arc in a circle is 360.

The number of radians of arc in a circle is $2\pi$.

GO ON TO THE NEXT PAGE

1. Tread depth is a measurement between the top of the rubber on a tire and the bottom of its deepest groove. The average tread depth on a new standard tire is $\frac{10}{32}$ inches. In most states, a tire is considered legally worn out, and therefore unsafe, when the tread depth reaches $\frac{2}{32}$ inches. Which inequality represents the range of safe tread depths, $d$, for a standard car tire?

   A) $\frac{2}{32} > d \le \frac{10}{32}$

   B) $\frac{2}{32} < d \ge \frac{10}{32}$

   C) $\frac{2}{32} < d \le \frac{10}{32}$

   D) $\frac{2}{32} > d \ge \frac{10}{32}$

2. If $x^2 - 8x = 48$ and $x < 0$, what is the value of $x + 10$?

   A) $-2$
   B) $4$
   C) $6$  $16 + 32$
   D) $8$

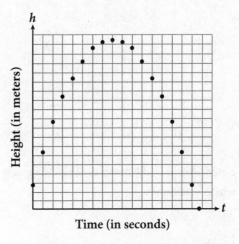

Time (in seconds)

3. A physics class is using simulation software to study water bottle rockets before attempting to build one for the National Physics Competition. Their first simulation is of a rocket without a parachute launched from the roof of the gymnasium. The scatterplot shows the approximate path of the rocket. The software program generates the equation $h = -4.9t^2 + 39.2t + 14$ to model the data, where $h$ is the height in meters of the rocket $t$ seconds after it was launched. What does the number 14 most likely represent in this equation?

   A) The number of seconds the rocket was in the air

   B) The height of the gymnasium from which the rocket was launched

   C) The number of seconds that it took the rocket to reach its maximum height

   D) The maximum height of the rocket

GO ON TO THE NEXT PAGE ▷

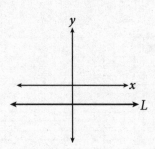

4. Line $L$ shown in the graph could be the graph of which equation?

   A) $x + y = -2$

   B) $x + y = 0$

   C) $x + y - 2 = x$

   D) $x + y + 2 = x$

$$\begin{cases} 2x + 5y = 8 \\ x + 3y = 3 \end{cases}$$

5. If $(x, y)$ is a solution to the system of equations above, what is the value of $y^2$?

   A) 4

   B) 9

   C) 25

   D) 81

6. An alloy is a metal made by mixing and melting two or more metals together. After the metals are mixed, the alloy must be cooled slowly to avoid crystallization. Suppose a metallurgist heats a mixture of metals to a temperature of 2,500°F and then removes the resulting alloy from the furnace. The alloy will then cool at a constant rate of 40°F every 15 minutes until it reaches room temperature. Which of the following functions represents the temperature $T$ of the alloy $h$ hours after it was removed from the furnace until it reaches room temperature?

   A) $T(h) = -15h + 2{,}500$

   B) $T(h) = -40h + 2{,}500$

   C) $T(h) = -160h + 2{,}500$

   D) $T(h) = -600h + 2{,}500$

7. If $\dfrac{3}{a - 1} = \dfrac{12}{w}$, such that $a \neq 1$ and $w \neq 0$, what is $w$ in terms of $a$?

   A) $4a - 4$

   B) $4a - 12$

   C) $12a - 4$

   D) $\dfrac{1}{4}a + 1$

$$\frac{4 - (1 - 3n)}{36} = \frac{2(n - 3) + 7}{12}$$

8. In the equation above, what is the value of $n$?

   A) 0

   B) 2

   C) 3

   D) There is no value of $n$ that satisfies the equation.

9. Which of the following functions has a domain of $x \geq 2$?

   A) $f(x) = -x^2 + 2$

   B) $g(x) = -\sqrt{x - 2}$

   C) $h(x) = -\sqrt{x} + 2$

   D) $k(x) = -|x - 2|$

10. If $\dfrac{1}{6}x - \dfrac{1}{2}y = 3$, what is the value of $x - 3y$?

   A) 6

   B) 12

   C) 18

   D) 36

GO ON TO THE NEXT PAGE ⇨

11. Suppose you know that $0° < m\angle\beta < 90°$ and $0 < m\angle\theta < 90°$, and that $\sin\beta = \cos\theta$. If $m\angle\beta = (7n - 12)°$ and $m\angle\theta = (3n - 8)°$, then what is the value of $n$?

A) 1

B) 5

C) 8

D) 11

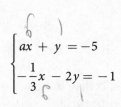

$$\begin{cases} ax + y = -5 \\ -\dfrac{1}{3}x - 2y = -1 \end{cases}$$

12. If the system of linear equations above has no solution, and $a$ is a constant, what is the value of $a$?

A) $-\dfrac{1}{3}$

B) $-\dfrac{1}{6}$

C) $\dfrac{1}{6}$

D) $\dfrac{1}{3}$

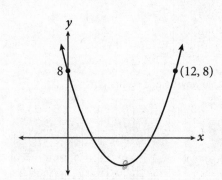

13. The range of the parabola shown in the graph is $y \geq -4$. If the equation $y = ax^2 + bx + c$ is used to represent the graph, what is the value of $a$?

A) $\dfrac{1}{3}$

B) $\dfrac{2}{3}$

C) $\dfrac{3}{2}$

D) 3

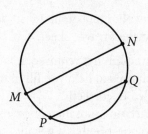

14. The circle shown has a radius of $r$ centimeters. If chord $PQ$ is parallel to diameter $MN$, and the length of chord $PQ$ is $\dfrac{3}{4}$ of the length of the diameter, what is the distance in centimeters between $\overline{MN}$ and $\overline{PQ}$ in terms of $r$?

A) $\dfrac{\sqrt{7}}{4}r$

B) $\dfrac{\sqrt{3}}{2}r$

C) $\dfrac{1}{4}\pi r$

D) $\dfrac{3}{4}\pi r$

15. Which of the following represents $16^{\frac{3}{2}}$ as an integer?

A) 4

B) 12

C) 48

D) 64

**GO ON TO THE NEXT PAGE**

**Directions:** For questions 16-20, solve the problem and enter your answer in the grid, as described below, on the answer sheet.

1. Although not required, it is suggested that you write your answer in the boxes at the top of the columns to help you fill in the circles accurately. You will receive credit only if the circles are filled in correctly.

2. Mark no more than one circle in any column.

3. No question has a negative answer.

4. Some problems may have more than one correct answer. In such cases, grid only one answer.

5. **Mixed numbers** such as $3\frac{1}{2}$ must be gridded as 3.5 or $\frac{7}{2}$.

   (If $3\frac{1}{2}$ is entered into the grid as $\boxed{3\ 1\ /\ 2}$, it will be interpreted as $\frac{31}{2}$, not $3\frac{1}{2}$.)

6. **Decimal answers:** If you obtain a decimal answer with more digits than the grid can accommodate, it may be either rounded or truncated, but it must fill the entire grid.

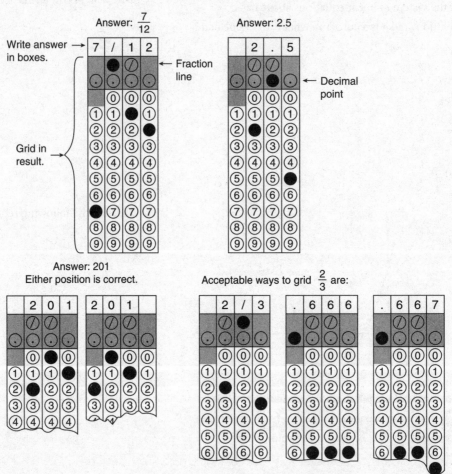

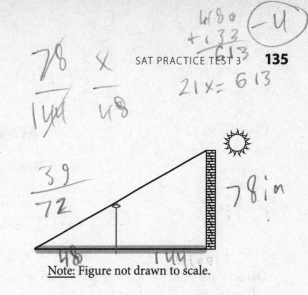

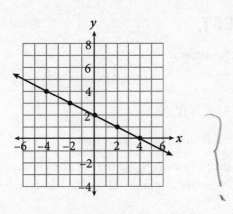

Note: Figure not drawn to scale.

16. If the equation that represents the graph shown above is written in standard form, $Ax + By = C$, and $A = 6$, what is the value of $B$?

17. If $\dfrac{1}{3} \leq 2 - \dfrac{d}{6} \leq \dfrac{5}{4}$, what is the minimum possible value of $d$?

$$g(x) = \begin{cases} x^2 - 1, \text{ if } x \leq 0 \\ \dfrac{x^2}{3} + 1, \text{ if } 0 < x \leq 3 \\ 5x + 3, \text{ if } x > 3 \end{cases}$$

18. For the piecewise-defined function $g(x)$ shown above, what is the value of $g(2)$?

19. A toy saber is stuck at a right angle into the ground 4 inches deep. It casts a shadow that is 4 feet long. The brick wall casts a shadow three times that long. If the wall is 7 feet 6 inches tall, how many inches long is the toy saber?

$$\dfrac{x}{x-1} - \dfrac{2}{x} = \dfrac{1}{x-1}$$

20. What is one possible solution to the rational equation given above?

# MATH TEST

### 55 Minutes—38 Questions

## CALCULATOR SECTION

Turn to Section 4 of your answer sheet to answer the questions in this section.

**Directions:** For this section, solve each problem and decide which is the best of the choices given. Fill in the corresponding oval on the answer sheet. You may use any available space for scratch work.

Notes:

1. Calculator use is permitted.
2. All numbers used are real numbers.
3. All figures used are necessary to solving the problems that they accompany. All figures are drawn to scale EXCEPT when it is stated that a specific figure is not drawn to scale.
4. Unless stated otherwise, the domain of any function $f$ is assumed to be the set of all real numbers $x$, for which $f(x)$ is a real number.

Information:

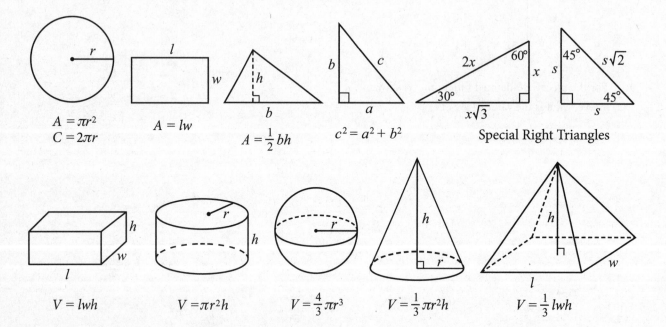

$A = \pi r^2$
$C = 2\pi r$

$A = lw$

$A = \frac{1}{2}bh$

$c^2 = a^2 + b^2$

Special Right Triangles

$V = lwh$

$V = \pi r^2 h$

$V = \frac{4}{3}\pi r^3$

$V = \frac{1}{3}\pi r^2 h$

$V = \frac{1}{3}lwh$

The sum of the degree measures of the angles in a triangle is 180.

The number of degrees of arc in a circle is 360.

The number of radians of arc in a circle is $2\pi$.

GO ON TO THE NEXT PAGE

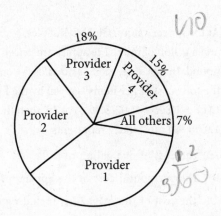

18%

Provider 3

15% Provider 4

Provider 2

All others 7%

Provider 1

1. A company's market share is the percent of consumers who utilize the services or buy the products of that company. The pie chart above shows the different market shares of cable providers in a certain region. If the ratio of the market shares of Provider 1 to Provider 2 is 3:2, what is Provider 1's market share?

   A) 24%

   B) 30%

   C) 36%

   D) 42%

2. Which of the following number lines represents the solution to the inequality $3x + 29 > 5 - x$?

   A)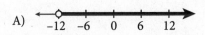
   −12  −6   0   6   12

   B)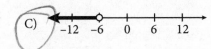
   −12  −6   0   6   12

   C)
   −12  −6   0   6   12

   D)
   −12  −6   0   6   12

3. Water is vital to human health. An average person should consume approximately 2.5 ounces of water per hour. However, because of the salt in it, seawater actually dehydrates the human body and should not be consumed. This is why boats must carry a supply of fresh water when embarking on long trips. Suppose a sailboat is traveling at an average speed of 4 nautical miles per hour with 3 people on board and the trip is 232 nautical miles. What is the minimum number of ounces of water the boat should stock before leaving?

   A) 69.6

   B) 145

   C) 435

   D) 1,113.6

4. If $a = 0$ and $b < 0$, then which of the following could be the graph of $f(x) = (x - a)(x - b)$?

   A)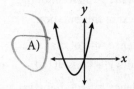

   B)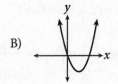

   C)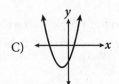

   D)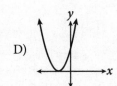

GO ON TO THE NEXT PAGE

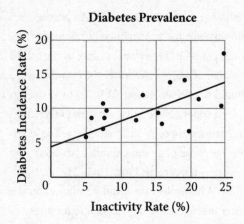

**Diabetes Prevalence**

5. Increased physical activity has been linked to a lower incidence rate of diabetes. The scatterplot above shows the relationship between the percent of people in a certain country whose daily activity qualifies them as "inactive" and the incidence rate of diabetes in that country. The line of best fit for the data is also shown. Which of the following best represents the meaning of the $y$-intercept of the line of best fit in the context of this question?

A) The predicted incidence rate of diabetes when the entire country is considered active

B) The predicted incidence rate of diabetes when the entire country is considered inactive

C) The predicted percent of people who will be active when the incidence rate of diabetes is 0%

D) The predicted percent of people who will be inactive when the incidence rate of diabetes is 0%

6. At the grocery store, Gigi buys apples, a magazine, and a gallon of milk. The apples are priced per pound. In her state, there is no sales tax on food. If the total cost of her items is given by the function $C(p) = 1.89p + 1.07(3.99) + 4.49$, then the term $1.07(3.99)$ most likely represents

A) the cost of one gallon of milk.

B) the per-pound cost of the apples.

C) the cost of the magazine, including tax.

D) the cost of the magazine, not including tax.

7. When a homeowner hires a contractor to renovate a bathroom, the homeowner is charged for both labor and materials. By law, the contractor can charge sales tax on the materials, but not on the labor. If the contractor quotes the homeowner $3,000 for materials and $40 per hour for labor, and sales tax in the homeowner's state is 5.5%, which equation represents the total cost for the bathroom renovation if it takes the contractor $h$ hours to complete the job?

A) $c = (40h + 3,000)(1.055)$

B) $c = 1.055(40 + 3,000)h$

C) $c = 40h(1.055) + 3,000$

D) $c = 40h + 1.055(3,000)$

8.  A picture-framing shop sells ready-made frames and also does custom framing using different kinds and widths of wood or metal. The shop has a three-day sale. During the sale, for an 11-inch × 14-inch frame, a ready-made frame costs $12 and a custom frame costs $30. Over the course of the three days, the shop sells ninety-two 11 × 14 frames and collects $1,788. Solving which system of equations would yield the number of 11 × 14 ready-made frames $r$ and the number of 11 × 14 custom frames $c$ that the shop sold during the three-day sale?

A)  $$\begin{cases} r+c=92 \\ 12r+30c=\dfrac{1,788}{3} \end{cases}$$

B)  $$\begin{cases} r+c=1,788 \\ 12r+30c=92\times3 \end{cases}$$

C)  $$\begin{cases} r+c=1,788 \\ 12r+30c=92 \end{cases}$$

D)  $$\begin{cases} r+c=92 \\ 12r+30c=1,788 \end{cases}$$

| City | Cost per Square Foot |
|---|---|
| Detroit | $62.45 |
| Atlanta | $74.19 |
| New York City | $288.58 |
| San Francisco | $420.99 |

9.  In real estate, location is often the number one determinant of home prices. The table above shows the average price per square foot of houses in four cities. Assuming an average home size of 1,500 to 2,000 square feet, which inequality represents how much more in dollars a house in New York City would cost than in Detroit?

A)  $x \geq 226.13$

B)  $62.45 \leq x \leq 288.58$

C)  $93,675 \leq x \leq 432,870$

D)  $339,195 \leq x \leq 452,260$

10. If $5n-3(n-1)=\dfrac{1}{2}(4n+16)-5$, what is the value of $n$?

A)  $n=1$

B)  $n=3$

C)  There is no value of $n$ for which the equation is true.

D)  There are infinitely many values of $n$ for which the equation is true.

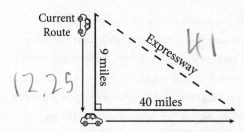

Note: Figure not drawn to scale.

11. The figure above shows the route that Max currently takes to work and back home every day. The city is planning to build an expressway that would cross through the city to help alleviate commuter traffic. Assuming an average gas consumption of 20 miles per gallon and a 5-day workweek, how many gallons of gas will Max save per week by taking the expressway to and from work each day instead of using his current route?

A)  2

B)  4

C)  8

D)  10.25

GO ON TO THE NEXT PAGE

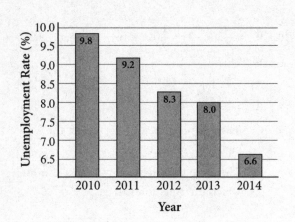

12. The bar graph shows the percent of the U.S. population that was unemployed as of January 1 on each of the years shown. A governmental agency wants to use the 5-year mean of the data to estimate how many people were unemployed in a certain geographic area between 2010 and 2014. If the total adult population of the area was 250,000, approximately how many adults were unemployed in that area during the indicated time period?

A) 16,950

B) 20,150

C) 20,950

D) 104,750

13. Which of the following expressions is equivalent to $(36x^4y^7)^{\frac{1}{2}}$ ?

A) $\dfrac{36x^4y^7}{2}$

B) $6xy^2\sqrt{y}$

C) $6x^2y^3\sqrt{y}$

D) $(36x^4y^7)^{-2}$

**Questions 14 and 15 refer to the following information.**

Use the data in the scatterplot and the line of best fit shown to answer the following questions.

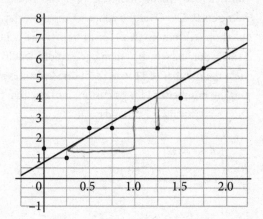

14. Which of the following values most accurately reflects the average rate of change of the data based on the line of best fit?

A) $\dfrac{3}{8}$

B) $\dfrac{3}{4}$

C) $\dfrac{4}{3}$

D) $\dfrac{8}{3}$

15. For how many of the data points is the difference between the actual $y$-value and the expected $y$-value greater than 2 ?

A) 3

B) 2

C) 1

D) 0

16. Which of the following are solutions to the quadratic equation $(x - 2)^2 = \dfrac{16}{25}$ ?

    A)  $x = \pm\sqrt{\dfrac{4}{5}}$

    B)  $x = -\dfrac{4}{5},\ x = \dfrac{4}{5}$

    C)  $x = \dfrac{6}{5},\ x = \dfrac{14}{5}$

    D)  $x = \dfrac{14}{5},\ x = -\dfrac{14}{5}$

17. If the slope of a line is $-\dfrac{5}{2}$ and a point on the line is $(2, -1)$, which of the following is the $y$-intercept of the line?

    A)  $-6$

    B)  $-\dfrac{1}{2}$

    C)  $4$

    D)  $6$

18. The Consumer Price Index (CPI) is a weighted average of the cost of certain categories of goods and services in the United States. It is one of the most widely used measures of inflation. According to the U.S. Census Bureau, the CPI was 130.7 in 1990 and was 218.1 in 2010. If the CPI continues to experience the same percent increase over the next 20 years, approximately what will the CPI be in 2030?

    A)  145.8

    B)  305.5

    C)  363.9

    D)  408.7

19. Given the function $f(x) = \dfrac{1}{4}x - 2$, what domain value corresponds to a range value of $-\dfrac{5}{3}$ ?

    A)  $-\dfrac{29}{12}$

    B)  $\dfrac{4}{3}$

    C)  $\dfrac{7}{3}$

    D)  $\dfrac{29}{12}$

$$T = 2\pi\sqrt{\dfrac{m}{k}}$$

20. When a spring is pressed tightly between two objects, it remains still. When one or both of those objects is disturbed, the spring starts to move. The equation above can be used to find the time period $T$ in which a mass $m$, attached to a spring, makes a single oscillation (going all the way down and then back up). The variable $k$ is a constant. Which of the following equations could be used to find the mass of the object?

    A)  $m = \dfrac{2\pi k}{T^2}$

    B)  $m = \dfrac{kT^2}{4\pi^2}$

    C)  $m = \dfrac{T^2}{4\pi^2 k}$

    D)  $m = \sqrt{\dfrac{T}{2\pi k}}$

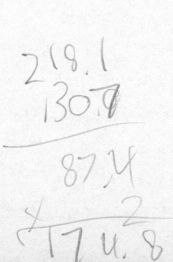

GO ON TO THE NEXT PAGE ⟩

21. An educational polling company wants to determine whether parents of high school-age children believe using an electronic tablet in the classroom will improve student learning. To do this, the company conducted a survey by sending 50,000 text messages across the entire United States to randomly selected phones with text-messaging capabilities. For every text that the company sent, it received a response to the survey. Which of the following best explains why this random sample is unlikely to be a good representative sample of parents' opinions on the use of tablets in the classroom?

A) Most parents don't care about this issue, and their attitude is likely to skew the results.

B) Surveys conducted via text messaging are illegal and therefore are not considered reliable.

C) There is no way to verify whether the responders to the survey were parents of high school age-children.

D) The survey was biased because parents who own a cell phone probably also have a tablet and would want their children to learn how to use it.

22. A company that makes shoelaces has two machines, both of which run 24 hours a day. The first machine can produce 36,000 shoelaces per day. The second machine can produce 28,800 shoelaces per day. How many more shoelaces can the first machine make than the second machine in 8 minutes?

A) 5

B) 40

C) 160

D) 200

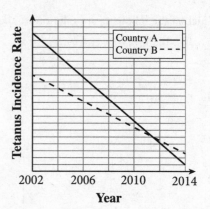

23. Tetanus is an infection of the body's nervous system. It is usually contracted by cutting oneself on a rusty metal object. In 2002, Country A started requiring students to have tetanus shots before entering public school. That same year, Country B started providing the vaccine free of charge to school-age children but has not required that they get it. The graph above shows the incidence rate of tetanus in these two countries starting in 2002. Which of the following statements is true?

A) Country A's vaccine requirement had a greater impact on the incidence rate than did Country B's free vaccines.

B) Country B's free vaccines had a greater impact on the incidence rate than did Country A's vaccine requirement.

C) Country A's vaccine requirement had about the same impact on the incidence rate as did Country B's free vaccines.

D) Because the countries started with different incidence rates, it is impossible to determine which country's actions had a greater impact.

GO ON TO THE NEXT PAGE

24. A college professor with several hundred students has office hours between classes to provide extra help when needed. His classes on Monday are from 9:00 AM to 10:45 AM and 2:30 PM to 3:45 PM. It takes him 5 minutes to walk from the classroom to his office, and he takes a lunch break from 12:00 PM to 1:00 PM. On a particular Monday, he plans to grade tests, which have all multiple-choice questions. If each test consists of 50 questions and it takes him 4 seconds to mark each question right or wrong, how many complete tests can he mark during his office hours if no students come for help? Assume that he does not take the time to add up the scores until after his afternoon class.

A) 46

B) 47

C) 54

D) 55

25. An optician charges $125 for an eye examination, frames, and clear glass lenses, but $197 for an eye examination, frames, and tinted glass lenses. If the tinted lenses cost three times as much as the clear lenses, how much do the clear glass lenses cost?

A) $24

B) $36

C) $48

D) $72

| Registered to Vote? | 1 | 2 | 3 | 4 | 5 | Total |
|---|---|---|---|---|---|---|
| Yes | 112 | 104 | 228 | 487 | 163 | 1,094 |
| No | 28 | 76 | 48 | 158 | 54 | 364 |
| Total | 140 | 180 | 276 | 645 | 217 | 1,458 |

26. An incumbent state senator (currently in office and running for an additional term) conducts a survey to see how favorably the people in her district view her. In the survey, responses of 1 or 2 represent an unfavorable view, a response of 3 is a neutral view, and responses of 4 or 5 are favorable. The results of the survey are recorded in the table. If one registered voter is chosen at random to attend a town hall meeting, what is the probability that the voter does not view the senator unfavorably?

A) 40.6%

B) 59.4%

C) 78.1%

D) 80.3%

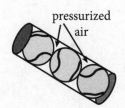

pressurized air

27. Higher-quality tennis balls are typically packaged in cylindrical cans, as shown above, which are pressurized with air to keep them fresh. If the can and the tennis balls have the same diameter, 2.6 inches, what is the volume in cubic inches of the air inside the can around the tennis balls? Assume that each tennis ball is tangent to the next and that the top and bottom tennis balls are tangent to the top and bottom of the can.

A) 4.4π

B) 8.1π

C) 10.3π

D) 29.3π

GO ON TO THE NEXT PAGE

28. If $h$ is a rational number such that $-1 < h < 0$, which of the following could be the graph of the equation $y = hy + hx + x - 4$?

A)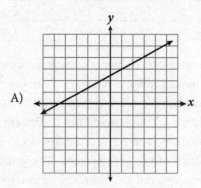

B)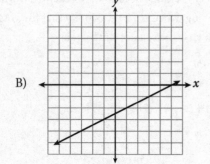

C)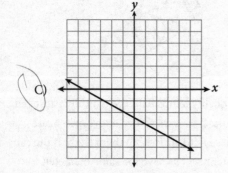

D)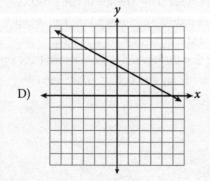

29. A scientist weighed a 1.0 cubic foot piece of granite and found that it weighed 168 pounds. The average density of Earth's inner core is approximately 12.8 g/cm³. How much denser, in g/cm³, is Earth's inner core than the piece of granite? Use any of the following conversions:

- 12 inches = 1 foot

- 16 ounces = 1 pound

- 1 inch = 2.54 cm

- 1 ounce = 28.35 grams

A) 2.7

B) 10.1

C) 15.55

D) 28.35

$$\dfrac{1}{\dfrac{1}{R_1} + \dfrac{1}{R_2}}$$

30. In electronic circuits, resistors are often paired to manage the flow of the electrical current. To find the total resistance of a pair of parallel resistors, electricians use the formula shown above, where $R_1$ is the resistance of the first resistor and $R_2$ is the resistance of the second resistor. Which of the following is another way to represent this formula?

A) $\dfrac{R_1 R_2}{R_1 + R_2}$

B) $\dfrac{R_1 + R_2}{R_1 R_2}$

C) $\dfrac{1}{R_2} - \dfrac{1}{R_1}$

D) $R_1 + R_2$

GO ON TO THE NEXT PAGE

**Directions:** For questions 31-38, solve the problem and enter your answer in the grid, as described below, on the answer sheet.

1. Although not required, it is suggested that you write your answer in the boxes at the top of the columns to help you fill in the circles accurately. You will receive credit only if the circles are filled in correctly.

2. Mark no more than one circle in any column.

3. No question has a negative answer.

4. Some problems may have more than one correct answer. In such cases, grid only one answer.

5. **Mixed numbers** such as $3\frac{1}{2}$ must be gridded as 3.5 or $\frac{7}{2}$.

   (If $3\frac{1}{2}$ is entered into the grid as $\boxed{3\ 1\ /\ 2}$, it will be interpreted as $\frac{31}{2}$, not $3\frac{1}{2}$.)

6. **Decimal answers:** If you obtain a decimal answer with more digits than the grid can accommodate, it may be either rounded or truncated, but it must fill the entire grid.

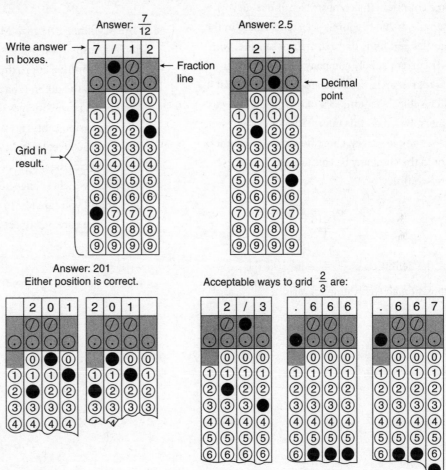

31. According to the U.S. Department of Agriculture, the linear equation $f = -3.7t + 872$ estimates the number of acres of farmland $f$ in the United States $t$ years after 2010, where $f$ is given in millions of acres. Based on this equation, at the start of what year will the amount of farmland be below 800 million acres?

32. If $g(x) = x^2 + 2x + 9$, what is $g(5) - g(-1)$?

33. A North Carolina agricultural supply company is hoping to expand its services to three counties in rural Virginia. According to its research, there is a total of approximately 1,200 farms in these three counties. The company sends out surveys to a sample of 200 randomly selected farmers in the counties and finds that 120 are not satisfied with their current supply company. Based on other market research, the company is confident that it will be able to acquire 75% of the dissatisfied customers. Based on this information and the results of the sample survey, about how many customers should the company be able to acquire in these three counties?

$$\frac{4 + \sqrt{-16}}{2 + \sqrt{-4}}$$

34. Use the definition $\sqrt{-1} = i$ to write the expression above in simplest form.

35. Sometimes, companies will buy stock in businesses owned by one or more of their competitors in order to gain some control over the competing companies. Suppose Company X buys stock in two of its competitors. The first competitor is a small regional company. Five hundred shares of its stock cost $25,000 less than half as much as 500 shares of the other competitor, which is a large national company. Together, Company X pays $155,000 for all the stock. How many more thousands of dollars did Company X spend on acquiring the stock of the national competitor than the regional one? Enter your answer in thousands of dollars. (For example, enter $15,000 as 15.)

36. The Mackinac Bridge in Michigan is one of the longest suspension bridges in the Western Hemisphere, spanning approximately 1.63 miles from one end to the other. It has several pieces that are connected by anchorages (large blocks to which the suspension cables are attached). The longest piece is 3,800 feet long. In a scale drawing on a poster board, the length of the bridge is 28 inches. How many inches long should the longest piece be? Round your answer to the nearest tenth of an inch. (There are 5,280 feet in 1 mile.)

GO ON TO THE NEXT PAGE

**Questions 37 and 38 refer to the following information.**

A restaurant sent out surveys to determine how long customers are willing to wait for a table on Friday night versus Saturday night. Participants randomly received either a Friday night or a Saturday night survey. Results are shown in the bar graph below.

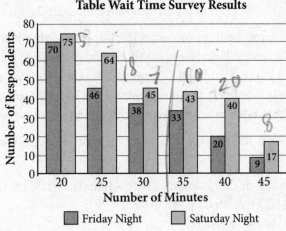

**Table Wait Time Survey Results**

37. If a customer is chosen at random from all of the survey respondents, what is the probability that the customer is willing to wait at least 30 minutes for a table?

38. On average, how many minutes longer are customers willing to wait for a table on Saturday night than on Friday night? Round your answer to the nearest whole minute.

# ESSAY TEST

## 50 Minutes

The essay gives you an opportunity to show how effectively you can read and comprehend a passage and write an essay analyzing the passage. In your essay, you should demonstrate that you have read the passage carefully, present a clear and logical analysis, and use language precisely.

Your essay must be written on the lines provided in your answer booklet; except for the planning page of the answer booklet, you will receive no other paper on which to write. You will have enough space if you write on every line, avoid wide margins, and keep your handwriting to a reasonable size. Remember that people who are not familiar with your handwriting will read what you write. Try to write or print so that what you are writing is legible to those readers.

You have 50 minutes to read the passage and write an essay in response to the prompt provided inside this booklet.

1. Do not write your essay in this booklet. Only what you write on the lined pages of your answer booklet will be evaluated.
2. An off-topic essay will not be evaluated.

---

As you read the passage below, consider how President Johnson uses

- evidence, such as facts or examples, to support claims.

- reasoning to develop ideas and to connect claims and evidence.

- stylistic or persuasive elements, such as word choice or appeals to emotion, to add power to the ideas expressed.

---

**Adapted from President Lyndon Johnson's Voting Rights Address, delivered March 15, 1965.**

1   I speak tonight for the dignity of man and the destiny of democracy.

2   I urge every member of both parties, Americans of all religions and of all races, from every section of this country, to join me in that cause.

3   At times history and fate meet at a single time in a single place to shape a turning point in man's unending search for freedom....

4   In our time we have come to live with moments of great crisis. Our lives have been marked with debate about great issues; issues of war and peace, issues of prosperity and depression. But rarely in any time does an issue lay bare the secret heart of America itself. Rarely are we met with a challenge, not to our growth or abundance, our welfare or our security, but rather to the values and the purposes and the meaning of our beloved Nation.

5   The issue of equal rights for African Americans is such an issue, and should we defeat every enemy, should we double our wealth and conquer the stars, and still be unequal to this issue, then we will have failed as a people and as a nation....

6   Many of the issues of civil rights are very complex and most difficult, but about this there can and should be no argument. Every American citizen must have an equal right to vote. There is no reason which can excuse the denial of that right. There is no duty which weighs more heavily on us than the duty we have to ensure that right.

GO ON TO THE NEXT PAGE

7    Yet the harsh fact is that in many places in this country men and women are kept from voting simply because they are black.

8    Every device of which human ingenuity is capable has been used to deny this right. The African American citizen may go to register only to be told that the day is wrong, or the hour is late, or the official in charge is absent; and if he persists, and if he manages to present himself to the registrar, he may be disqualified because he did not spell out his middle name or because he abbreviated a word on the application.

9    And if he manages to fill out an application he is given a test. The registrar is the sole judge of whether he passes this test. He may be asked to recite the entire Constitution, or explain the most complex provisions of state law. And even a college degree cannot be used to prove that he can read and write.

10   Experience has clearly shown that the existing process of law cannot overcome systematic and ingenious discrimination. No law that we now have on the books—and I have helped to put three of them there—can ensure the right to vote when local officials are determined to deny it.

11   In such a case our duty must be clear to all of us. The Constitution says that no person shall be kept from voting because of his race. We have all sworn an oath before God to support and to defend that Constitution. We must now act in obedience to that oath....

12   It is wrong—deadly wrong—to deny any of your fellow Americans the right to vote in this country....

13   We cannot, we must not, refuse to protect the right of every American to vote in every election that he may desire to participate in; and we ought not and we cannot and we must not wait another eight months before we get a bill. We have already waited a hundred years and more, and the time for waiting is gone....

14   Because it is not just African Americans, but really it is all of us, who must overcome the crippling legacy of bigotry and injustice—and we shall overcome.

15   As a man whose roots go deeply into Southern soil, I know how agonizing racial feelings are. I know how difficult it is to reshape the attitudes and the structure of our society.

16   But a century has passed, more than a hundred years, since the slave was freed, and he is not fully free tonight.

17   It was more than a hundred years ago that Abraham Lincoln, a great President of another party, signed the Emancipation Proclamation, but emancipation is a proclamation and not a fact.

> Write an essay in which you explain how President Johnson builds an argument to persuade his audience that "emancipation is a proclamation and not a fact." In your essay, analyze how he uses one or more of the features listed in the box that precedes the passage (or features of your own choice) to strengthen the logic and persuasiveness of his argument. Be sure that your analysis focuses on the most relevant features of the passage.
>
> Your essay should not explain whether you agree with Johnson's claims, but rather explain how he builds an argument to persuade his audience.

**IF YOU FINISH BEFORE TIME IS CALLED, YOU MAY CHECK YOUR WORK ON THIS SECTION ONLY. DO NOT TURN TO ANY OTHER SECTION IN THE TEST.**  **STOP**

# SAT®
## Practice Test 4

# READING TEST

## 65 Minutes—52 Questions

Turn to Section 1 of your answer sheet to answer the questions in this section.

Directions: Each passage or pair of passages below is followed by a number of questions. After reading each passage or pair, choose the best answer to each question based on what is stated or implied in the passage or passages and in any accompanying graphics (such as a table or graph).

**Questions 1-10 are based on the following passage.**

The following passage is adapted from Willa Cather's 1918 novel *My Ántonia*. In this excerpt, the boy narrator, Jim Burden, has traveled from Virginia to his grandparents' Nebraska farm to spend the rest of his childhood there. On his first Nebraska morning, he goes outdoors to observe the landscape.

As I looked about me I felt that the grass was the country, as the water is the sea. The red of the grass made all the great prairie the colour of winestains,
*Line* or of certain seaweeds when they are first washed
(5) up. And there was so much motion in it; the whole country seemed, somehow, to be running.

I had almost forgotten that I had a grandmother, when she came out, her sunbonnet on her head, a grain-sack in her hand, and asked me if I did not
(10) want to go to the garden with her to dig potatoes for dinner. . . .

I can remember exactly how the country looked to me as I walked beside my grandmother along the faint wagon-tracks on that early September morning.
(15) Perhaps the glide of long railway travel was still with me, for more than anything else I felt motion in the landscape; in the fresh, easy-blowing morning wind, and in the earth itself, as if the shaggy grass were a sort of loose hide, and underneath it herds of wild
(20) buffalo were galloping, galloping. . . .

Alone, I should never have found the garden—except, perhaps, for the big yellow pumpkins that lay about unprotected by their withering vines—and I felt very little interest in it when I got there.
(25) I wanted to walk straight on through the red grass and over the edge of the world, which could not be very far away. The light air about me told me that

the world ended here: only the ground and sun and sky were left, and if one went a little farther there
(30) would be only sun and sky, and one would float off into them, like the tawny hawks which sailed over our heads making slow shadows on the grass. While grandmother took the pitchfork we found standing in one of the rows and dug potatoes, while I picked
(35) them up out of the soft brown earth and put them into the bag, I kept looking up at the hawks that were doing what I might so easily do.

When grandmother was ready to go, I said I would like to stay up there in the garden awhile.
(40) She peered down at me from under her sunbonnet. "Aren't you afraid of snakes?"

"A little," I admitted, "but I'd like to stay, anyhow." . . .

Grandmother swung the bag of potatoes over
(45) her shoulder and went down the path, leaning forward a little. The road followed the windings of the draw; when she came to the first bend, she waved at me and disappeared. I was left alone with this new feeling of lightness and content.
(50) I sat down in the middle of the garden, where snakes could scarcely approach unseen, and leaned my back against a warm yellow pumpkin. There were some ground-cherry bushes growing along the furrows, full of fruit. I turned back the papery triangular
(55) sheaths that protected the berries and ate a few. All about me giant grasshoppers, twice as big as any I had ever seen, were doing acrobatic feats among the dried vines. The gophers scurried up and down the ploughed ground. There in the sheltered draw-
(60) bottom the wind did not blow very hard, but I could hear it singing its humming tune up on the level, and I could see the tall grasses wave. The earth was warm under me, and warm as I crumbled it through my

GO ON TO THE NEXT PAGE ⇨

fingers. Queer little red bugs came out and moved
(65) in slow squadrons around me. Their backs were
polished vermilion, with black spots. I kept as still as
I could. Nothing happened. I did not expect anything to happen. I was something that lay under the
sun and felt it, like the pumpkins, and I did not want
(70) to be anything more. I was entirely happy. Perhaps
we feel like that when we die and become a part of
something entire, whether it is sun and air, or good-
ness and knowledge. At any rate, that is happiness;
to be dissolved into something complete and great.
(75) When it comes to one, it comes as naturally as sleep.

1. According to the passage, why is Jim's grandmother initially concerned about leaving him in
the garden?

   A) Jim doesn't know the way back home.

   B) She is worried he will encounter snakes.

   C) A bad storm is brewing on the horizon.

   D) She hoped Jim would help her cook dinner.

2. As used in line 51, "scarcely" most nearly means

   A) not easily.

   B) rapidly.

   C) with fear.

   D) narrowly.

3. Based on information in the passage, it can reasonably be inferred that

   A) the prairie reminds Jim of the landscape
   back in his native Virginia.

   B) the snakes and coyotes make the prairie a
   dangerous place.

   C) growing crops on the prairie is extremely
   difficult for farmers.

   D) it is very easy to get lost because there are
   few landmarks.

4. Which choice provides the best evidence for the
answer to the previous question?

   A) Lines 1-2 ("As I looked . . . sea")

   B) Lines 21-24 ("Alone . . . there")

   C) Lines 46-48 ("The road . . . disappeared")

   D) Lines 50-52 ("I sat . . . pumpkin")

5. The central claim of the passage is that

   A) confronting fears allows a person to move
   forward in life.

   B) nature, though beautiful, can present many
   hidden dangers.

   C) family relationships can help a person
   adjust to new places.

   D) a natural setting can have a transforming
   effect on a person.

6. Based on information in the passage, it can reasonably be inferred that Jim's personality could best be
described as

   A) aggressive.

   B) introspective.

   C) regretful.

   D) ambivalent.

7. Which choice provides the best evidence for the
answer to the previous question?

   A) Lines 7-11 ("I had . . . for dinner")

   B) Lines 12-14 ("I can . . . morning")

   C) Lines 38-52 ("When grandmother . . .
   pumpkin")

   D) Lines 70-73 ("Perhaps we . . . knowledge")

GO ON TO THE NEXT PAGE ⟩

8.  As used in line 74, "dissolved" most nearly means

    A)  assimilated.

    B)  destroyed.

    C)  disintegrated.

    D)  terminated.

9.  The repetition of "galloping" in line 20 ("herds of . . . galloping, galloping") mainly serves to emphasize how

    A)  fast the wind moved against the grass.

    B)  much the Nebraska landscape seems like a dream.

    C)  the recurrent motion of the landscape.

    D)  wild buffalo and wild horses on the prairie are similar.

10.  Through the perspective of a first-person narrator, the author is able to

    A)  focus attention on the main character rather than on his grandmother.

    B)  limit what we learn about the main character.

    C)  describe in detail the thoughts and experiences of the main character.

    D)  distance herself from her main character.

**Questions 11-20 are based on the following passage.**

The following passage is adapted from an open letter to the United Nations, written by Danish physicist and Nobel Prize winner Niels Bohr. Bohr completed important work on atomic structure long before World War II. After fleeing Denmark to escape the Nazis, he eventually went to work with the British as an adviser to U.S. scientists developing the first atomic bomb. The atomic bomb was then used to bring an end to World War II.

I address myself to the organization, founded for the purpose to further co-operation between nations. . . .

*Line*  The fear of being left behind was a strong
(5)  incentive in various countries to explore, in secrecy,

the possibilities of using such energy sources for military purposes. The joint American-British project remained unknown to me until, after my escape from occupied Denmark in the autumn of
(10)  1943, I came to England at the invitation of the British government. At that time I was taken into confidence about the great enterprise which had already then reached an advanced stage.

Everyone associated with the atomic energy
(15)  project was, of course, conscious of the serious problems which would confront humanity once the enterprise was accomplished. . . .

It certainly surpasses the imagination of anyone to survey the consequences of the project in years
(20)  to come, where in the long run the enormous energy sources which will be available may be expected to revolutionize industry and transport. The fact of immediate preponderance is, however, that a weapon of an unparalleled power is being
(25)  created which will completely change all future conditions of warfare.

This situation raises a number of problems which call for most urgent attention. Unless, indeed, some agreement about the control of the
(30)  use of the new active materials can be obtained in due time, any temporary advantage, however great, may be outweighed by a perpetual menace to human security.

When the war ended and the great menaces
(35)  of oppression to so many peoples had disappeared, an immense relief was felt all over the world. Nevertheless, the political situation was fraught with ominous forebodings. Divergences in outlook between the victorious nations inevitably
(40)  aggravated controversial matters arising in connection with peace settlements. Contrary to the hopes for future fruitful co-operation, expressed from all sides and embodied in the Charter of the United Nations, the lack of mutual confidence soon
(45)  became evident.

The creation of new barriers, restricting the free flow of information between countries, further increased distrust and anxiety. . . .

The very fact that knowledge is in itself the
(50)  basis for civilization points directly to openness as the way to overcome the present crisis. Whatever

GO ON TO THE NEXT PAGE ▷

judicial and administrative international authorities may eventually have to be created in order to stabilize world affairs, it must be realized that full
(55) mutual openness, only, can effectively promote confidence and guarantee common security.

Any widening of the borders of our knowledge imposes an increased responsibility on individuals and nations through the possibilities it gives for
(60) shaping the conditions of human life. The forceful admonition in this respect which we have received in our time cannot be left unheeded and should hardly fail in resulting in common understanding of the seriousness of the challenge with which our
(65) whole civilization is faced. It is just on this background that quite unique opportunities exist to-day for furthering co-operation between nations on the progress of human culture in all its aspects.

11. The main purpose of this letter is to

A) discuss the implications of the military use of atomic energy.

B) explore the industrial potential of atomic energy development.

C) compare the shared atomic energy goals of members of the United Nations.

D) clarify the role of the United Nations in overseeing atomic energy use.

12. Which choice provides the best evidence for the answer to the previous question?

A) Lines 7-11 ("The joint . . . government")

B) Lines 11-13 ("At that time . . . stage")

C) Lines 14-17 ("Everyone . . . accomplished")

D) Lines 18-22 ("It certainly . . . transport")

13. As used in line 23, "preponderance" most nearly means

A) eminence.

B) importance.

C) majority.

D) prestige.

14. The passage most clearly suggests that Bohr's work before World War II

A) began as a nonmilitary pursuit.

B) led to the outbreak of the war.

C) resulted from industrialization.

D) undermined efforts to reach peace.

15. Which choice provides the best evidence for the answer to the previous question?

A) Lines 4-7 ("The fear . . . purposes")

B) Lines 7-11 ("The joint . . . government")

C) Lines 23-26 ("The fact of . . . warfare")

D) Lines 27-28 ("This situation . . . attention")

16. As used in line 38, "divergences" most nearly means

A) differences.

B) misinterpretations.

C) perspectives.

D) rebellions.

17. In lines 41-42, the the author mentions "contrary to the hopes for fruitful co-operation" primarily to show that what happened after World War II?

A) Countries decided to form the United Nations.

B) Knowledge became the driving force behind civilization.

C) Trust among nations declined because of political disagreements.

D) New judicial and administrative authorities were established.

GO ON TO THE NEXT PAGE

18. The reference to knowledge in lines 49-51 ("The very fact . . . present crisis") mainly serves to

    A) explain the important uses of atomic energy.

    B) highlight the role of learning in societal progress.

    C) posit the benefits of regulating scientific investigation.

    D) justify the need for transparency among nations.

19. Based on information in the passage, it can reasonably be inferred that the author would most likely support international

    A) laws restricting the testing of nuclear bombs.

    B) monitoring of countries' nuclear technologies.

    C) regulation of nuclear power plants and materials.

    D) sanctions on nations with nuclear weapons.

20. The sentence in lines 60-65 ("The forceful admonition . . . is faced") mainly serves to

    A) emphasize the significance of the author's purpose.

    B) explain the author's credentials regarding the subject.

    C) offer evidence for a contrary point of view.

    D) summarize the author's arguments and evidence.

**Questions 21-31 are based on the following passage and supplementary material.**

The following passage is adapted from an article about the evolution of computers.

*Line*

(5)

(10)

(15)

(20)

(25)

If you had to count every person who lived in the United States, and there were neither calculators nor computers of any kind to help you, how would you do it?

That's the puzzle that nineteen-year-old engineer Herman Hollerith was faced with in the 1880s when he was employed by the U.S. Census Bureau. His solution was to invent a machine that stored information by putting patterns of holes in stiff pasteboard—an idea that Hollerith struck upon by observing the Jacquard loom, an automatic weaving machine that was controlled by specially coded punch cards. The machine, called the Hollerith tabulating machine and sorting box, was used to record the 1890 population census and shortened what had been a seven-year job to just three months.

Because Hollerith's machine used mechanical counters operated by electromagnets and circuits, it is considered the very first computer. Go anywhere today—a grocery store, an office, a school—and you see one of its many descendants, such as the calculator, personal computer, iPad, and smartphone. Though Hollerith retired to work at a cattle farm in Maryland, in 1924 the company he founded was renamed International Business Machines (IBM), which is still one of the largest technology corporations in the world.

**Data Storage**

(30)

(35)

As a data storage medium, Hollerith's invention was revolutionary, but one problem with it was the physical size and quantities of cards, each punch card holding only 960 bits of information. Many types of companies needed to hold more data in a smaller space. A big leap was made in the 1950s with the invention of magnetic tape, which consisted of long strips of plastic with a magnetized coating that could store as much data as 10,000 punch cards. A single reel was about the size of a dinner plate, and could be read from and written

*(40)* to rapidly. In 1963, Philips introduced magnetized tape in a small cassette, which became a popular choice for businesses to store data using computers.

Nevertheless, tapes were still cumbersome, and they would degrade over time. Then came the hard *(45)* drive. IBM made one of the first, in 1956, called 305 RAMAC. It was bigger than a refrigerator and contained fifty discs, each two feet in diameter. The 305 RAMAC could store 4.4 megabytes of data. By comparison, at about the size of a wallet, three *(50)* floppy discs, a popular medium from the 1980s and 1990s, held the same amount of information.

Hard drives have been constantly improving ever since, getting smaller, faster, and more energy-efficient. With the invention of the flash drive *(55)* and the micro-SD card, our information storage platforms are almost too small to handle with our bare hands.

Over the years, the price of data storage space has decreased exponentially. In 1984, a 5-megabyte *(60)* drive cost $1,400, or $280 per megabyte. Within five years, this was cut in half, and since then, the popularity of personal computers for home and business has driven the price even lower. In 2010, the cost per megabyte was less than ten cents.

### Microprocessors

*(65)* The microprocessor, or Central Processing Unit (CPU), is the brain inside every computer, tablet, and smartphone. It's a silicon semiconductor chip that contains the basic logic and arithmetic functions that the device needs in order to run. *(70)* The CPU receives and decodes instructions from keyboards, touch screens, and Wi-Fi adapters and sends signals out in a timed sequence to devices such as monitors, printers, and networks.

The first microprocessor was devised in 1971 *(75)* and called the Intel 4004. Measuring just 1/8" by 1/16", it was as powerful as the electronic computer of 25 years prior, which weighed 30 tons and used 18,000 vacuum tubes. It was said about that computer that the lights of Philadelphia dimmed when *(80)* it was turned on.

And yet, as fast as the Intel 4004 was, today's CPUs are thousands of times faster. One way that chips get faster is by the addition of more, and

smaller, transistors. Though the Intel 4004 proces-*(85)* sor held 2,300 transistors, a typical Intel processor today, with a 32-nanometer processing die, holds 560,000,000 transistors. (One nanometer equals one-billionth of a meter.)

Manufacturers of microprocessors also speed up *(90)* chips by making circuits smaller; when the circuits are more compact, the microprocessors become faster because electrons have less distance to travel. As chips get smaller, more of them can be etched onto the same diameter silicon wafer by improved fabrication *(95)* equipment. Consequently, computers that used to require warehouses now fit in the palm of our hands.

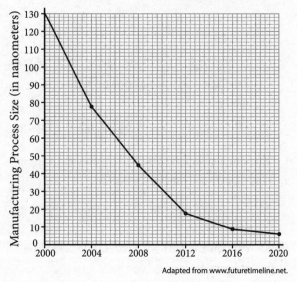

**Microchip Transistor Sizes, 2000-2020**

Adapted from www.futuretimeline.net.

21. Which choice best describes the narrator's view of technology?

A) A computer industry spokesperson explaining why innovation is good for the economy.

B) A consumer advocate explaining why the price of computers continues to fall.

C) A columnist outlining the evolution of computer speed and storage over time.

D) An efficiency expert discussing how the Census Bureau can improve its performance.

**GO ON TO THE NEXT PAGE**

22. An unstated assumption made by the author about Hollerith's invention is that

    A) the invention of the Jacquard loom was inspired by the success of Hollerith's machine.

    B) subsequent technological innovations were based on Hollerith's original design.

    C) the success of the 1890 census propelled IBM to the forefront of the computer industry.

    D) Hollerith's mechanical counters continued to be used years after their original debut.

23. Which choice provides the best evidence for the answer to the previous question?

    A) Lines 13-17 ("The machine . . . three months")

    B) Lines 18-20 ("Because Hollerith's . . . computer")

    C) Lines 20-24 ("Go anywhere . . . smart-phone")

    D) Lines 24-28 ("Though Hollerith . . . world")

24. As used in line 43, "cumbersome" most nearly means

    A) awkward.

    B) bulky.

    C) heavy.

    D) ponderous.

25. The main purpose of the opening sentence of the passage is to help readers

    A) understand the enormity of Hollerith's initial task.

    B) relive the bygone era in which Hollerith lived.

    C) appreciate the job of the U.S. Census Bureau.

    D) acknowledge how important computers are.

26. The passage most strongly suggests that

    A) the 1980s saw the most significant innovations in the history of personal computing.

    B) the price of data storage space has risen due to consumer demand for personal computers.

    C) continued innovation in data storage devices has resulted in increased value for consumers.

    D) computer industry profits have fallen as a result of decreased costs related to data storage.

27. Which choice provides the best evidence for the answer to the previous question?

    A) Lines 54-57 ("With the . . . hands")

    B) Lines 59-60 ("In 1984 . . . megabyte")

    C) Lines 60-63 ("Within five . . . lower")

    D) Lines 63-64 ("In 2010 . . . ten cents")

28. Data in the graph provide most direct support for which idea in the passage?

    A) The greatest decrease in microchip transistor sizes occurred between 2000 and 2008.

    B) The decline in microchip transistor sizes will most likely level out after the year 2020.

    C) Microchip transistor sizes are expected to increase to approximately 10 nanometers by the year 2020.

    D) The difference in microchip transistor sizes from 2004 and 2012 is 40 nanometers.

29. As used in line 44, "degrade" most nearly means

    A) corrupt.

    B) decay.

    C) humiliate.

    D) lower.

GO ON TO THE NEXT PAGE ⇨

30. The description of how a computer in the 1940s dimmed the lights of Philadelphia (lines 78-80) mainly serves to demonstrate the relationship between

    A) the size of the Intel 4004 and of its predecessor.

    B) the speed of contemporary CPUs and of the Intel 4004.

    C) the manufacturing process in the 1970s and that of today.

    D) the number of transistors in the Intel 4004 and in CPUs today.

31. It can most reasonably be inferred from the passage and graphic that

    A) Herman Hollerith's ideas influenced contemporary computers and other devices.

    B) The price of data storage space has fallen in the face of continual consumer demand.

    C) Increased consumer demand corresponds to a decrease in transistor sizes in the 2000s.

    D) Smaller transistors have exponentially increased the processing speed of today's CPUs.

**Questions 32-42 are based on the following passages.**

The following passages discuss solar farming.

**Passage 1**

The largest solar farm in the world, known as Topaz, opened in late 2014. The plant, which cost $2.5 billion dollars to build, generates a whopping
Line 550 megawatts of power. To put this number into
(5) perspective, this amount of power will be used to supply 160,000 homes. This switch from fossil fuels to solar power will save the environment exposure to approximately 377,000 tons of carbon dioxide emissions per year, which is the equivalent of
(10) retiring 73,000 cars.

The benefits of constructing such a large-scale solar farm are not only environmental. There are also significant economic benefits. Over 400 construction jobs were added to the area during
(15) the construction phase. $192 million in income was pumped into the local economy as a result. Economic benefits haven't stopped since the plant opened. Local energy suppliers are now able to enjoy $52 million in economic output.
(20) Located in San Luis Obispo County in California, the area where Topaz was built is part of California's Carrizo Plain. The plain is an area of native grassland northwest of Los Angeles. The land on which the plant sits was used as farmland
(25) in the past. Because of this, no new land disturbance was required in order to complete this large project. The land was no longer suitable for farming due to irrigation practices that stripped the soil of its nutrients. The 4,700 private acres provided
(30) the perfect setting for a solar plant, meeting the developer's standards for low-impact development, which was a priority considering the site's proximity to the Carrizo Plain National Monument, a protected area home to native species and plants.
(35) The plant's setup includes 460 panels mounted on steel support posts. The sunlight taken in by these panels is fed to power conversion stations. Each panel has its own conversion station. Made up of two inverters and a transformer each, the
(40) conversion stations are needed to make the power usable. The power is then sent to a substation that transforms it from 35.5 kilovolts to the standard 230 kilovolts. The Pacific Gas and Electric Company (PG&E) built a new switching station next to
(45) the solar farm. It is here that the power is looped into the grid that supplies neighboring areas.

Topaz will only remain the world's largest solar farm for a short period of time. The plant's owner, First Solar, is currently developing an even larger
(50) plant, also in California.

**Passage 2**

With more and more large-scale solar farms being developed in the sunny southwestern United States, researchers and conservationists alike are beginning to notice surprising environmental
(55) effects. While solar energy is known for its positive environmental impacts, officials at the National Fish and Wildlife Forensics Laboratory have come to

GO ON TO THE NEXT PAGE

recognize one of its significant downsides: Some species of birds that live in close proximity to large solar
(60) plants are dying off, including endangered birds.

A recent federal investigation recovered 233 birds that had been killed as a direct result of solar plants. Researchers believe that some of the affected birds have mistaken the large, reflective
(65) areas of the solar panels for bodies of water. This is a phenomenon referred to by scientists as "lake effect." The birds are drawn to what they assume to be water. They home in on the area and slam into the panels with great force. It is thought that the
(70) insects that birds eat fall victim to "lake effect" as well, leading the birds into the panels.

Researchers estimate that between 1,000 and 28,000 birds are killed as a result of harvesting solar energy. The number of birds affected by wind
(75) farming is much greater, ranging from 140,000 to 328,000. Coal-fired electricity has the largest negative effect on birds, killing nearly 8 million a year. These numbers make solar farming seem like the best option. However, conservationists
(80) are quick to point out that the areas where solar is expected to boom between 2015 and 2020 are home to some of the rarest birds in the United States. This could put specific bird species at risk of extinction.

(85) There exists a state mandate in California that 20 percent of all electricity sold must be renewable by the year 2017. This has been one driving force behind the rapid development of huge solar farms. The industry, which is expecting to boom as a
(90) result of this shift to renewable energy, is facing newly filed lawsuits by conservationist groups, citing the negative impact on wildlife. These lawsuits could prolong the approval process for the planned solar developments across the Southwest.

32. The central claim of Passage 1 is that solar farms

A) are an accepted form of generating energy because of their benefits.

B) were first thought impractical ways to generate energy.

C) help to improve the environment.

D) need large amounts of land to be developed.

33. In Passage 2, which choice best describes the narrator's view of solar farms?

A) Using solar farms is the most viable way to create energy.

B) More birds are endangered by wind farms than solar farming.

C) Solar farms may not be as friendly to the environment as many people believe.

D) Scientists need to find ways to discourage "lake effect" caused by solar farms.

34. It can most reasonably be inferred from Passage 1 that

A) solar farms will most likely only be built in the state of California.

B) the developer of Topaz is respectful of the environment.

C) not many studies have been done on the impact of solar farms on the environment.

D) the consumption of energy continues to grow greater each year.

35. Which choice provides the best evidence for the answer to the previous question?

A) Lines 6-10 ("This switch . . . cars")

B) Lines 13-15 ("Over 400 . . . phase")

C) Lines 29-34 ("The 4,700 . . . and plants")

D) Lines 47-48 ("Topaz will . . . of time")

GO ON TO THE NEXT PAGE

36. Passage 2 most strongly suggests that

    A) wind farms do less harm to the environment than solar farms.

    B) there are ways to create energy that do not harm wildlife.

    C) the life of solar farms will be short-lived because of their cost.

    D) birds can be easily confused by human-made structures.

37. Which choice provides the best evidence for the answer to the previous question?

    A) Lines 63-65 ("Researchers . . . of water")

    B) Lines 74-76 ("The number . . . 328,000")

    C) Lines 85-87 ("There exists . . . 2017")

    D) Lines 92-94 ("These lawsuits . . . Southwest")

38. Which of the following best describes the passages' central ideas?

    A) Passage 1 aims to convince readers that solar farming will be the primary form of developing energy in the future, while Passage 2 aims to show the limited benefits of solar farms.

    B) The purpose of Passage 1 is to show the many benefits of solar farming, while Passage 2 concentrates on the negative side effects of solar farming.

    C) Passage 1 discusses current research into the benefits of solar farms, while Passage 2 relates why solar farms are not practical in all locations.

    D) The purpose of Passage 1 is to show that producing energy is vital to the economy, while Passage 2 explains the ways in which solar farms can be developed.

39. As used in line 16 of Passage 1, "pumped" most nearly means

    A) drained.

    B) encouraged.

    C) extracted.

    D) funneled.

40. As used in line 58 of Passage 2, "recognize" most nearly means

    A) appreciate.

    B) credit.

    C) distinguish.

    D) realize.

41. In Passage 2, the word "surprising" (line 54) most directly suggests that

    A) solar farms require a lengthy development period.

    B) most people would be shocked by the size of solar farms.

    C) solar energy panels look strange to most people.

    D) most people think that solar energy is very beneficial.

42. On which of the following points would the authors of both passages most likely agree?

    A) Solar farms have effects that disturb some conservationists.

    B) Solar farms are an accepted way to generate electricity.

    C) All of the ways to create energy have negative side effects.

    D) Finding sites for solar farms is difficult to accomplish.

GO ON TO THE NEXT PAGE

**Questions 43-52 are based on the following passage and supplementary material.**

The following passage is adapted from an article about carbon dioxide in the atmosphere.

The concentration of carbon dioxide in our atmosphere has been steadily increasing since about 1750. Carbon dioxide lets in sun energy and
Line then traps it as heat energy, so the more carbon
(5)  dioxide in the atmosphere, the higher the average global temperature. Scientists are concerned that even slight increases in global temperatures will significantly affect plant and animal life on Earth.

In the past, photosynthesis has been able to keep
(10)  the level of carbon dioxide in the air at a lower level. Plants and algae convert water and carbon dioxide into oxygen and glucose, using the sun's energy. Carbon from carbon dioxide becomes trapped or "fixed" as the plant uses glucose to build
(15)  cellulose and starches, which make up most of the plant's structure.

Human industry is the main cause of increased carbon dioxide in the atmosphere. Cutting down forests to make room for expanding cities or farm-
(20)  land reduces the amount of carbon dioxide being removed. The wood is also often burned, releasing more carbon dioxide into the air. Burning fossil fuels for energy releases even more carbon dioxide that had previously been locked up in the coal, oil,
(25)  or gas underground.

We can reduce the amount of carbon dioxide by reducing how much we release, either by burning fewer fossil fuels or by removing carbon dioxide as the fuel is being burned. We can burn fewer
(30)  fossil fuels by switching to other forms of power that don't release carbon dioxide, such as solar or wind power, but these methods are more expensive. We can "scrub" the carbon dioxide from the air at the power plant where the fuel is burned, but
(35)  that is also expensive. It also does not work for the carbon dioxide produced by cars, trucks, and airplanes. Reducing our output of carbon diox-

ide, though a commendable idea, may not reduce the levels enough to have a meaningful impact.
(40)  We might need to go one step farther and try to remove carbon dioxide from the air.

Many research and development companies are now developing systems that will act like artificial "trees" and remove carbon dioxide from the atmos-
(45)  phere. Several built their approach on a method used in submarines and space vehicles. They combine the carbon dioxide with a strong base called sodium hydroxide to produce sodium bicarbonate, also known as baking soda. Bubbling air through
(50)  a solution of sodium hydroxide works well enough for the small amount of air in a space vehicle or submarine, but this would be a slow way to process a large amount of air.

One researcher found a way to make a plastic
(55)  with hydroxide components that would remove carbon dioxide from air as it passes over the surface of the plastic. Filters made out of long strands of this plastic can then remove carbon dioxide as wind pushes the air through the strands. The filters,
(60)  therefore, act much like leaves in a tree.

This plastic is inexpensive, but making it into filters, building towers that contain many "leaves" of the filters, and processing the plastic to remove the carbon dioxide so the plastic can be reused
(65)  is currently very expensive. To pay for the cost, gasoline would end up increasing in price. If manufacturers could get the cost of this method down to $100 per metric ton of carbon dioxide removed, for example, the price of gas would still
(70)  have to increase by about 88 cents to cover the cost. Researchers are optimistic that they could actually get the cost down to $25 per metric ton. If they achieve this goal, we someday may see artificial trees in our cities, assisting the real trees in clean-
(75)  ing the air.

GO ON TO THE NEXT PAGE ▷

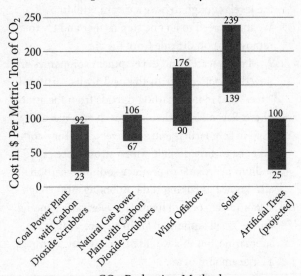

**CO$_2$ Reduction Costs by Method**

CO$_2$ Reduction Methods

Adapted from the Global CSS Institute.

43. The central claim of the passage is that

 A) methods to help remove carbon dioxide from the air are being developed.

 B) problems are caused by cutting down forests to make cities larger.

 C) increased levels of carbon dioxide in the atmosphere are a danger to humans.

 D) increased global temperatures will affect humans, plants, and animals.

44. Which choice provides the best evidence for the answer to the previous question?

 A) Lines 1-3 ("The concentration . . . 1750")

 B) Lines 11-13 ("Plants and . . . energy")

 C) Lines 17-18 ("Human industry . . . atmosphere")

 D) Lines 42-45 ("Many research . . . atmosphere")

45. In paragraph 2, the author helps structure the passage's claim by providing

 A) a detailed description of how real trees are different from artificial trees.

 B) examples of current methods of removing carbon dioxide from the air.

 C) an explanation of how carbon dioxide is naturally removed from the air.

 D) details about how the level of carbon dioxide in the air has been steadily increasing.

46. According to the passage, how do the filters described in paragraph 6 act like leaves in a tree?

 A) They contain long strands like veins in a leaf.

 B) They remove carbon dioxide from the air.

 C) They release oxygen into the atmosphere.

 D) They branch out from the plastic-like leaves.

47. Which of the following examples of evidence would most strengthen the author's line of reasoning?

 A) Details about the type of consequences plant and animal life could face if global temperatures increase in paragraph 1

 B) How many acres of forest are cut down each year to make room for bigger cities and more farmland in paragraph 3

 C) Descriptions of how solar and wind energy are harvested and converted to electricity in paragraph 4

 D) An analysis of how much people would be willing to pay for gas to offset the cost of plastic used to remove carbon dioxide from the air in paragraph 7

**GO ON TO THE NEXT PAGE**

48. As used in line 11, "convert" most nearly means

    A) control.

    B) transform.

    C) substitute.

    D) adjust.

49. The passage most strongly suggests that

    A) solar and wind energy would become less expensive if more people used these forms of energy.

    B) technology that removes carbon dioxide from the air would not be necessary if more people rode bikes.

    C) global temperatures could reach levels dangerous to plant and animal life in the next 50 years.

    D) people will resist technology that removes carbon dioxide from the air if it is too expensive.

50. Which choice provides the best evidence for the answer to the previous question?

    A) Lines 3-6 ("Carbon dioxide . . . temperature")

    B) Lines 26-29 ("We can . . . burned")

    C) Lines 61-65 ("This plastic . . . very expensive")

    D) Lines 71-75 ("Researchers . . . the air")

51. As used in line 38, "commendable" most nearly means

    A) convincing.

    B) hopeful.

    C) admirable.

    D) effective.

52. Data in the graph provide most direct support for which idea in the passage?

    A) Solar and wind energy are the most expensive methods of reducing carbon dioxide emissions.

    B) Artificial trees remove more carbon dioxide from the air than scrubbers at power plants.

    C) Natural gas power plants with scrubbers provide the least expensive method of reducing carbon dioxide emissions.

    D) Coal power plants with scrubbers cost more to operate than natural gas power plants with scrubbers.

**IF YOU FINISH BEFORE TIME IS CALLED, YOU MAY CHECK YOUR WORK ON THIS SECTION ONLY. DO NOT TURN TO ANY OTHER SECTION IN THE TEST.**    **STOP**

# WRITING AND LANGUAGE TEST

### 35 Minutes—44 Questions

Turn to Section 2 of your answer sheet to answer the questions in this section.

**Directions:** Each passage below is accompanied by a number of questions. For some questions, you will consider how the passage might be revised to improve the expression of ideas. For other questions, you will consider how the passage might be edited to correct errors in sentence structure, usage, or punctuation. A passage or a question may be accompanied by one or more graphics (such as a table or graph) that you will consider as you make revising and editing decisions.

Some questions will direct you to an underlined portion of a passage. Other questions will direct you to a location in a passage or ask you to think about the passage as a whole.

After reading each passage, choose the answer to each question that most effectively improves the quality of writing in the passage or that makes the passage conform to the conventions of standard written English. Many questions include a "NO CHANGE" option. Choose that option if you think the best choice is to leave the relevant portion of the passage as it is.

**Questions 1-11 are based on the following passage.**

## Vitamin C—Essential Nutrient or Wonder Drug?

Vitamin C has been considered a wonder drug by many people, including a two-time Nobel Prize winner. Unfortunately, although it is **1** so very essential for many growth and repair activities in the body, vitamin C does not live up to most other claims.

Linus Pauling was one of the earliest, and most famous, of the vitamin C supporters. He was a brilliant chemist and **2** deferential humanitarian who won both the Nobel Prize in Chemistry and the Nobel Peace Prize for his work. His later work on vitamin C still serves for many as proof that vitamin C is a wonder drug; **3** as a result, his work never supported his theories.

1. A) NO CHANGE
   B) very essential
   C) important and essential
   D) essential

2. A) NO CHANGE
   B) dedicated
   C) good
   D) loyal

3. A) NO CHANGE
   B) because
   C) however,
   D) so

GO ON TO THE NEXT PAGE

**4** [1] In 1932, vitamin C was identified as the nutrient that prevents scurvy. [2] The symptoms of scurvy are caused mainly by the body's inability to repair and replace damaged cells. [3] The word "scurvy" has been in use since the 1500s and is believed to have Dutch and French origins. [4] These symptoms appear after months without sufficient vitamin C, usually because of a poor diet. [5] Getting enough vitamin C is therefore essential to good health. [6] Pauling and others **5** implied that increasing vitamin C intake beyond the amount found in a balanced diet could do more than just maintain good health.

For example, Pauling was certain that high doses of vitamin C could cure cancer. His research with cancer patients did not reveal any conclusive support **6** for his theory, very high doses of vitamin C slowed the growth of certain tumors but did not shrink them. The high levels of vitamin C were also dangerous and actually interfered with other cancer treatments.

Pauling and others were also convinced that high doses of vitamin C could prevent and cure colds. Research has shown that people with a high vitamin C intake recover from colds slightly faster than people with a normal intake. **7** However, for the average person, who gets a few a year, this means reducing sick days a little bit. Also, increasing levels of vitamin C in the body once a person has already come down with a cold unfortunately makes no difference.

4. Which choice provides the least relevant detail?

A) Sentence 1

B) Sentence 2

C) Sentence 3

D) Sentence 5

5. A) NO CHANGE

B) reasoned

C) judged

D) philosophized

6. A) NO CHANGE

B) for this theory, so very high doses

C) for his theory very high doses

D) for his theory; very high doses

7. Which choice most effectively supports the claim that vitamin C has only a slight effect on people's ability to recover from colds?

A) However, for most people, who get colds around 3 times a year, the reduced time frame is not that significant.

B) However, for an average person, who gets colds every year, this amounts to only about two or three days a year.

C) However, for most people, who get a lot of colds each year, this doesn't add up to be much time.

D) However, for the average person, who gets about 3 colds a year, this means reducing sick days from about 6 to about 4.

GO ON TO THE NEXT PAGE ▷

The recommended daily intake of vitamin C for adult males is 90 mg, and for women it is 75 mg. Amounts up to twice that much can be absorbed well by the digestive system, but anything beyond those amounts cannot. People who take high doses are able to absorb only about 50 percent of the vitamin. **8** The unabsorbed vitamin will have caused digestive problems, such as nausea, **9** diarrhea; and abdominal cramps. The slightly shorter cold duration obtained at high doses is not worth the possible side effects.

Vitamin C is important for **10** good health. People should make sure they get the recommended amount by eating a balanced diet. However, a person who takes higher doses through supplements will see almost no additional benefit, and may, in fact, feel worse from the side effects. **11** Vitamin C may not be a "wonder" drug, but it is an essential nutrient for all of us.

8. A) NO CHANGE
   B) The unabsorbed vitamin can cause digestive problems,
   C) The unabsorbed vitamin has caused digestive problems,
   D) The unabsorbed vitamin could have caused digestive problems,

9. A) NO CHANGE
   B) diarrhea—and abdominal cramps.
   C) diarrhea, and abdominal cramps.
   D) diarrhea, and, abdominal cramps.

10. Which choice most effectively combines the sentences at the underlined portion?
    A) good health, making sure
    B) good health, but people should make sure
    C) good health, and people should make sure
    D) good health; however making sure

11. The author wants a conclusion that summarizes the main point of the passage. Which choice accomplishes that goal?
    A) NO CHANGE
    B) Vitamin C is found in fruits and vegetables, such as oranges, peppers, tomatoes, and broccoli.
    C) Vitamin C supplements have always been accompanied by false claims, so choose one carefully.
    D) Vitamin C supplements are sold in a pharmacy or health food store near you.

GO ON TO THE NEXT PAGE

**Questions 12-22 are based on the following passage.**

## The Familiar Myth

Jermaine typed "Joseph Campbell" into his Internet browser. His teacher had said that Campbell's research held the key to understanding the universal motifs of literature from around the world. He clicked on a web page dedicated to the man's life and work. The first thing Jermaine noted was that American mythologist and author Joseph Campbell wrote in his **12** seminal work, *The Hero with a Thousand Faces*, "Myth is the secret opening through which the inexhaustible energies of the cosmos pour into human cultural manifestation." Online, Jermaine learned that **13** Campbell showcases what he calls the "monomyth" in this work. "Monomyth" is a term Campbell borrowed from fellow author James Joyce,

12. A) NO CHANGE
    B) initial
    C) primary
    D) fictitious

13. A) NO CHANGE
    B) Campbell is showcasing what he calls the "monomyth"
    C) Campbell showcased what he calls the "monomyth"
    D) Campbell showcased what he called the "monomyth"

GO ON TO THE NEXT PAGE

referring to a story pattern that has served as the basis for many pieces of literature from around the world. The monomyth is often referred to as the "hero's journey."

Next, Jermaine clicked to view a graphic representation of the story structure. A plot diagram detailed the typical events of **14** a heros' journey. The start of the journey is referred to as "the call to adventure." It is followed by several challenges and encounters with people who appear to help him. The hero experiences revelations along the way, and these revelations are the catalyst for transformation. Most heroes undergo this transformation in order to reach **15** the end of there journey.

**16** Jermaine sought out famous stories and myths to help him better understand the monomyth concept. Jermaine clicked a link titled "Cultural Representations." He learned that throughout time, many cultures have expressed their worldview through myths. While some of these stories are representative of humanity as a whole, the monomyth prominently featured one hero working for the good of all humans, experiencing **17** hardships, challenges, and will triumph. Two very recognizable instances of this structure from modern

14. A) NO CHANGE
    B) a hero's journey.
    C) a heroes journey.
    D) a heroes' journey.

15. A) NO CHANGE
    B) the journey they are ending.
    C) the end of their journey.
    D) the end of they're journey.

16. Which choice most effectively sets up the information that follows?

    A) NO CHANGE
    B) Jermaine wanted to write about the very first monomyth, so he chose to focus his research on that.
    C) Jermaine decided that religious figures were the best way to explore the monomyth concept.
    D) Jermaine didn't quite understand the progression of the hero's journey.

17. A) NO CHANGE
    B) hardships, challenges, and is triumphant.
    C) hardships, challenges, and triumph.
    D) hardships, challenges, and triumphs.

**GO ON TO THE NEXT PAGE**

times are the stories of superheroes found in comic **18** books. Such as Superman and Batman.

Jermaine then read monomyths found in other cultures. He learned about the Kayapo Indians and their myth about a boy who stole fire from a jaguar. The boy brought this fire to his people, enabling them to cook their food. To a large extent, this hero brought more to his people than just the **19** use of fire—in this story, fire symbolized civilization. Similarly, in Greek mythology, Prometheus also stole fire to bring to his people. In the mythology of the Daribi people, native to Papua New Guinea, Souw, a wanderer, brought his people livestock and crops. These stories are similar **20** not only in its structure but also in its symbolism. **21**

The monomyth, Jermaine learned, is a structure that people across all cultures are familiar and comfortable with to the point that they can picture themselves as the heroes in their own stories. It is because of this that the monomyth will continue to be a **22** timely story structure moving forward.

18. A) NO CHANGE
    B) books. And Superman and Batman.
    C) books, such as Superman and Batman.
    D) books, as well as Superman and Batman.

19. A) NO CHANGE
    B) use of fire, in this story,
    C) use of fire. In this story,
    D) use of fire: in this story,

20. A) NO CHANGE
    B) not only in their structure but also in their symbolism.
    C) not only in structure but also in its symbolism.
    D) not only in each structure but also symbolism.

21. Which detail, if added here, would best complete the paragraph?
    A) A description of a villain in a modern fairy tale
    B) The name of the website where Jermaine found this information
    C) The importance of animal figures in myths
    D) The location of the Kayapo Indians' homeland

22. A) NO CHANGE
    B) prevalent
    C) distinguished
    D) requisite

GO ON TO THE NEXT PAGE

**Questions 23-33 are based on the following passage and supplementary material.**

## America's Love for Streetcars

The history of the electric trolley car can be traced to 1887, the era when electric motor technology was perfected. The street railway industry immediately hailed the new mode of public transport as a solution to horsecars, which were horse-drawn vehicles that ran on rails. Extremely popular, trolley lines had a large impact on cities such as San Francisco.

A streetcar, or trolley, is an electric vehicle that runs on rails; **23** they connect to form a system, typically providing public access to urban centers. Besides transportation, other benefits of the new technology abounded—for example, by World War I, streetcars had become America's fifth largest industry, employing over 100,000 workers nationwide.

**24** People loved the trolleys. During the summer, special open trolleys called "breezers" allowed riders to enjoy cool air on hot days, but the main attraction was that electric cars **25** were faster, more speedy, and arrived sooner than the previous horsecars. The demand resulted in the creation of larger and more powerful trolleys, such as double-deckers.

The public's desire to travel between cities prompted a change in the late 1800s to intercity trolleys, also known as "interurbans." These electric trolleys were economical and thus were less expensive to ride than steam railroads. **26** Trolley routes within cities nonetheless continued to be common, however.

23. A) NO CHANGE
    B) these rails
    C) it
    D) which

24. Which choice most effectively sets up the information that follows?
    A) NO CHANGE
    B) Most people today have never seen a trolley in person.
    C) Trolleys remain popular outside America.
    D) The popularity of trolleys did not last in the United States.

25. A) NO CHANGE
    B) were faster and speedier
    C) were faster
    D) were faster, speedier, and arrived sooner

26. Which choice provides the most relevant detail?
    A) NO CHANGE
    B) Decades later, long-distance buses would become the transportation of choice.
    C) Although some still viewed railroads romantically, their time was coming to an end.
    D) Farmers saved money by using interurbans to get products to markets in large cities.

GO ON TO THE NEXT PAGE ⟩

[1] As more automobiles became available, the competition caused trolley companies to cut back. [2] Henry Ford, however, changed the world with the 1908 introduction of the Model T, a car the average worker could afford. [3] Ultimately, this major factor led to the demise of such lines. [4] The World War II years ignited renewed interest in, and use of, some interurban lines, because gasoline and tire **27** rationalizing limited the use of automobiles. [5] This **28** resumption was short-lived, though, because once new cars hit the post-war market, people again chose mobility over scheduled public transportation. **29**

A modern resurgence in electric trolleys began in 2009, when federal funding became available for streetcar projects in key cities such as Atlanta. **30** Critics argue that modern streetcars aren't any faster than local buses. Critics argue that this is the reason modern streetcars will never be cost-effective. They also point out that a lot of streetcar projects start as economic development projects rather than as transit projects.

27. A) NO CHANGE
    B) rationing
    C) reasoning
    D) rating

28. A) NO CHANGE
    B) reparation
    C) renaissance
    D) renovation

29. To make this paragraph most logical, sentence 2 should be placed
    A) where it is now.
    B) before sentence 1.
    C) after sentence 3.
    D) after sentence 4.

30. Which choice most effectively combines the sentences at the underlined portion?
    A) Critics argue that modern streetcars aren't any faster than local buses and therefore will never be cost-effective.
    B) Critics argue that modern streetcars aren't any faster than local buses and that they will never be cost-effective.
    C) Critics argue that modern streetcars aren't any faster than local buses and critics argue they will never be cost-effective.
    D) Critics argue that modern streetcars aren't any faster than local buses, so critics say they will never be cost-effective.

GO ON TO THE NEXT PAGE

Today, most commuters still get to work by car; **31** in fact, very few Americans in any metropolitan area use public transportation. Some communities are **32** embracing a revival, with light rail systems as the second generation of streetcars. Portland, Oregon, for example, boasts a successful light rail system serving the broad metropolitan area with an annual ridership of 39.12 million residents interested in car-free living.

From trolleys to light rail, the evolution of public transportation shows that if it is **33** reliable convenient comfortable, and fast, it's on the right track.

31. Which choice offers an accurate interpretation of the data in the chart?

A) NO CHANGE

B) however, public transportation is crucial to some cities.

C) it is only in rural areas that public transportation is still a valuable service.

D) nonetheless, public transportation use is on the rise in all metro areas.

32. A) NO CHANGE

B) accepting

C) tolerating

D) understanding

33. A) NO CHANGE

B) reliable—convenient, comfortable, and fast,

C) reliable; convenient, comfortable and fast

D) reliable, convenient, comfortable, and fast,

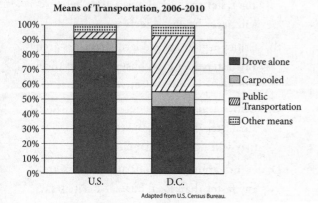

Means of Transportation, 2006-2010

Adapted from U.S. Census Bureau.

GO ON TO THE NEXT PAGE ⟹

**Questions 34-44 are based on the following passage and supplementary material.**

## Educating Early

Early childhood education (ECE) is the field **34** formed by those who teach young children, typically between ages three and five. Preschool teachers, teaching assistants, and childcare workers are today's most common ECE job titles. **35** Careers in ECE involve reward and challenge, as well as a healthy measure of fun.

For those interested in working with children up to about age eight, it is perhaps as important to develop nurturing skills as it is to undergo the proper training. Early childhood **36** educators must be patient, gentle, creative, and physically, energetic in order to address the many needs of young children. **37** Varying levels of educational training are also required for some entry-level childcare positions. A high school diploma is sufficient. For most teaching jobs, though, an associate's or bachelor's degree in an ECE-related discipline is expected. Some of these jobs also require staff to obtain credentials as Child Development Associates (CDA) or Child Care Professionals (CCP). Due to these variations in qualifications, it is important that anyone pursuing ECE find out specific expectations for the job of their choice.

The daily demands of ECE are multifaceted. Educators conscientiously interact with both children and parents and must plan in advance for the day's activities. They teach at the unique level of the children under

34. A) NO CHANGE
    B) consisting of
    C) epitomized by
    D) exclusive of

35. A) NO CHANGE
    B) Careers in ECE involve reward and challenge. As well as a healthy measure of fun.
    C) Careers in ECE involve reward and challenge; as well as a healthy measure of fun.
    D) Careers in ECE involve reward and challenge, as well as: a healthy measure of fun.

36. A) NO CHANGE
    B) educators must be patient, gentle, creative, and physically energetic
    C) educators must be: patient gentle creative and physically energetic
    D) educators must be, patient, gentle, creative, and physically energetic

37. A) NO CHANGE
    B) Varying levels of educational training are also required, for some entry-level childcare positions, a high school diploma is sufficient.
    C) Varying levels of educational training are also required. For some entry-level childcare positions, a high school diploma is sufficient.
    D) Varying levels of educational training are also required: for some entry-level childcare positions a high school diploma is sufficient.

GO ON TO THE NEXT PAGE

their care, continually working to prepare them for many coming years of formal education. Introducing concepts such as storytelling, reading, basic sciences, arts, and math, as well as healthy physical, social, and emotional activities, **38** these teachers instruct children listening, learning, and enjoying school. The vital lessons taught to the preschool-aged child **39** equips young learners to succeed in kindergarten and beyond.

**40** The field presents a challenging career path. The U.S. Department of Labor expects ECE jobs to grow moderately over the coming decade. As research continues to confirm early education's positive impact on children's lives, the U.S. government is spending more money to improve and expand opportunities. Parents and guardians of any socioeconomic status are urged to consider preschool because of **41** their influence on the future of both the individual child and the nation as a whole. These developments indicate **42** a ceaseless job market for early childhood educators. **43** Early childhood educators often choose to pursue graduate studies in fields such as education and psychology.

38. A) NO CHANGE
   B) these teachers instruct children in listening, learning, and enjoying school.
   C) these teachers instruct children to listen, how to learn, and how to enjoy school.
   D) these teachers instruct children to listen, to learn, and enjoy of school.

39. A) NO CHANGE
   B) has equipped
   C) equipping
   D) equip

40. Which choice most effectively sets up the information that follows?
   A) NO CHANGE
   B) Job security in ECE is promising.
   C) The field is booming internationally.
   D) Unfortunately, pay for ECE positions is low.

41. A) NO CHANGE
   B) it's
   C) its
   D) they're

42. A) NO CHANGE
   B) an erratic
   C) an eternal
   D) an enduring

43. Which choice provides the most relevant detail?
   A) NO CHANGE
   B) Recent years have seen an increase in federal funding to preschool programs offered to low-income families.
   C) In Sweden, preschool is compulsory and is fully funded by the government.
   D) The benefits of preschool are apparent in longitudinal studies focusing on child development.

**GO ON TO THE NEXT PAGE** ⇨

Those pursuing ECE should anticipate a lower average yearly income than that of some other jobs. For those who love young children, activity, and an interactive, eventful, and playful workplace, however, this career offers what many would find to be a rewarding and stimulating life. The Bureau of Labor Statistics bears this out, **44** as schools and day care centers continue to be the most common places of employment for workers in ECE. The influence of such educators is irreplaceable. Inviting children each day to craft and imagine, these teachers form the minds that will someday imagine and craft the future of this world.

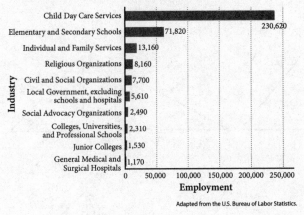

**Industries with the Highest Employment Level for Preschool Teachers, Except Special Education, May 2013**

Child Day Care Services — 230,620
Elementary and Secondary Schools — 71,820
Individual and Family Services — 13,160
Religious Organizations — 8,160
Civil and Social Organizations — 7,700
Local Government, excluding schools and hospitals — 5,610
Social Advocacy Organizations — 2,490
Colleges, Universities, and Professional Schools — 2,310
Junior Colleges — 1,530
General Medical and Surgical Hospitals — 1,170

Industry / Employment (0, 50,000, 100,000, 150,000, 200,000, 250,000)

Adapted from the U.S. Bureau of Labor Statistics.

44. Which choice offers an accurate interpretation of the data in the chart?

A) NO CHANGE

B) as civic and social organizations have seen a rapid decline in the number of ECE-trained employees.

C) as most students pursuing careers in ECE can anticipate finding work in the fast-paced medical field.

D) as the majority of ECE graduates find employment in rewarding local government positions.

# MATH TEST

### 25 Minutes—20 Questions

## NO-CALCULATOR SECTION

Turn to Section 3 of your answer sheet to answer the questions in this section.

**Directions:** For this section, solve each problem and decide which is the best of the choices given. Fill in the corresponding oval on the answer sheet. You may use any available space for scratch work.

Notes:

1. Calculator use is NOT permitted.
2. All numbers used are real numbers.
3. All figures used are necessary to solving the problems that they accompany. All figures are drawn to scale EXCEPT when it is stated that a specific figure is not drawn to scale.
4. Unless stated otherwise, the domain of any function $f$ is assumed to be the set of all real numbers $x$, for which $f(x)$ is a real number.

Information:

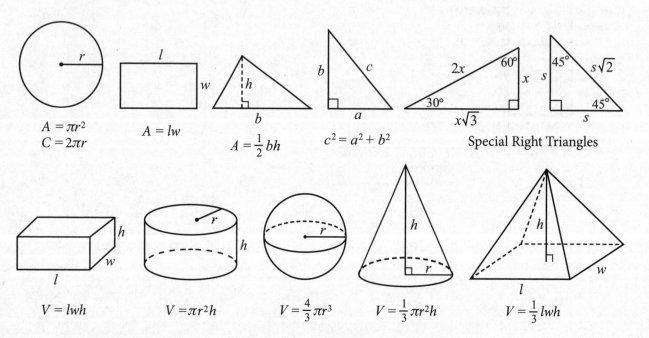

$A = \pi r^2$
$C = 2\pi r$

$A = lw$

$A = \frac{1}{2}bh$

$c^2 = a^2 + b^2$

Special Right Triangles

$V = lwh$

$V = \pi r^2 h$

$V = \frac{4}{3}\pi r^3$

$V = \frac{1}{3}\pi r^2 h$

$V = \frac{1}{3}lwh$

The sum of the degree measures of the angles in a triangle is 180.

The number of degrees of arc in a circle is 360.

The number of radians of arc in a circle is $2\pi$.

GO ON TO THE NEXT PAGE

$$a = \frac{b - 3}{c}$$

1. In a certain board game, where playing involves a specific number of cards and a specific number of players, three cards are removed from the deck and kept in an envelope, while the rest of the cards are distributed equally among the players. The scenario can be represented by the equation given above. What does the variable $c$ represent in this scenario?

   A) The number of players

   B) The number of cards left over

   C) The number of cards in the deck

   D) The number of cards dealt to each player

2. A hospital hosts an annual charity drive in which volunteers sell first aid kits to raise money for the pediatric ward. The hospital ordered too many kits last year, so it already has some to start this year's drive with. The project manager estimates, based on last year's sales, that the hospital needs to order an additional 50 boxes of kits. The function $k(b) = 12b + 32$, where $b$ is the number of boxes ordered, represents the number of kits the hospital will have after the order arrives. When the project manager places the order, she is told that the company has changed the number of kits per box to 8. How many more boxes will she need to order to end up with the same number of kits that she had originally planned for?

   A) 25

   B) 32

   C) 75

   D) 200

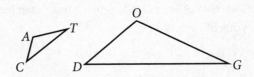

Note: Figure not drawn to scale.

3. If $\triangle CAT$ shown above is similar to $\triangle DOG$, and the ratio of the length of $\overline{TC}$ to $\overline{GD}$ is 2:7, which of the following ratios must also be equal to 2:7?

   A) $\overline{CA} : \overline{DG}$

   B) $m\angle C : m\angle D$

   C) area of $\triangle CAT$ : area of $\triangle DOG$

   D) perimeter of $\triangle CAT$ : perimeter of $\triangle DOG$

4. Which of the following expressions is equivalent to $\sqrt{16x^9 y^6}$ ?

   A) $4x^2 y^3$

   B) $4x^3 y^2$

   C) $4xy\sqrt{xy}$

   D) $4x^4 y^3 \sqrt{x}$

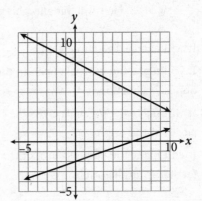

5. What is the solution to the system of equations shown in the graph?

   A) $(11, 1.5)$

   B) $(12, 2)$

   C) $(13, 2.5)$

   D) $(14, 2.75)$

GO ON TO THE NEXT PAGE

6. The value of $7x^2 + 3$ is how much more than the value of $7x^2 - 9$ ?

A) 6

B) 12

C) $7x^2 - 6$

D) $7x^2 + 12$

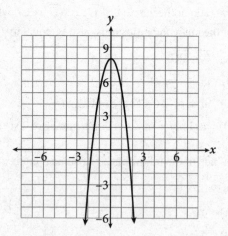

7. Vadim graphs the equation $y = -3x^2 + 8$, which is shown in the figure above. He realizes, however, that he miscalculated and should have graphed $y = -\frac{1}{3}x^2 + 8$. How will this affect his graph?

A) It will change the $y$-intercept.

B) It will make the parabola open in the opposite direction.

C) It will make the parabola cross the $x$-axis closer to the origin.

D) It will make the parabola cross the $x$-axis farther from the origin.

8. Which value of $x$ makes the equation $\frac{9}{4}\left(x - \frac{7}{3}\right) = 5$ true?

A) $-\frac{1}{9}$

B) $\frac{41}{9}$

C) $\frac{163}{12}$

D) $\frac{67}{3}$

9. An egg farmer packs his eggs in standard 12-hole cartons and then packs the cartons in large shipping boxes. The number of boxes needed, $b$, to transport $c$ cartons of eggs can be found using the function $b(c) = \frac{c}{40}$. If the carton-packing machine can pack a maximum of 4,000 cartons per day, and it does not pack partial boxes, what is the range of the function in this context?

A) All integers from 0 to 100

B) All integers from 0 to 4,000

C) All integers greater than or equal to 40

D) All integers greater than or equal to 100

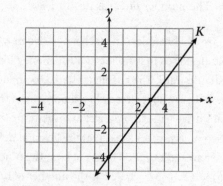

10. Where will the graph of $y = \frac{4}{3}x + 8$ intersect line $K$ shown above?

A) $(-3, 4)$

B) $(9, 20)$

C) The graphs will never intersect.

D) It is not possible to determine where the graphs will intersect because the $y$-intercept of the given line does not fit on the coordinate plane.

**GO ON TO THE NEXT PAGE**

11. Some herbicides are more effective at killing weeds than others, relative to the amount of the herbicide needed to produce results. Which graph could represent the effectiveness of a more-effective herbicide, $m$, and a less-effective herbicide, $l$?

A)
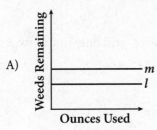

B)
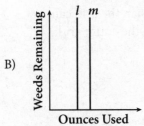

C)
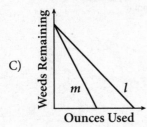

D)
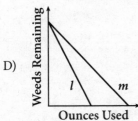

12. Which of the following values satisfies the inequalities $t - \dfrac{3}{4} > \dfrac{3}{2}$ and $\dfrac{t}{4} - \dfrac{1}{3} < \dfrac{5}{12}$?

A) 1.75

B) 2.25

C) 2.75

D) 3.25

13. If $p(x)$ is a polynomial function that has a simple zero at $x = 4$ and a double zero at $x = -\dfrac{1}{3}$, which of the following could be the factored form of $p(x)$?

A) $p(x) = (x - 4)(x + 3)^2$

B) $p(x) = (x - 4)(3x + 1)^2$

C) $p(x) = 2(x - 4)(x + 3)$

D) $p(x) = 2(x - 4)(3x + 1)$

14. Triangle $ABC$ (not shown) is a right triangle, with $AB < AC < BC$. If the length of side $AB$ is 6 and the length of side $BC$ is 10, what is the area, in square units, of triangle $ABC$?

A) 24

B) 30

C) 48

D) 60

15. Water from rivers and streams is often unsafe to drink because of sediments and contaminants. One primitive way that water has been filtered in the past (and is still occasionally employed by avid campers and survivalists) is to use a charcoal filter, through which the water is allowed to trickle. Suppose three campers each make a charcoal filter. The first two campers make their filters using water bottles, each of which can filter enough water for all three campers in 8 hours. The third filter is made from a two-liter soda bottle and can filter the same amount of water in 4 hours. How long will it take the three filters working together to filter enough water for all three campers?

A) $\dfrac{1}{2}$ hour

B) 1 hour

C) $1\dfrac{1}{2}$ hours

D) 2 hours

GO ON TO THE NEXT PAGE

**Directions:** For questions 16-20, solve the problem and enter your answer in the grid, as described below, on the answer sheet.

1. Although not required, it is suggested that you write your answer in the boxes at the top of the columns to help you fill in the circles accurately. You will receive credit only if the circles are filled in correctly.

2. Mark no more than one circle in any column.

3. No question has a negative answer.

4. Some problems may have more than one correct answer. In such cases, grid only one answer.

5. **Mixed numbers** such as $3\frac{1}{2}$ must be gridded as 3.5 or $\frac{7}{2}$.

   (If $3\frac{1}{2}$ is entered into the grid as 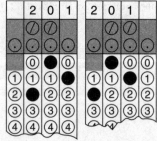, it will be interpreted as $\frac{31}{2}$, not $3\frac{1}{2}$.)

6. **Decimal answers:** If you obtain a decimal answer with more digits than the grid can accommodate, it may be either rounded or truncated, but it must fill the entire grid.

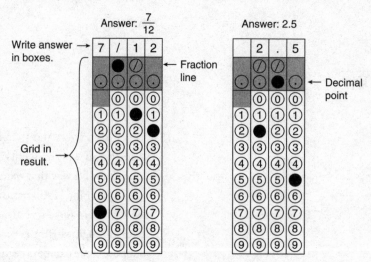

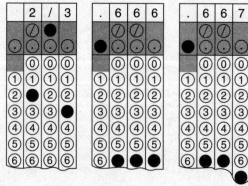

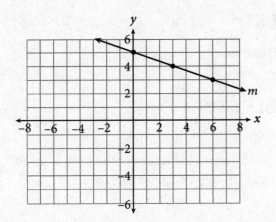

16. If line $m$ shown above is reflected over the $x$-axis, what is the slope of the new line?

$$0 \leq \frac{1-k}{2} < \frac{7}{8}$$

17. If $k$ lies within the solution set of the inequality shown above, what is the maximum possible value of $k$?

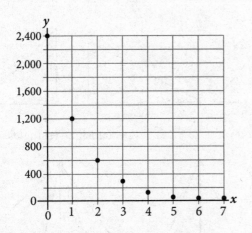

18. If an exponential function of the form $h(x) = a(b)^x$ is used to model the data shown in the graph above, what is the value of $b$?

19. What is the value of the complex number $\frac{1}{4}i^{42} + i^{60}$?

20. In medicine, when a drug is administered in pill form, it takes time for the concentration in the bloodstream to build up, particularly for pain medications. Suppose for a certain pain medication, the function $C(t) = \frac{1.5t}{t^2 + 4}$ is used to model the concentration, where $t$ is the time in hours after the patient takes the pill. For this particular medication, the concentration reaches a maximum level of 0.375 about two hours after it is administered and then begins to decrease. If the patient isn't allowed to eat or drink until the concentration drops back down to 0.3, how many hours after taking the pill must the patient wait before eating or drinking?

# MATH TEST

**55 Minutes—38 Questions**

## CALCULATOR SECTION

Turn to Section 4 of your answer sheet to answer the questions in this section.

**Directions:** For this section, solve each problem and decide which is the best of the choices given. Fill in the corresponding oval on the answer sheet. You may use any available space for scratch work.

Notes:

1. Calculator use is permitted.
2. All numbers used are real numbers.
3. All figures used are necessary to solving the problems that they accompany. All figures are drawn to scale EXCEPT when it is stated that a specific figure is not drawn to scale.
4. Unless stated otherwise, the domain of any function $f$ is assumed to be the set of all real numbers $x$, for which $f(x)$ is a real number.

Information:

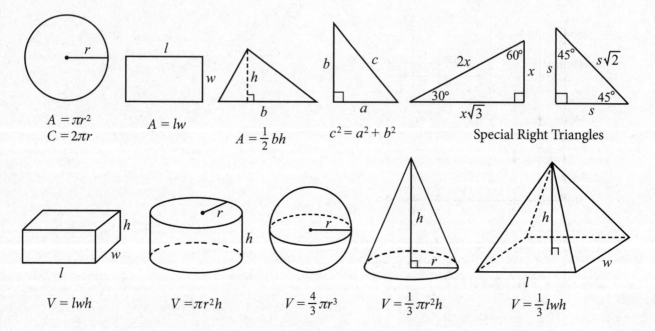

$A = \pi r^2$
$C = 2\pi r$

$A = lw$

$A = \frac{1}{2} bh$

$c^2 = a^2 + b^2$

Special Right Triangles

$V = lwh$

$V = \pi r^2 h$

$V = \frac{4}{3} \pi r^3$

$V = \frac{1}{3} \pi r^2 h$

$V = \frac{1}{3} lwh$

The sum of the degree measures of the angles in a triangle is 180.

The number of degrees of arc in a circle is 360.

The number of radians of arc in a circle is $2\pi$.

GO ON TO THE NEXT PAGE

| Rating Score | 1 | 2 | 3 | 4 | 5 |
|---|---|---|---|---|---|
| Frequency | 0 | 4 | 6 | 8 | 2 |

1.  In a market where approximately 44% of all book purchases are made online, customer reviews are extremely important from a sales and marketing perspective. Early reviews are most important, as they help or hinder a book's momentum in the marketplace. The frequency table shown above gives the first 20 customer ratings for a certain book sold online. What is the mean rating for this book?

    A)  3

    B)  3.4

    C)  3.7

    D)  4

2.  Hardwood trees take much longer to grow than softwood trees. Once harvested, however, hardwood is much stronger and more durable. Because of its higher density, a piece of hardwood that is the same size as a piece of softwood weighs considerably more. A lumberyard ships both kinds of wood to home improvement stores. The cost $C$, in dollars, to ship a pallet of wood weighing $p$ pounds can be found using the equation $C = 6.5p + 16$. What is the cost difference to ship a pallet of hardwood weighing 170 pounds versus a pallet of softwood weighing 80 pounds?

    A)  $90

    B)  $325

    C)  $585

    D)  $715

3.  The First Transcontinental Railroad, which was 1,907 miles long, was completed in 1869 to connect the West Coast of the United States to the existing rail system that ran from the Missouri River to the East Coast. During the early years after building the railroad, dangerous conditions and mechanical problems could delay the train significantly. For a person traveling from one end of the First Transcontinental Railroad to the other, which inequality represents all possible values of $t$, where $t$ is the time it took to complete the journey, if, while in motion, the train traveled at an average speed of $m$ miles per hour?

    A)  $t \geq \dfrac{m}{1,907}$

    B)  $t \geq \dfrac{1,907}{m}$

    C)  $t \geq 1,907m$

    D)  $t \geq 1,907 + m$

$$\frac{3x + 7}{x - 2} = 16$$

4.  Which value of $x$ satisfies the equation given above?

    A)  $\dfrac{9}{19}$

    B)  $\dfrac{9}{13}$

    C)  2

    D)  3

| | Bargain | High-End |
|---|---|---|
| Price (per sq. ft) | $1.89 | $5.49 |
| Rating | 2.8 | 8.2 |
| Life Expectancy | 5 years | |

5. The table above shows the price per square foot, the average customer rating (out of 10), and the life expectancy (before needing replacement) of the bargain version and the high-end version of carpet at a flooring warehouse. If the ratio of the life expectancies is roughly the same as the ratios of the prices and the ratings, about how many years can the high-end carpet be expected to last?

A) 10

B) 12

C) 15

D) 18

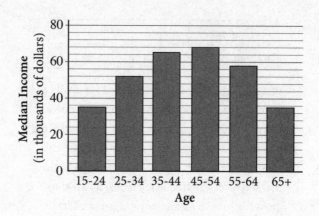

6. The bar graph shows median household incomes in a certain geographic region according to the age of the highest earner in the household. When presenting the data, the researcher who compiled the data decides to exclude the first age bracket (15-24), because it includes minors, which will likely skew the results because most minors do not have full-time jobs. The researcher also decides to exclude the last age bracket (65+) because it includes retirees, which is again likely to skew the results for the same reason. Which of the following statements most likely describes how this will affect the data overall?

A) It will significantly change the median, but not the mean.

B) It will significantly change the mean, but not the median.

C) There will be no significant change to either the mean or the median.

D) There is not enough information to determine what effect, if any, it will have on either the median or the mean.

7. If the graph of $y = mx + b$ passes through quadrants I, III, and IV on a coordinate plane, which of the following must be true about $m$ and $b$?

A) $m < 0, b < 0$

B) $m < 0, b > 0$

C) $m > 0, b < 0$

D) $m > 0, b > 0$

GO ON TO THE NEXT PAGE

The graph shows Expenses (in thousands of dollars) on the y-axis ranging from 0 to 200, and Units Produced (in thousands) on the x-axis ranging from 0 to 100. Two lines are shown, labeled 2013 (dashed, starting at about 80) and 2014 (solid, starting at about 40).

$$\begin{cases} y = \dfrac{1}{4}x - 3 \\ y = -\dfrac{5}{2}x + 8 \end{cases}$$

9. Which of the following is the y-coordinate of the solution to the system of equations given above?

   A) −8
   B) −2
   C) 2
   D) 4

8. Manufacturing companies typically have a number of fixed costs (such as rent, machinery, insurance, etc.), which do not depend on output, and variable costs (such as wages, utilities, materials, etc.), which vary with output, usually at a constant rate. The graph shows a company's costs for manufacturing a particular product over the course of two years. Which of the following could explain the difference between the 2013 and 2014 costs?

   A) The company reduced its fixed costs by 50%.

   B) The company reduced its variable costs by 50%.

   C) The company reduced the number of units produced by 50%.

   D) The company reduced its fixed costs, variable costs, and the number of units produced by 50%.

10. Premature babies are typically born underweight and are cared for in a neonatal intensive care unit (NICU). At a certain NICU, the mean weight of all the male babies is 4 pounds, and the mean weight of all the female babies is 3.6 pounds. Which of the following must be true about the mean weight $w$ of the combined group of male and female babies at this NICU?

    A) $w = 3.8$
    B) $w > 3.8$
    C) $w < 3.8$
    D) $3.6 < w < 4$

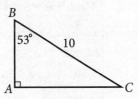

11. Given that $\sin 53° \approx 0.8$, what is the approximate length of side $AB$ in the figure above?

    A) 6
    B) 7.2
    C) 8
    D) 8.5

12. When most people buy a house, they take out a mortgage to cover at least part of the cost of the home and then pay the loan back over time. The most common kind of mortgage is a 30-year loan. A couple buys a home and takes out a 30-year loan in the amount of $220,000 (called the principal). They decide they want to pay it off early to save money on interest. They set a goal of reducing the principal amount of the loan to $170,000 in four years. Suppose during the first two years of their four-year timeline, the couple pays down the loan by 10%. By what percent do they need to pay down the rest of the loan to reach their overall goal?

A) 10%

B) 14%

C) 18%

D) 20%

| $x$ | 1 | 2 | 3 | 4 | 5 | 6 |
|------|-----|---|------|----|------|----|
| $f(x)$ | 3.5 | 0 | −2.5 | −4 | −4.5 | −4 |

13. The table above shows several points through which the graph of a quadratic function $f(x)$ passes. One of the $x$-intercepts for the graph is given in the table. What is the other $x$-intercept for the graph?

A) (−2, 0)

B) (5, 0)

C) (8, 0)

D) (10, 0)

**Questions 14 and 15 refer to the following information.**

A college cafeteria received a petition from students to offer healthier meat, vegetarian, and vegan dishes. In response to the petition, the cafeteria conducted an analysis of its existing menu to determine the current state of those options. The results are summarized in the table below. The analyst used a sliding scale based on the nutrient levels compared against calorie, sugar, and sodium counts to determine the health score, a score of 1 being the least healthy and 5 being the healthiest.

| Health Score | Meat Dishes | Vegetarian Dishes | Vegan Dishes |
|--------------|-------------|-------------------|--------------|
| 1 | 3 | 1 | 1 |
| 2 | 4 | 3 | 1 |
| 3 | 8 | 5 | 4 |
| 4 | 5 | 4 | 2 |
| 5 | 0 | 1 | 0 |

14. What fraction of the vegetarian and vegan dishes received a health score greater than 2 ?

A) $\dfrac{7}{22}$

B) $\dfrac{8}{21}$

C) $\dfrac{8}{11}$

D) $\dfrac{11}{21}$

15. If a student chooses a dish at random for lunch one day, what is the probability that it will be a meat dish with a health score of at least 4 ?

A) $\dfrac{5}{42}$

B) $\dfrac{6}{21}$

C) $\dfrac{1}{4}$

D) $\dfrac{13}{42}$

$$r = \sqrt[4]{\frac{8kl}{\pi R}}$$

16. Ideally, blood should flow smoothly through the arteries in our bodies. When there are problems, or as a natural part of aging, there is an increased amount of resistance to blood flow. *Viscosity* is a term used to describe the thickness or stickiness of the blood and is directly related to this resistance, as are the radius and the length of the artery through which the blood flows. The formula given above relates the radius ($r$) of an artery to the viscosity ($k$), resistance ($R$), and length ($l$) of that artery. Which of the following represents the viscosity in terms of the other variables?

A) $k = \dfrac{r^4 \pi R}{8l}$

B) $k = \sqrt[4]{\dfrac{8l}{\pi R r}}$

C) $k = \dfrac{1}{2} r \pi R l$

D) $k = \left(\dfrac{8l}{\pi R r}\right)^4$

17. Two muffins and a carton of milk cost \$3.35. If five muffins and a carton of milk cost \$5.60, what is the cost of two cartons of milk?

A) \$0.75

B) \$1.50

C) \$1.85

D) \$3.70

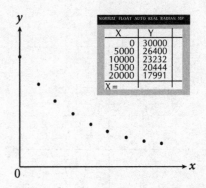

18. The calculator screenshot above shows the $x$- and $y$-values for the first few data points shown in the scatterplot, which can be modeled using an exponential function. Which of the following scenarios could be represented by this function?

A) The resale value of a car is cut in half for every 3,600 miles driven.

B) The resale value of a car decreases by \$5,000 for every 3,600 miles driven.

C) The resale value of a car decreases by \$3,600 for every 5,000 miles driven.

D) The resale value of a car decreases by approximately 12% for every 5,000 miles driven.

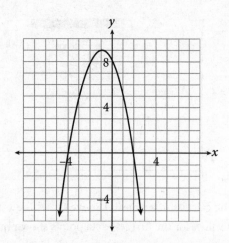

19. The graph of the function $f(x) = -x^2 - 2x + 8$ is shown in the figure above. For what values of $x$ does $f(x) = 5$?

    A) −4 and 2

    B) −3 and 1

    C) −1 and 9

    D) 5 and 8

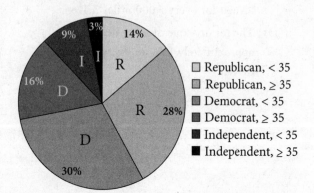

20. The pie chart above shows the distribution of registered voters in a certain district in Illinois by party and by age. If there are 8,640 voters in the district, what is the ratio of Republicans to Independents?

    A) 3:1

    B) 7:2

    C) 22:3

    D) 23:6

21. A DVD rental kiosk dispenses movies for $1 for a 24-hour rental. After the initial rental period has expired, customers are charged a $0.50 late fee for every 24 hours that the movie is returned late. If a customer rents four movies at one time, which of the following graphs represents the total possible charges in late fees, assuming he returns all the movies together?

A)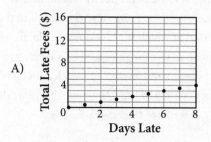

B)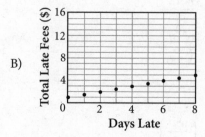

C)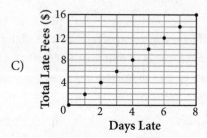

D)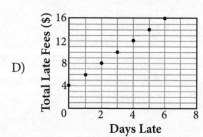

GO ON TO THE NEXT PAGE

22. There are many ways to defrost a turkey. One way is to let it thaw slowly in the refrigerator, at a thaw rate of about 4 pounds per day. Another way is to submerge the turkey in cold water, which thaws it at a rate of 1 pound per 30 minutes. Approximately how many more ounces of turkey can the cold-water method thaw in 2 hours than the refrigerator method? (1 pound = 16 ounces)

A) 16
B) 27
C) 32
D) 59

23. A freight train operator knows that on a 200-mile trip, if the freight cars are not fully loaded, she can save 1 hour of travel time by increasing her normal speed by 10 miles per hour. What is her normal speed in miles per hour?

A) 40
B) 45
C) 55
D) 60

24. A cable company offers movie rental packages. If you join the Movie Fan club, you get 10 movies for $20 and each movie after that costs $2.50. If you join the Movie Super Fan club, you get unlimited movies for a year for $75. How many movies would a person need to rent for each package to cost the same amount over a one-year period?

A) 22
B) 30
C) 32
D) 57

25. Many wholesale businesses charge customers less per item when they buy those items in bulk. Suppose a baseball cap distributor charges $6 per cap for the first 25 caps the customer purchases, $5 per cap for the next 75 purchased, and $4 per cap for all additional caps over 100. Which of the following piecewise functions represents this scenario, where $C$ represents the total cost and $n$ represents the number of caps purchased?

A) $C(n) = \begin{cases} 6n, & \text{if } n \leq 25 \\ 5n, & \text{if } 25 < n \leq 100 \\ 4n, & \text{if } n > 100 \end{cases}$

B) $C(n) = \begin{cases} 6n, & \text{if } n < 25 \\ 5n, & \text{if } 25 \leq n < 100 \\ 4n, & \text{if } n \geq 100 \end{cases}$

C) $C(n) = \begin{cases} 6n, & \text{if } n \leq 25 \\ 150 + 5(n - 25), & \text{if } 25 < n \leq 100 \\ 500 + 4(n - 100), & \text{if } n > 100 \end{cases}$

D) $C(n) = \begin{cases} 6n, & \text{if } n \leq 25 \\ 150 + 5(n - 25), & \text{if } 25 < n \leq 100 \\ 525 + 4(n - 100), & \text{if } n > 100 \end{cases}$

26. The decline of a certain animal species' population, currently estimated to be 22,000, can be modeled using the quadratic function $p(x) = -0.5x^2 + 22{,}000$, where $x$ is the number of years after 2015. Based on only this information, and assuming no intervention to change the path of the population, which of the following statements must be true?

A) This species will be extinct by the end of the year 2225.

B) The animal population for this species is decreasing at a constant rate.

C) In approximately 100 years, the animal population for this species will be about half what it was in 2015.

D) The animal population will increase or decrease from the initial 2015 level, depending on the year after 2015.

GO ON TO THE NEXT PAGE

27. In geology, the water table is the level below which the ground is saturated with water. Wells must be dug below this point to bring water up into the well. Except in cases of severe flooding, the water level in a well does not rise above the water table. Suppose a cylindrical well is 6 feet wide and 60 feet deep in an area where the water table is 40 feet below ground level. Assuming no unusual circumstances, what is the volume in cubic feet of the water in the well at any given time?

A) $180\pi$

B) $360\pi$

C) $540\pi$

D) $720\pi$

28. Ramon graphed a line that has a slope of $-2$. The line he graphed passes through the point $(3, 5)$. If Ramon doubles the slope of his line and then shifts it down 1 unit, through which point will the line pass?

A) $(3, -2)$

B) $(3, 9)$

C) $(6, 4)$

D) $(10, 2)$

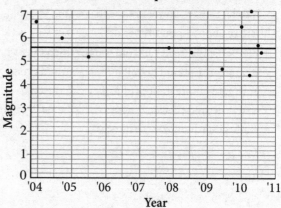

**California Earthquakes, 2003-2010**

29. Earthquakes occur when energy is released from deep inside the earth, causing friction between the tectonic plates of the earth's crust. The magnitude, or intensity, of the earthquake is measured on the Richter scale. The scatterplot above shows the earthquakes experienced by California between December 2003 and December 2010. The line of best fit, which has a slope of 0, is a fairly good indicator in California. Approximately what percent of the earthquakes in California during this time period differed by 1 point or more on the Richter scale from the magnitude predicted by the line of best fit?

A) 22%

B) 27%

C) 33%

D) 36%

30. If the equation $\frac{2}{9}x^2 + \frac{8}{3}x - 7 = 3$ has solutions $x_1$ and $x_2$, what is the product of $x_1$ and $x_2$?

A) $-45$

B) $-15$

C) $-5$

D) $3$

GO ON TO THE NEXT PAGE ⟶

**Directions:** For questions 31-38, solve the problem and enter your answer in the grid, as described below, on the answer sheet.

1. Although not required, it is suggested that you write your answer in the boxes at the top of the columns to help you fill in the circles accurately. You will receive credit only if the circles are filled in correctly.

2. Mark no more than one circle in any column.

3. No question has a negative answer.

4. Some problems may have more than one correct answer. In such cases, grid only one answer.

5. **Mixed numbers** such as $3\frac{1}{2}$ must be gridded as 3.5 or $\frac{7}{2}$.

    (If $3\frac{1}{2}$ is entered into the grid as $\boxed{3\ 1\ /\ 2}$, it will be interpreted as $\frac{31}{2}$, not $3\frac{1}{2}$.)

6. **Decimal answers:** If you obtain a decimal answer with more digits than the grid can accommodate, it may be either rounded or truncated, but it must fill the entire grid.

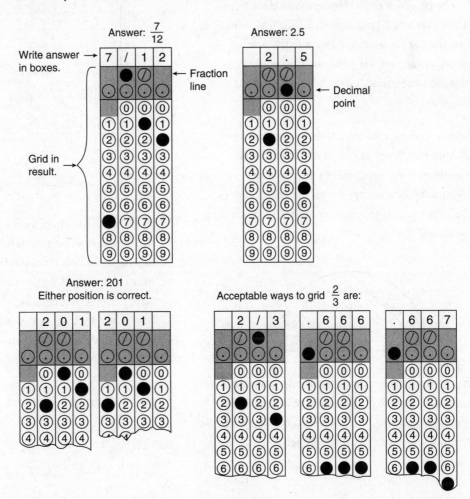

GO ON TO THE NEXT PAGE

31. If $-10 < 14 - 2p < 6$, what is the greatest possible integer value of $7 - p$?

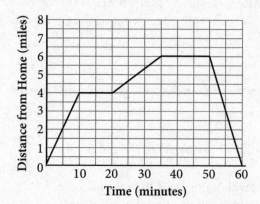

32. The graph above shows Umberto's distance from home over a one-hour period, during which time he first went to the bank, then went to the post office, and then returned home. How many minutes did Umberto spend at the bank and at the post office combined?

33. Selena is taking a 90-minute test that consists of 50 multiple-choice questions and 30 true-false questions. If she completes 48 questions in 50 minutes, how many seconds per question does she have on average to answer each of the remaining questions?

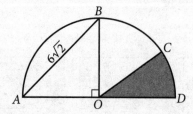

34. If $\overline{AD}$ is a diameter of the semicircle shown above, and the arc length of $CD$ is $\pi$, what is the area of the shaded region? Use 3.14 to approximate $\pi$ and round your answer to the nearest tenth.

35. A bag valve mask is used to resuscitate patients who have stopped breathing. It consists primarily of a bag attached to a mask. The mask is fitted to the patient's nose and mouth. Squeezing the bag pushes air through the mask and into the patient's lungs. For sanitary reasons, most of these masks are disposable. Suppose a hospital's mask supplier sells them in boxes of 48 or 144, and the supplier has 35 boxes in stock. If the supplier has 2,832 total masks in stock, how many masks would the hospital receive if it ordered all of the boxes of 144 that the supplier has in stock?

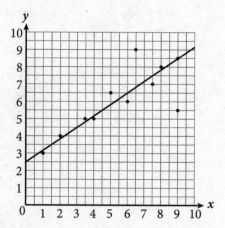

36. Patricia collected data for a school project, plotted the information on a scatterplot (shown above), and drew the line of best fit. In reviewing her notes, she realized that one of her data points was wrong, so she eliminated that point and redrew the line of best fit. If the new $y$-intercept of her line is 2 and the slope is steeper than before, what was the $y$-value of the point she eliminated?

GO ON TO THE NEXT PAGE

**Questions 37 and 38 refer to the following information.**

A company sponsors a health program for its employees by partnering with a local gym. If employees pay for a year-long membership at this gym, then for every day the employee uses his or her swipe card to enter the gym (and work out), the company reimburses the employee 0.2% of the cost of the $220 membership. Additionally, any employee who goes to the gym more than 60% of the days in the year gets one bonus paid day off of work. The company uses a 365-day year.

37. If 246 employees participate in the program and they each go to the gym an average of 84 days per year, how much money in membership reimbursements will the company pay out? Round your answer to the nearest whole dollar.

38. Giving employees additional paid time off also costs the company money because it is paying the salary of an employee who is not actually doing any work on that day. The pie graph below shows gym usage for the 246 employees who participated in the health program.

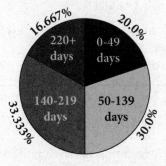

If the average salary of workers who participated was $14.90 per hour and one day off equals 8 hours, how much did the health program day-off benefit cost the company? Round your answer to the nearest whole dollar.

# ESSAY TEST

## 50 Minutes

The essay gives you an opportunity to show how effectively you can read and comprehend a passage and write an essay analyzing the passage. In your essay, you should demonstrate that you have read the passage carefully, present a clear and logical analysis, and use language precisely.

Your essay must be written on the lines provided in your answer booklet; except for the planning page of the answer booklet, you will receive no other paper on which to write. You will have enough space if you write on every line, avoid wide margins, and keep your handwriting to a reasonable size. Remember that people who are not familiar with your handwriting will read what you write. Try to write or print so that what you are writing is legible to those readers.

You have 50 minutes to read the passage and write an essay in response to the prompt provided inside this booklet.

1. Do not write your essay in this booklet. Only what you write on the lined pages of your answer booklet will be evaluated.
2. An off-topic essay will not be evaluated.

---

As you read the passage below, consider how Winston Churchill uses

- evidence, such as facts or examples, to support claims.

- reasoning to develop ideas and to connect claims and evidence.

- stylistic or persuasive elements, such as word choice or appeals to emotion, to add power to the ideas expressed.

---

**Adapted from Winston Churchill's speech "The Defence of Freedom and Speech (The Lights Are Going Out),"**
**broadcast by radio to the United States and London, October 16, 1938.**

1    I avail myself with relief of the opportunity of speaking to the people of the United States. I do not know how long such liberties will be allowed. The stations of uncensored expression are closing down; the lights are going out; but there is still time for those to whom freedom and parliamentary government mean something, to consult together. Let me, then, speak in truth and earnestness while time remains. . . .

2    The American people have, it seems to me, formed a true judgment upon the disaster which has befallen Europe. They realise, perhaps more clearly than the French and British publics have yet done, the far-reaching consequences of the abandonment and ruin of the Czechoslovak Republic. . . .

3    Has any benefit or progress ever been achieved by the human race by submission to organised and calculated violence? As we look back over the long story of the nations we must see that, on the contrary, their glory has been founded upon the spirit of resistance to tyranny and injustice, especially when these evils seemed to be backed by heavier force. Since the dawn of the Christian era a certain way of life has slowly been shaping itself among the Western peoples, and certain standards of conduct and government have come to be esteemed. After many miseries and prolonged confusion, there arose into the broad light of day the conception of the right of the individual; his right to be consulted in the government of his country; his right to invoke the law even against the State itself. . . .

GO ON TO THE NEXT PAGE ⟹

4    We are confronted with another theme. It is not a new theme; it leaps out upon us from the Dark Ages—racial persecution, religious intolerance, deprivation of free speech, the conception of the citizen as a mere soulless fraction of the State. To this has been added the cult of war. Children are to be taught in their earliest schooling the delights and profits of conquest and aggression. A whole mighty community has been drawn painfully, by severe privations, into a warlike frame. They are held in this condition, which they relish no more than we do, by a party organisation, several millions strong, who derive all kinds of profits, good and bad, from the upkeep of the regime. Like the Communists, the Nazis tolerate no opinion but their own. Like the Communists, they feed on hatred. Like the Communists, they must seek, from time to time, and always at shorter intervals, a new target, a new prize, a new victim. The Dictator, in all his pride, is held in the grip of his Party machine. . . .

5    The culminating question to which I have been leading is whether the world as we have known it—the great and hopeful world of before the war, the world of increasing hope and enjoyment for the common man, the world of honoured tradition and expanding science—should meet this menace by submission or by resistance. Let us see, then, whether the means of resistance remain to us today. We have sustained an immense disaster; the renown of France is dimmed. In spite of her brave, efficient army, her influence is profoundly diminished. No one has a right to say that Britain, for all her blundering, has broken her word—indeed, when it was too late, she was better than her word. Nevertheless, Europe lies at this moment abashed and distracted before the triumphant assertions of dictatorial power. In the Spanish Peninsula, a purely Spanish quarrel has been carried by the intervention, or shall I say the "non-intervention" (to quote the current Jargon) of Dictators into the region of a world cause.

6    Is this a call to war? Does anyone pretend that preparation for resistance to aggression is unleashing war? I declare it to be the sole guarantee of peace. We need the swift gathering of forces to confront not only military but moral aggression; the resolute and sober acceptance of their duty by the English-speaking peoples and by all the nations, great and small, who wish to walk with them. Their faithful and zealous comradeship would almost between night and morning clear the path of progress and banish from all our lives the fear which already darkens the sunlight to hundreds of millions of men.

> Write an essay in which you explain how Winston Churchill builds an argument to persuade his audience that the United States and Britain must mobilize their forces in preparation to resist the military aggression of Nazi Germany and its allies. In your essay, analyze how he uses one or more of the features listed in the box that precedes the passage (or features of your own choice) to strengthen the logic and persuasiveness of his argument. Be sure that your analysis focuses on the most relevant features of the passage.
>
> Your essay should not explain whether you agree with Churchill's claims, but rather explain how he builds an argument to persuade his audience.

# Answer Grids and Essay Practice Test Comment Forms

**SECTION**

**5**

Name

EID

Name _____

EID _____

_____

_____

_____

_____

_____

_____

_____

_____

_____

_____

_____

_____

_____

_____

_____

_____

_____

_____

_____

_____

_____

Name

EID

# SAT Essay Practice Test Comments

Your SAT Essay will be graded in three areas: Reading, Analysis, and Writing. Here are some comments from your Kaplan grader based on the College Board's criteria to help you improve your essay writing.

| | |
|---|---|
| **Reading** | ☐ This essay demonstrates a thorough comprehension of the source text.<br>☐ Explain how the central idea(s) and important details interrelate.<br>☐ Cite important details from the source text.<br>☐ Use textual evidence from the source text.<br>☐ Read the source text again; this essay contains errors of fact. |
| **Analysis** | ☐ This essay offers insightful analysis of the source text and demonstrates a sophisticated understanding of the analytical task.<br>☐ Focus only on the features of the text that are most relevant to the task.<br>☐ Explain the importance of the features you include in your response.<br>☐ Choose features that are most relevant to addressing the task.<br>☐ Provide support for your claims and points.<br>☐ Read the task again; this is a summary, not an analysis. |
| **Writing** | ☐ This essay is cohesive and demonstrates a highly effective command of language.<br>☐ Spelling **and** ☐ grammar usage are satisfactory.<br>☐ Use of vocabulary **and** ☐ sentence structure are varied.<br>☐ Make a stronger central claim/thesis.<br>☐ Create an outline before you write.<br>☐ Write a stronger introduction **and** ☐ conclusion.<br>☐ Use a formal style and objective tone.<br>☐ Proofread; remember to budget your time. |

## Additional Comments:

## Administrative Purposes:

Student's Name: _____  ID Number: _____

Test:        1     2     3     4

Reading:   1     2     3     4
Analysis:   1     2     3     4
Writing:    1     2     3     4
(These scores are **doubled** on your score report.)

# SAT PRACTICE TEST 2 ANSWER SHEET

**Remove (or photocopy) this answer sheet and use it to complete the test.**

Start with number 1 for each section. If a section has fewer questions than answer spaces, leave the extra spaces blank.

**SECTION 1**

| | | | |
|---|---|---|---|
| 1. Ⓐ Ⓑ Ⓒ Ⓓ | 14. Ⓐ Ⓑ Ⓒ Ⓓ | 27. Ⓐ Ⓑ Ⓒ Ⓓ | 40. Ⓐ Ⓑ Ⓒ Ⓓ |
| 2. Ⓐ Ⓑ Ⓒ Ⓓ | 15. Ⓐ Ⓑ Ⓒ Ⓓ | 28. Ⓐ Ⓑ Ⓒ Ⓓ | 41. Ⓐ Ⓑ Ⓒ Ⓓ |
| 3. Ⓐ Ⓑ Ⓒ Ⓓ | 16. Ⓐ Ⓑ Ⓒ Ⓓ | 29. Ⓐ Ⓑ Ⓒ Ⓓ | 42. Ⓐ Ⓑ Ⓒ Ⓓ |
| 4. Ⓐ Ⓑ Ⓒ Ⓓ | 17. Ⓐ Ⓑ Ⓒ Ⓓ | 30. Ⓐ Ⓑ Ⓒ Ⓓ | 43. Ⓐ Ⓑ Ⓒ Ⓓ |
| 5. Ⓐ Ⓑ Ⓒ Ⓓ | 18. Ⓐ Ⓑ Ⓒ Ⓓ | 31. Ⓐ Ⓑ Ⓒ Ⓓ | 44. Ⓐ Ⓑ Ⓒ Ⓓ |
| 6. Ⓐ Ⓑ Ⓒ Ⓓ | 19. Ⓐ Ⓑ Ⓒ Ⓓ | 32. Ⓐ Ⓑ Ⓒ Ⓓ | 45. Ⓐ Ⓑ Ⓒ Ⓓ |
| 7. Ⓐ Ⓑ Ⓒ Ⓓ | 20. Ⓐ Ⓑ Ⓒ Ⓓ | 33. Ⓐ Ⓑ Ⓒ Ⓓ | 46. Ⓐ Ⓑ Ⓒ Ⓓ |
| 8. Ⓐ Ⓑ Ⓒ Ⓓ | 21. Ⓐ Ⓑ Ⓒ Ⓓ | 34. Ⓐ Ⓑ Ⓒ Ⓓ | 47. Ⓐ Ⓑ Ⓒ Ⓓ |
| 9. Ⓐ Ⓑ Ⓒ Ⓓ | 22. Ⓐ Ⓑ Ⓒ Ⓓ | 35. Ⓐ Ⓑ Ⓒ Ⓓ | 48. Ⓐ Ⓑ Ⓒ Ⓓ |
| 10. Ⓐ Ⓑ Ⓒ Ⓓ | 23. Ⓐ Ⓑ Ⓒ Ⓓ | 36. Ⓐ Ⓑ Ⓒ Ⓓ | 49. Ⓐ Ⓑ Ⓒ Ⓓ |
| 11. Ⓐ Ⓑ Ⓒ Ⓓ | 24. Ⓐ Ⓑ Ⓒ Ⓓ | 37. Ⓐ Ⓑ Ⓒ Ⓓ | 50. Ⓐ Ⓑ Ⓒ Ⓓ |
| 12. Ⓐ Ⓑ Ⓒ Ⓓ | 25. Ⓐ Ⓑ Ⓒ Ⓓ | 38. Ⓐ Ⓑ Ⓒ Ⓓ | 51. Ⓐ Ⓑ Ⓒ Ⓓ |
| 13. Ⓐ Ⓑ Ⓒ Ⓓ | 26. Ⓐ Ⓑ Ⓒ Ⓓ | 39. Ⓐ Ⓑ Ⓒ Ⓓ | 52. Ⓐ Ⓑ Ⓒ Ⓓ |

# correct in Section 1

# incorrect in Section 1

**SECTION 2**

| | | | |
|---|---|---|---|
| 1. Ⓐ Ⓑ Ⓒ Ⓓ | 12. Ⓐ Ⓑ Ⓒ Ⓓ | 23. Ⓐ Ⓑ Ⓒ Ⓓ | 34. Ⓐ Ⓑ Ⓒ Ⓓ |
| 2. Ⓐ Ⓑ Ⓒ Ⓓ | 13. Ⓐ Ⓑ Ⓒ Ⓓ | 24. Ⓐ Ⓑ Ⓒ Ⓓ | 35. Ⓐ Ⓑ Ⓒ Ⓓ |
| 3. Ⓐ Ⓑ Ⓒ Ⓓ | 14. Ⓐ Ⓑ Ⓒ Ⓓ | 25. Ⓐ Ⓑ Ⓒ Ⓓ | 36. Ⓐ Ⓑ Ⓒ Ⓓ |
| 4. Ⓐ Ⓑ Ⓒ Ⓓ | 15. Ⓐ Ⓑ Ⓒ Ⓓ | 26. Ⓐ Ⓑ Ⓒ Ⓓ | 37. Ⓐ Ⓑ Ⓒ Ⓓ |
| 5. Ⓐ Ⓑ Ⓒ Ⓓ | 16. Ⓐ Ⓑ Ⓒ Ⓓ | 27. Ⓐ Ⓑ Ⓒ Ⓓ | 38. Ⓐ Ⓑ Ⓒ Ⓓ |
| 6. Ⓐ Ⓑ Ⓒ Ⓓ | 17. Ⓐ Ⓑ Ⓒ Ⓓ | 28. Ⓐ Ⓑ Ⓒ Ⓓ | 39. Ⓐ Ⓑ Ⓒ Ⓓ |
| 7. Ⓐ Ⓑ Ⓒ Ⓓ | 18. Ⓐ Ⓑ Ⓒ Ⓓ | 29. Ⓐ Ⓑ Ⓒ Ⓓ | 40. Ⓐ Ⓑ Ⓒ Ⓓ |
| 8. Ⓐ Ⓑ Ⓒ Ⓓ | 19. Ⓐ Ⓑ Ⓒ Ⓓ | 30. Ⓐ Ⓑ Ⓒ Ⓓ | 41. Ⓐ Ⓑ Ⓒ Ⓓ |
| 9. Ⓐ Ⓑ Ⓒ Ⓓ | 20. Ⓐ Ⓑ Ⓒ Ⓓ | 31. Ⓐ Ⓑ Ⓒ Ⓓ | 42. Ⓐ Ⓑ Ⓒ Ⓓ |
| 10. Ⓐ Ⓑ Ⓒ Ⓓ | 21. Ⓐ Ⓑ Ⓒ Ⓓ | 32. Ⓐ Ⓑ Ⓒ Ⓓ | 43. Ⓐ Ⓑ Ⓒ Ⓓ |
| 11. Ⓐ Ⓑ Ⓒ Ⓓ | 22. Ⓐ Ⓑ Ⓒ Ⓓ | 33. Ⓐ Ⓑ Ⓒ Ⓓ | 44. Ⓐ Ⓑ Ⓒ Ⓓ |

# correct in Section 2

# incorrect in Section 2

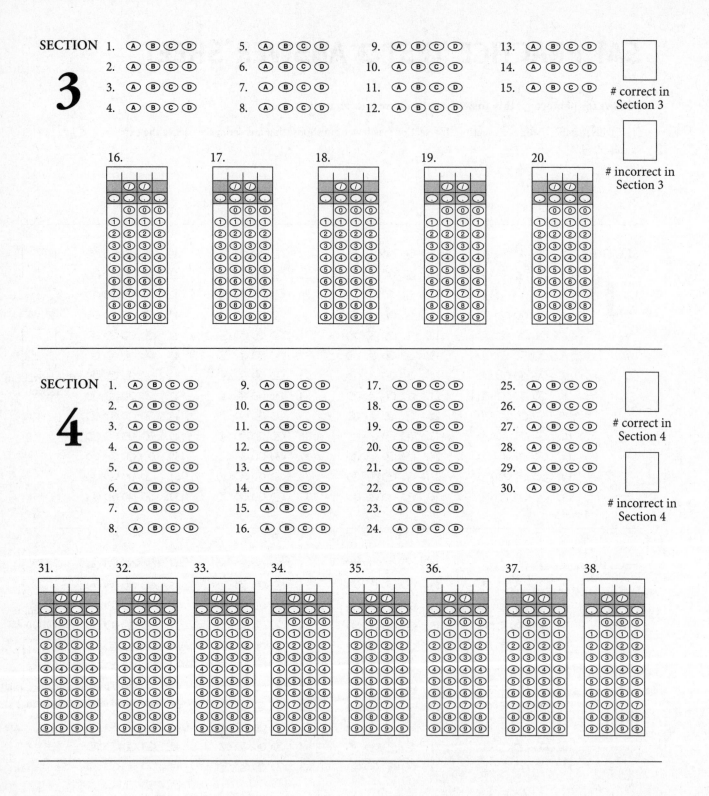

**SECTION**

**5**

Name

EID

Name

EID

Name _____

EID _____

_____

_____

_____

_____

_____

_____

_____

_____

_____

_____

_____

_____

_____

_____

_____

_____

_____

_____

_____

_____

_____

_____

_____

**KAPLAN** TEST PREP

## SAT Essay Practice Test Comments

Your SAT Essay will be graded in three areas: Reading, Analysis, and Writing. Here are some comments from your Kaplan grader based on the College Board's criteria to help you improve your essay writing.

| | |
|---|---|
| **Reading** | ☐ This essay demonstrates a thorough comprehension of the source text. <br> ☐ Explain how the central idea(s) and important details interrelate. <br> ☐ Cite important details from the source text. <br> ☐ Use textual evidence from the source text. <br> ☐ Read the source text again; this essay contains errors of fact. |
| **Analysis** | ☐ This essay offers insightful analysis of the source text and demonstrates a sophisticated understanding of the analytical task. <br> ☐ Focus only on the features of the text that are most relevant to the task. <br> ☐ Explain the importance of the features you include in your response. <br> ☐ Choose features that are most relevant to addressing the task. <br> ☐ Provide support for your claims and points. <br> ☐ Read the task again; this is a summary, not an analysis. |
| **Writing** | ☐ This essay is cohesive and demonstrates a highly effective command of language. <br> ☐ Spelling **and** ☐ grammar usage are satisfactory. <br> ☐ Use of vocabulary **and** ☐ sentence structure are varied. <br> ☐ Make a stronger central claim/thesis. <br> ☐ Create an outline before you write. <br> ☐ Write a stronger introduction **and** ☐ conclusion. <br> ☐ Use a formal style and objective tone. <br> ☐ Proofread; remember to budget your time. |

## Additional Comments:

## Administrative Purposes:

Student's Name: _____ ID Number: _____

Test:          1    2    3    4

Reading:      1    2    3    4
Analysis:     1    2    3    4
Writing:      1    2    3    4
(These scores are **doubled** on your score report.)

**SECTION**

**5**

Name _____

EID _____

Name

EID

Name _____

EID _____

_____

_____

_____

_____

_____

_____

_____

_____

_____

_____

_____

_____

_____

_____

_____

_____

_____

_____

_____

_____

_____

# SAT Essay Practice Test Comments

Your SAT Essay will be graded in three areas: Reading, Analysis, and Writing. Here are some comments from your Kaplan grader based on the College Board's criteria to help you improve your essay writing.

| | |
|---|---|
| **Reading** | ☐ This essay demonstrates a thorough comprehension of the source text.<br>☐ Explain how the central idea(s) and important details interrelate.<br>☐ Cite important details from the source text.<br>☐ Use textual evidence from the source text.<br>☐ Read the source text again; this essay contains errors of fact. |
| **Analysis** | ☐ This essay offers insightful analysis of the source text and demonstrates a sophisticated understanding of the analytical task.<br>☐ Focus only on the features of the text that are most relevant to the task.<br>☐ Explain the importance of the features you include in your response.<br>☐ Choose features that are most relevant to addressing the task.<br>☐ Provide support for your claims and points.<br>☐ Read the task again; this is a summary, not an analysis. |
| **Writing** | ☐ This essay is cohesive and demonstrates a highly effective command of language.<br>☐ Spelling **and** ☐ grammar usage are satisfactory.<br>☐ Use of vocabulary **and** ☐ sentence structure are varied.<br>☐ Make a stronger central claim/thesis.<br>☐ Create an outline before you write.<br>☐ Write a stronger introduction **and** ☐ conclusion.<br>☐ Use a formal style and objective tone.<br>☐ Proofread; remember to budget your time. |

## Additional Comments:

## Administrative Purposes:

Student's Name: _____  ID Number: _____

Test:           1     2     3     4

Reading:        1     2     3     4
Analysis:       1     2     3     4
Writing:        1     2     3     4

(These scores are **doubled** on your score report.)

# SAT PRACTICE TEST 4 ANSWER SHEET

**Remove (or photocopy) this answer sheet and use it to complete the test.**

Start with number 1 for each section. If a section has fewer questions than answer spaces, leave the extra spaces blank.

**SECTION 1**

1. Ⓐ Ⓑ Ⓒ Ⓓ
2. Ⓐ Ⓑ Ⓒ Ⓓ
3. Ⓐ Ⓑ Ⓒ Ⓓ
4. Ⓐ Ⓑ Ⓒ Ⓓ
5. Ⓐ Ⓑ Ⓒ Ⓓ
6. Ⓐ Ⓑ Ⓒ Ⓓ
7. Ⓐ Ⓑ Ⓒ Ⓓ
8. Ⓐ Ⓑ Ⓒ Ⓓ
9. Ⓐ Ⓑ Ⓒ Ⓓ
10. Ⓐ Ⓑ Ⓒ Ⓓ
11. Ⓐ Ⓑ Ⓒ Ⓓ
12. Ⓐ Ⓑ Ⓒ Ⓓ
13. Ⓐ Ⓑ Ⓒ Ⓓ

14. Ⓐ Ⓑ Ⓒ Ⓓ
15. Ⓐ Ⓑ Ⓒ Ⓓ
16. Ⓐ Ⓑ Ⓒ Ⓓ
17. Ⓐ Ⓑ Ⓒ Ⓓ
18. Ⓐ Ⓑ Ⓒ Ⓓ
19. Ⓐ Ⓑ Ⓒ Ⓓ
20. Ⓐ Ⓑ Ⓒ Ⓓ
21. Ⓐ Ⓑ Ⓒ Ⓓ
22. Ⓐ Ⓑ Ⓒ Ⓓ
23. Ⓐ Ⓑ Ⓒ Ⓓ
24. Ⓐ Ⓑ Ⓒ Ⓓ
25. Ⓐ Ⓑ Ⓒ Ⓓ
26. Ⓐ Ⓑ Ⓒ Ⓓ

27. Ⓐ Ⓑ Ⓒ Ⓓ
28. Ⓐ Ⓑ Ⓒ Ⓓ
29. Ⓐ Ⓑ Ⓒ Ⓓ
30. Ⓐ Ⓑ Ⓒ Ⓓ
31. Ⓐ Ⓑ Ⓒ Ⓓ
32. Ⓐ Ⓑ Ⓒ Ⓓ
33. Ⓐ Ⓑ Ⓒ Ⓓ
34. Ⓐ Ⓑ Ⓒ Ⓓ
35. Ⓐ Ⓑ Ⓒ Ⓓ
36. Ⓐ Ⓑ Ⓒ Ⓓ
37. Ⓐ Ⓑ Ⓒ Ⓓ
38. Ⓐ Ⓑ Ⓒ Ⓓ
39. Ⓐ Ⓑ Ⓒ Ⓓ

40. Ⓐ Ⓑ Ⓒ Ⓓ
41. Ⓐ Ⓑ Ⓒ Ⓓ
42. Ⓐ Ⓑ Ⓒ Ⓓ
43. Ⓐ Ⓑ Ⓒ Ⓓ
44. Ⓐ Ⓑ Ⓒ Ⓓ
45. Ⓐ Ⓑ Ⓒ Ⓓ
46. Ⓐ Ⓑ Ⓒ Ⓓ
47. Ⓐ Ⓑ Ⓒ Ⓓ
48. Ⓐ Ⓑ Ⓒ Ⓓ
49. Ⓐ Ⓑ Ⓒ Ⓓ
50. Ⓐ Ⓑ Ⓒ Ⓓ
51. Ⓐ Ⓑ Ⓒ Ⓓ
52. Ⓐ Ⓑ Ⓒ Ⓓ

☐ # correct in Section 1

☐ # incorrect in Section 1

**SECTION 2**

1. Ⓐ Ⓑ Ⓒ Ⓓ
2. Ⓐ Ⓑ Ⓒ Ⓓ
3. Ⓐ Ⓑ Ⓒ Ⓓ
4. Ⓐ Ⓑ Ⓒ Ⓓ
5. Ⓐ Ⓑ Ⓒ Ⓓ
6. Ⓐ Ⓑ Ⓒ Ⓓ
7. Ⓐ Ⓑ Ⓒ Ⓓ
8. Ⓐ Ⓑ Ⓒ Ⓓ
9. Ⓐ Ⓑ Ⓒ Ⓓ
10. Ⓐ Ⓑ Ⓒ Ⓓ
11. Ⓐ Ⓑ Ⓒ Ⓓ

12. Ⓐ Ⓑ Ⓒ Ⓓ
13. Ⓐ Ⓑ Ⓒ Ⓓ
14. Ⓐ Ⓑ Ⓒ Ⓓ
15. Ⓐ Ⓑ Ⓒ Ⓓ
16. Ⓐ Ⓑ Ⓒ Ⓓ
17. Ⓐ Ⓑ Ⓒ Ⓓ
18. Ⓐ Ⓑ Ⓒ Ⓓ
19. Ⓐ Ⓑ Ⓒ Ⓓ
20. Ⓐ Ⓑ Ⓒ Ⓓ
21. Ⓐ Ⓑ Ⓒ Ⓓ
22. Ⓐ Ⓑ Ⓒ Ⓓ

23. Ⓐ Ⓑ Ⓒ Ⓓ
24. Ⓐ Ⓑ Ⓒ Ⓓ
25. Ⓐ Ⓑ Ⓒ Ⓓ
26. Ⓐ Ⓑ Ⓒ Ⓓ
27. Ⓐ Ⓑ Ⓒ Ⓓ
28. Ⓐ Ⓑ Ⓒ Ⓓ
29. Ⓐ Ⓑ Ⓒ Ⓓ
30. Ⓐ Ⓑ Ⓒ Ⓓ
31. Ⓐ Ⓑ Ⓒ Ⓓ
32. Ⓐ Ⓑ Ⓒ Ⓓ
33. Ⓐ Ⓑ Ⓒ Ⓓ

34. Ⓐ Ⓑ Ⓒ Ⓓ
35. Ⓐ Ⓑ Ⓒ Ⓓ
36. Ⓐ Ⓑ Ⓒ Ⓓ
37. Ⓐ Ⓑ Ⓒ Ⓓ
38. Ⓐ Ⓑ Ⓒ Ⓓ
39. Ⓐ Ⓑ Ⓒ Ⓓ
40. Ⓐ Ⓑ Ⓒ Ⓓ
41. Ⓐ Ⓑ Ⓒ Ⓓ
42. Ⓐ Ⓑ Ⓒ Ⓓ
43. Ⓐ Ⓑ Ⓒ Ⓓ
44. Ⓐ Ⓑ Ⓒ Ⓓ

☐ # correct in Section 2

☐ # incorrect in Section 2

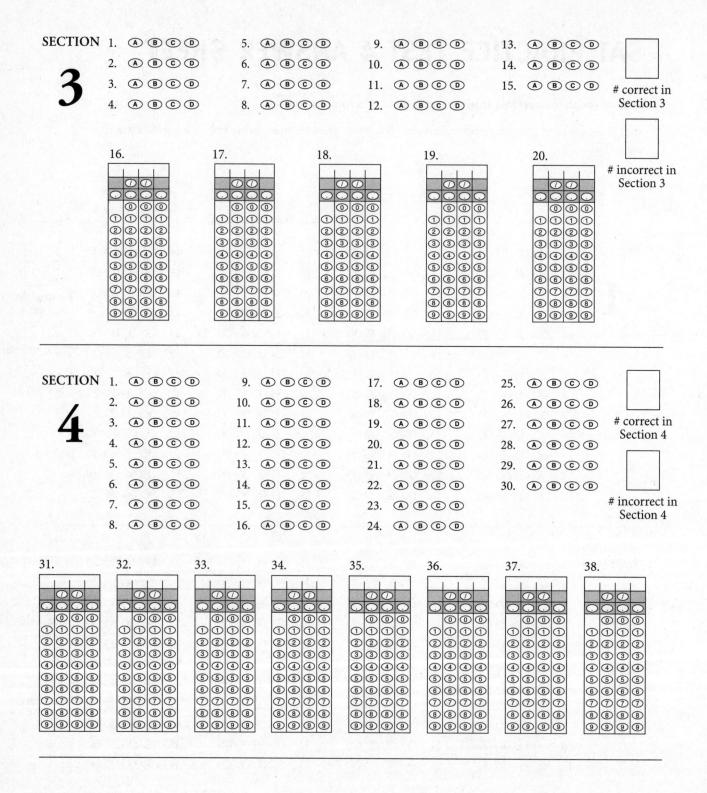

**SECTION**

**5**

Name _____

EID _____

_____

_____

_____

_____

_____

_____

_____

_____

_____

_____

_____

_____

_____

_____

_____

_____

_____

_____

_____

_____

_____

_____

_____

Name

EID

Name

EID

# SAT Essay Practice Test Comments

Your SAT Essay will be graded in three areas: Reading, Analysis, and Writing. Here are some comments from your Kaplan grader based on the College Board's criteria to help you improve your essay writing.

| | |
|---|---|
| **Reading** | ☐ This essay demonstrates a thorough comprehension of the source text.<br>☐ Explain how the central idea(s) and important details interrelate.<br>☐ Cite important details from the source text.<br>☐ Use textual evidence from the source text.<br>☐ Read the source text again; this essay contains errors of fact. |
| **Analysis** | ☐ This essay offers insightful analysis of the source text and demonstrates a sophisticated understanding of the analytical task.<br>☐ Focus only on the features of the text that are most relevant to the task.<br>☐ Explain the importance of the features you include in your response.<br>☐ Choose features that are most relevant to addressing the task.<br>☐ Provide support for your claims and points.<br>☐ Read the task again; this is a summary, not an analysis. |
| **Writing** | ☐ This essay is cohesive and demonstrates a highly effective command of language.<br>☐ Spelling **and** ☐ grammar usage are satisfactory.<br>☐ Use of vocabulary **and** ☐ sentence structure are varied.<br>☐ Make a stronger central claim/thesis.<br>☐ Create an outline before you write.<br>☐ Write a stronger introduction **and** ☐ conclusion.<br>☐ Use a formal style and objective tone.<br>☐ Proofread; remember to budget your time. |

## Additional Comments:

## Administrative Purposes:

Student's Name: _____  ID Number: _____

Test:       1    2    3    4

Reading:    1    2    3    4
Analysis:   1    2    3    4
Writing:    1    2    3    4

(These scores are **doubled** on your score report.)